HALLDÓR LAXNESS

by

PETER HALLBERG

This is the first full-length study of Halldór Laxness, Iceland's Nobel Prize-winning novelist, to appear in English. Dr. Hallberg traces Laxness's literary development through its three main stages. After a brief introduction to Iceland's history, Dr. Hallberg examines Laxness's two most important early works, the first of which reflects his attraction to Catholicism, and the second his engagement with social problems.

The author then discusses the epic novels of the thirties—*Salka Valka*, *Independent People* and *World Light*—in which Laxness develops his earlier themes, and the element of religious fervour combines with his stern social criticism. The second stage of his career also includes *Iceland's Bell* (1943-46), which is based on Icelandic history of the seventeenth and eighteenth centuries; *The Atom Station* (1948), a satire on life in post-war Reykjavík; and *The Happy Warriors* (1952), in which the heroic ideals of the Saga Age are subjected to bitter criticism.

Laxness had published three plays when he received the Nobel Prize for Literature in 1955, and three more have since followed. The current stage of his development is discussed in the final chapter. In the plays and two of his recent novels, *The Fish can Sing* (1957) and *Paradise Reclaimed* (1960) Laxness's work has mellowed, and shows a sceptical attitude to ideologies of all kinds.

The author thus gives a clear picture of Laxness's artistic development. The plots of the major novels are summarized, and a wealth of quotations is given. This book is a fascinating introduction to the work of Iceland's greatest writer in modern times.

ABOUT THE AUTHOR

Peter Hallberg was born in Gothenburg, Sweden, in 1916, and was educated in Gothenburg, Copenhagen and Reykjavík. From 1944-47 he was a lecturer at the University of Iceland, and since 1951 he has been a docent in literary history at the University of Gothenburg.

His many publications include *Den store vävaren* (1954), a study of Laxness's early works, and *Skaldens hus* (1956), an examination of Laxness's writings from *Salka Valka* to *The Happy Warriors. Den isländska sagan*, which has been translated into English (*The Icelandic Saga*, translated by Paul Schach, University of Nebraska Press, Lincoln 1962) also appeared in 1956, and was followed by its companion volume, *Den fornisländska poesien* (Old Icelandic Poetry) in 1962. Two of his books on Old Icelandic literature, *Snorri Sturluson och Egils saga Skallagrimssonar* (1962) and *Ólafr Þórðarson hvítaskáld, Knytlinga saga och Laxdæla saga* (1963) are provided with summaries in English. His most recent contribution to Old Norse studies is *Stilsignalement och författarskap i norrön sagalitteratur* (1968), a detailed investigation of the stylistic features of the sagas and the problems of their authorship.

ABOUT THE TRANSLATOR

Rory McTurk was born in Surrey, England, in 1942, and was educated in Scotland and at University College, Oxford. He studied Icelandic at the University of Iceland. Returning to Oxford, he worked for two years as lecturer in English at the University of Lund, Sweden, and now holds a similar position at the University of Copenhagen.

TWAYNE'S WORLD AUTHORS SERIES

A Survey of the World's Literature

Sylvia E. Bowman, Indiana University
GENERAL EDITOR

ICELAND

Leif Sjöberg, State University of New York, Stony Brook
EDITOR

Halldór Laxness

(TWAS 89)

TWAYNE'S WORLD AUTHORS SERIES (TWAS)

The purpose of TWAS is to survey the major writers—novelists, dramatists, historians, poets, philosophers, and critics—of the nations of the world. Among the national literatures covered are those of Australia, Canada, China, Eastern Europe, France, Germany, Greece, India, Italy, Japan, Latin America, New Zealand, Poland, Russia, Scandinavia, Spain, and the African nations, as well as Hebrew, Yiddish, and Latin Classical literatures. This survey is complemented by Twayne's United States Authors Series and English Authors Series.

The intent of each volume in these series is to present a critical analytical study of the works of the writer; to include biographical and historical material that may be necessary for understanding, appreciation, and critical appraisal of the writer; and to present all material in clear, concise English—but not to vitiate the scholarly content of the work by doing so.

Halldór Laxness

By PETER HALLBERG

UNIVERSITY OF GOTHENBURG

Translated by Rory McTurk

Twayne Publishers, Inc. :: New York

Preface

As an Icelander and a member of a very small Scandinavian nation with an ancient and unique literary culture, Halldór Laxness has rather special qualifications as a writer. Throughout the period of his literary achievement, which has now continued for almost half a century, the Icelandic heritage has constantly been a living force in his work, contrasting or combining in various ways with his modernism and preoccupation with the problems of his time. The tension between the native and the foreign, the national and the cosmopolitan, has formed one of the fruitful contrasts which run through all his writing. I have therefore found it suitable to include a short introductory chapter giving a brief outline of the history of Iceland and its cultural tradition.

Today, at the age of sixty-five, Laxness is still a productive writer. What is more, his literary output, for all its continuity, reveals an unflagging interest in experimenting with new forms. Since 1955, when he received the Nobel Prize for his "vividly descriptive epic works, which have given new life to the great Icelandic art of storytelling"—to quote the reasons given by the Swedish Academy for its choice—he has especially concentrated his energies on writing plays of an extremely original and somewhat bizarre character. A brief but comprehensive assessment of his contribution may therefore be of a merely preliminary nature; surprising features may yet reveal themselves in works still unwritten. The literary historian awaits with especial eagerness a sequel to Laxness' memoirs as a writer; the part published so far, *Skáldatími* (A Writer's Schooling, 1963) covers approximately the period between the two World Wars.

The present study is to a large extent chronologically arranged, in the form of a series of chapters on each of the essential works—a plan which in some measure can be said to have Laxness' own approval, for he readily emphasizes that every literary work is a world in itself, obeying its own inherent laws. Three stages in his development may be fairly clearly distinguished. The first is characterized by his attempts as a young man to find his way among conceptions of life and literary trends in Europe after the First World War. It is a period of vehement and restless searching, which finds its artistic liberation in the cosmopolitan novel of ideas *Vefarinn mikli frá Kasmír* (The Great Weaver from Kashmir, 1927). After a few years' stay in America, mostly at Los Angeles, from 1927 to 1929, Laxness began his long succession of novels with subjects drawn from the social life of Iceland, past and present. This stage, with *Gerpla* (The Happy Warriors, 1952), as its last great literary manifestation, is in part quite strongly colored by the writer's involvement in political and social life, and by his socialistic criticism of society. In his present phase, finally, which began around the time of the Nobel Prize award, his creative powers have, as already mentioned, been directed in no small measure towards the drama. But the novels and short stories written in these later years also differ in tone and spirit from his earlier epic works. They have become "de-ideologized" and have, on the whole, a more calmly retrospective and chronicle-like character; their relation to Icelandic tradition seems to be more free of tension, more conservative.

The three stages that I have outlined here are not, of course, separated by rigid dividing lines. On the contrary, as soon as one penetrates a little below the surface it becomes clear that they are closely linked and develop organically out of each other. Indeed, it could be maintained that *Vefarinn mikli,* the great work of Laxness' youth, contains *in nuce* almost everything that Laxness has later come to write, despite the fact that the book otherwise differs strongly—in setting, style, and choice of subject—from all his other novels. I hope that this unity amid variety, and this basic attitude lying behind what appear to be sudden turns and changes of thought will be clearly discernible in the form I have chosen for my own account of Halldór Laxness and his work.

PETER HALLBERG

Acknowledgments

The author and the translator are grateful to Mrs. Margaret Brittingham Callery, of Wilmington, Delaware; to Gylfi Gíslason, Icelandic Minister of Education, Reykjavík; to Dr. Per-Axel Hildeman of the Swedish Institute, Stockholm; and to The American-Scandinavian Foundation, New York, for generous financial grants. The translator is grateful to Dr. Finnbogi Guðmundsson for a generous loan of books from the National Library of Iceland, Reykjavík; to Magnus Magnusson, of Glasgow, for help and advice concerning some difficult words in *Heimsljós* and for invaluable help with the bibliographical lists; and to a number of friends and colleagues at the University of Lund, Sweden, for help with translation difficulties.

Translator's Note

All Icelandic words and proper names, whether ancient or modern, are given in Modern Icelandic spelling where they occur in the text—except in certain cases where Laxness' spelling is deliberately archaic (as in the title of his autobiographical manuscript *Heiman ek fór,* for instance, or in the book title *Eldur í Kaupinhafn*). Where the Icelandic name of a person or thing is interesting or important in itself, a short explanation of its meaning is given in brackets. In the rare cases where there are examples of Laxness' idiosyncratic spelling differing from normal modern usage, his own spelling has been used. For a detailed guide to the pronunciation and grammar of Modern Icelandic, the reader is referred to Stefán Einarsson's *Icelandic. Grammar, Texts, Glossary* (Baltimore, 1949).

In translating the quotations I have been greatly assisted by the author's Swedish rendering of the original Icelandic, and have relied on these for my English versions of passages quoted from letters and from certain relatively "minor" works of Laxness, where I have not had access to the original. The existing English translations of Laxness' works, which are listed at the end of this book, have also been a great help to me, and I freely acknowledge my debt to them—even if the author and I have not always agreed with their interpretations.

The page reference after each quotation refers to the first Icelandic edition of the work in question.

R. W. MCTURK

Contents

Chronology

1902   Halldór Guðjónsson is born April 23 in Reykjavík, Ice-
        land, the son of the road construction foreman Guðjón
        Helgi Helgason, and his wife Sigríður Halldórsdóttir.

1905   The family moves to the farm of Laxnes in Mosfells-
        sveit, just northeast of Reykjavík, and takes up farming.

1919   Guðjón Helgi dies. Halldór breaks off his schooling in
        Reykjavík High School and travels abroad for the first
        time, primarily to Copenhagen. Publishes the short novel
        Barn náttúrunnar (Child of Nature) under the pen
        name of Halldór frá Laxnes:.

1921–   Goes abroad again, and stays mainly in Germany and
1922   Austria, working on a "philosophical" book, never printed,
        called *Rauða kverið* (The Red Booklet).

1922–   With the help of Johannes Jörgensen, the Danish writer
1923   and Catholic, Halldór is given a place as a guest at the
        Benedictine monastery of Saint Maurice de Clervaux in
        the Grand Duchy of Luxembourg, some time in Novem-
        ber, 1922. Is baptized and confirmed in the Catholic faith
        by the Bishop of Luxembourg at a solemn Mass in the
        monastery church on January 6, 1922, and takes at his
        baptism the names Kiljan Marie Pierre. At the same time
        he adopts the family name of Laxness, after his father's
        farm, and this is later legalized by the Icelandic author-
        ities. During his time in the monastery he keeps a diary,
        which is still preserved. Publishes in 1923 the collection
        of short stories *Nokkrar sögur* (Some Stories).

1924   Publishes the novel *Undir Helgahnúk* (Under the Holy
        Mountain). Works on the manuscript of his stylized
        autobiography, *Heiman ek fór* (From Home I Went),
        which is not published until 1952.

1925   Publishes the apologetic *Kaþólsk viðhorf* (From a Catholic
        Point of View).

1927   Makes his "breakthrough" with the publication of his novel *Vefarinn mikli frá Kasmír* (The Great Weaver from Kashmir).

1927–
1929 Travels in Canada and the United States, studies the cinema world in Los Angeles, and becomes acquainted with Upton Sinclair.

1929 Publishes *Alþýðubókin* (The Book of the People), a collection of radical essays, which marks a decisive readjustment of his interests from religious to social problems.

1930 Marries Ingibjörg (Inga) Einarsdóttir. Publishes *Kvæðakver* (Poems), his only collection of poems to date.

1931 Publishes *Þú vínviður hreini* (O Thou Pure Vine), the first part of the novel about Salka Valka, the fishergirl.

1932 Publishes *Fuglinn í fjörunni* (The Bird on the Beach), the second and final part of the novel about Salka Valka. Travels in the autumn in the Soviet Union.

1933 Publishes *Í Austurvegi* (Going East), an eyewitness account of his journey to the Soviet Union, and the collection of short stories *Fótatak manna* (Steps of Men).

1934 Publishes the first part of the novel *Sjálfstætt fólk* (Independent People), and the play *Straumrof* (Short Circuit).

1935 Publishes the second and final part of the novel *Sjálfstætt fólk*.

1937 Publishes *Ljós heimsins* (The Light of the World), the first part of the novel tetralogy—later known as *Heimsljós* (World Light)—about Ólafur Kárason, the parish pauper and folk poet; and the collection of essays *Dagleið á fjöllum* (A Day's Journey in the Mountains).

1937–
1938 Travels during the winter months in the Soviet Union.

1938 Publishes *Gerska æfintýrið* (The Russian Adventure), an account of his travels in the Soviet Union, and *Höll sumarlandsins* (The Palace of the Summerland), the second part of the novel tetralogy about Ólafur Kárason.

1939 Publishes *Hús skáldsins* (The House of the Poet), the third part of the Ólafur Kárason tetralogy.

1940 Is divorced from Ingibjörg Einarsdóttir. Publishes *Fegurð himinsins* (The Beauty of the Skies), the final part of the Ólafur Kárason tetralogy.

1941 Publishes *Vopnin kvödd,* a translation of Hemingway's *A Farewell to Arms* (1929).

1942 Publishes the collection of short stories *Sjö töframenn* (Seven Enchanters), and *Vettvangur dagsins* (The Contemporary Scene), a collection of essays and articles.

1943 Publishes *Íslandsklukkan* (Iceland's Bell), the first part of a trilogy of novels.

1944 Publishes *Hið ljósa man* (The Bright Maid), the second part of the novel trilogy.

1945 Marries Auður Sveinsdóttir. Moves into Gljúfrasteinn, his villa in the neighborhood of Laxnes, his parents' farm, and publishes *Birtíngur,* a translation of Voltaire's *Candide.*

1946 Publishes *Eldur í Kaupinhafn* (Fire in Copenhagen), the final part of the novel trilogy, and *Sjálfsagðir hlutir* (Obvious Things), a collection of essays and articles.

1948 Publishes the novel *Atómstöðin* (The Atom Station).

1950 Publishes *Reisubókarkorn* (A Little Diary of Travels), a collection of essays and articles, and the play *Snæfríður Íslandssól* (Snæfríður, Iceland's Sun), which is based on the novel trilogy of 1943–46.

1952 Publishes *Heiman eg fór* (From Home I Went), the autobiographical manuscript of 1924, and the novel *Gerpla* (The Happy Warriors).

1954 Publishes the play *Silfurtúnglið* (The Silver Moon).

1955 Publishes *Dagur í senn* (A Day at a Time), a collection of articles and speeches. Is awarded the year's Nobel Prize for Literature.

1957 Publishes the novel *Brekkukotsannáll* (The Fish can Sing).

1957– Makes a world tour, visiting the United States, China, and
1958 India.

1959 Publishes *Gjörníngabók* (Documents), a collection of articles and speeches.

1960 Publishes the novel *Paradísarheimt* (Paradise Reclaimed).

1961 Publishes the play *Strompleikurinn* (The Chimney Play).

1962 Publishes the play *Prjónastofan Sólin* (The Knitting Workshop called "The Sun").

1963 Publishes the book of memoirs *Skáldatími* (A Writer's Schooling).

1964 Publishes the collection of short stories *Sjöstafakverið* (The Book of Seven Signs).

1965 Publishes *Upphaf mannúðarstefnu* (The Beginning of Humanism), a collection of essays and articles.

1966 Publishes the play *Dúfnaveislan* (The Pigeon Banquet), and *Veisla í farángrinum,* a translation of Hemingway's *A Moveable Feast* (1964).

1967 Publishes *Íslendíngaspjall* (An Essay on Icelanders), a short account of the author's special experiences as an Icelandic writer and primarily conceived as a complement to *Skáldatími* (A Writer's Schooling), the book of memoirs published in 1963.

1968 Publishes the novel *Kristnihald undir Jökli* (Christianity in Snæfellsnes).

1968 Publishes *Svavar Guðnason,* an essay in Danish, with illustrations, on a modern Icelandic painter (= Vor Tids Kunst. 67. Gyldendal, Copenhagen).

1969 Publishes *Vínlandspúnktar* (Some Remarks on Vinland), four essays on Old Icelandic matters.

1970 Publishes *Innansveitarkronika* (A Parish Chronicle), a story from the author's home district, Mosfellssveit.

CHAPTER 1

The Icelandic Background

I Early History and Literature

THE origin and history of Iceland as a nation are so unique as to give the Icelanders an exceptional position among the peoples of Scandinavia. The remote island in the North Atlantic was colonized by Scandinavians—by far the greater part of them from Norway—in the decades just before and after the year 900. The first settler is reported to have been Ingólfur Arnarson, who took up his abode in 874 at the site of the country's present capital, Reykjavík—which derives its name, "Smoky Bay," from the steam coming from the hot springs in that area.

The story of the settlement (Icel. *landnám*) is told in the remarkable *Landnámabók* (Book of Settlements), which is thought to have been compiled in the twelfth century. It gives a systematic account of the settlement along the coast and inwards from the coast to the glens and valleys round the whole island; more than 3,000 people and 1,400 places are mentioned in connection with the colonization of Iceland. The extensive genealogies in this work are quite often obscured by the confused myth and legend of ancient times, but to Icelanders the book has been of enormous importance in strengthening their feelings of national self-esteem and solidarity.

In the new society some organization was of course needed to handle the general affairs of the community. Thus in the year 930 the Icelandic General Assembly (*alþingi*) was established, with its meeting place at Þingvellir by the country's largest lake, Þingvallavatn. The *alþingi* met annually in June. Its foremost official was the Lawspeaker (*lögsögumaður*), who was chosen for a period of three years, had to know the code of laws by heart, and also had to recite them in their entirety, at meetings of the *alþingi,* during his three-year term of office; for at that time the laws were not yet written down and had to be preserved in memory.

In founding the *alþingi* the Icelanders had created a legislative and judicial authority, but no administrative or executive one. This strange feature has left its mark on the many descriptions of legal disputes and acts of vengeance in the Sagas of Icelanders. If a plaintiff managed to secure the conviction of his opponent, it was his own business to see the sentence carried out. The frequent result of this, of course, was that power and strength became the deciding factors. The lack of a central administrative and executive authority was to show itself fatal to Iceland's continuance as an independent state. In the long run it undermined powers of resistance both to internal disintegration and to external pressures.

The hundred years from the origin of the *alþingi* until 1030 are sometimes called the "Saga Age" (*söguöld*) in the history of Iceland; for during those years the events related in such Icelandic Family Sagas as *Egils saga Skalla-Grímssonar, Laxdæla saga, Eyrbyggja saga, Njáls saga* and *Grettis saga Ásmundarsonar* —to name just a few of the greatest and best known—are supposed to have taken place. These suggestively realistic and carefully localized narratives were earlier regarded, both in Iceland and elsewhere, as true stories taken from life. More recently, however, scholars have been able to show that, to a large extent at least, the sagas are not so much historical documents as remarkable works of fiction.

However this may be, the *söguöld* was, in reality too, a time of greatness for Iceland. The sons of the settlers showed the same bold spirit of discovery as their fathers. In 982 the Icelanders made their way to Greenland and founded an Icelandic settlement there. Leifur Eiríksson, a son of the first European to settle in Greenland, was driven off course on a sea voyage in the year 1000 and landed on a foreign coast, which he called Vínland. This was America—which was thus discovered by an Icelandic seafarer nearly 500 years before Columbus. As is well known, the description given of Vínland in the Icelandic sagas has aroused great interest not only among students of literature, but also among archeologists, geographers, and cartographers.

The year 1000 was also an important milestone in the internal history of Iceland in that Christianity was then adopted, by decree of the *alþingi*, as the official religion of the country. In its earliest days the Icelandic church differed greatly from its Catholic mother church in Europe. It was far from having the independent position of a kind of state within the state, with legislative and judicial authority in its own affairs. In Iceland the church never gained the same firm hold on the people as it did in other countries. Yet no real gulf arose, either, between the ordinary people and the clergy, between layman and cleric. This is one aspect of the strikingly democratic nature of the Icelandic social system which has been preserved to the present day.

The Icelandic Commonwealth consisted of independent farmers who, in theory at least, were each other's equals. No formal class distinction existed among them, and no privileged nobility ever arose in Iceland. The very precondition for such a development—a monarch surrounded by a court, an official hierarchy, and an army—was also lacking.

Nevertheless, the balance of power originally shared by the local chieftains gradually became unhinged; a local chieftain (*goði*) represented, within his sphere of dominion (*goðorð*), both secular and—before the introduction of Christianity—religious authority. A few great families succeeded independently in gaining domination in different parts of the country, and waged with each other a violent struggle for supremacy. This period of unrest, which lasted from the middle of the twelfth century to the fall of the Icelandic Commonwealth in the year 1262, is known as the Age of the Sturlungs (*Sturlungaöld*) after one of the leading families. The most famous representative of this family, which is named after Sturla, its founding father, was the chieftain and historian Snorri Sturluson (1179–1241).

Iceland now paid the price of having no national government. From the very beginning the kings of Norway had had designs on Iceland and had made a number of attempts to gain control of the island. In medieval Europe a nation with no head of state was evidently regarded as something of an anomaly. A cardinal visiting Norway in the middle of the thirteenth century found it "unseemly" that Iceland "was not subject to a king, like all other countries in the world."[1] In their mutual struggles

Icelandic chieftains now began to look to the Norwegian king for support against each other, and to refer the final decision in these conflicts to him. Finally, the Icelanders had to swear allegiance to King Hákon Hákonarson and were made to pay taxes to the crown of Norway (1262–64).

Thus the Icelandic Commonwealth came to an end. The feuds of the Age of the Sturlungs give ample evidence of ruthless self-assertion, low cunning, and cruelty. But this period of unrest in the history of Iceland, when the freedom of the nation was lost, was accompanied by a unique efflorescence of literature. *Sturlunga saga,* the sternly realistic chronicle of contemporary history, was written by men who in many cases had themselves played an active part in the events there described. The principal author of the work was Sturla Þórðarson (1214–84), a nephew of Snorri Sturluson. But writers also turned to the past, and gave historical accounts of the kings and jarls of Norway and Denmark. Snorri's *Heimskringla,* which dates from around 1230, stands out as the great crowning achievement of this historical genre. The most original contributions to the art of prose, however, are undoubtedly the abovementioned Family Sagas or Sagas of Icelanders *(Íslendingasögur),* in which anonymous Icelandic authors cause their forefathers from the *söguöld* to rise up again in all the changing scenes of life, from its small everyday anxieties to its great tragic conflicts. It was also during this period, the thirteenth century, that the old Norse poems of gods and heroes, the socalled "Eddic" poems, were collected and written down in Iceland.

It was not until the seventeenth century that this remarkable literature became known in the other Scandinavian countries. Then it aroused great interest, primarily in being regarded as history. Here were new vistas to stir the imagination, opening out onto an ancient Scandinavian past, previously unknown— an age of heroic deeds, of saga and song. Classical Icelandic literature thus became a powerful stimulus to Scandinavians in strengthening their feelings of self-awareness as members of the Northern nations, and has frequently provided writers of later times with subject matter and inspiration. Examples from the Romantic period are Adam Oehlenschläger (1779–1850) in Denmark and Esaias Tegnér (1782-1846) in Sweden; while later in the nineteenth century, Longfellow (1807–82) in America and William Morris (1834–96) in England translated and interpreted in their own way certain poems and sagas from early Icelandic literature.

Above all, however, this Golden Age of literature acquired a national and cultural importance for the Icelandic people themselves—an importance which can hardly be overestimated. In the following dark centuries of poverty and foreign rule in Iceland people could seek comfort and self-confidence in the sagas which told of their forefathers' exploits and glorious lives. For the fact remained that mighty champions such as Egill Skalla-Grímsson and Gunnar of Hlíðarendi, a man of wisdom such as Njáll, and beautiful women such as Guðrún Ósvífsdóttir and Helga the Fair had lived and been active here in Iceland and nowhere else. Icelandic people still lived and moved, every day, in the surroundings which formed the setting for the sagas; they were well acquainted with the names and geographical features of the places where the events related in the sagas were supposed to have happened. In such places both imagination and longing could call forth with ease the shades of the past.

Thus the classical literature of medieval Iceland has undoubtedly been of moral significance in the Icelandic people's struggle for existence. But it has also left its mark, in a decisive way, on the Icelandic language and literary tradition, as can still be seen today. In the prose of the sagas the written language was fixed earlier in Iceland than elsewhere in the North in such a way as to provide a linguistic standard. This—together, perhaps, with certain other factors such as the geographical isolation of the country—has undoubtedly contributed to the fact that modern Icelandic has preserved the structure and vocabulary originally characteristic of Old Norse, and has done so incomparably better than any of the other Scandinavian languages. Thus an Icelandic child who has learned to read can without much difficulty read the classical sagas in the language in which they were written in the thirteenth century—provided, of course, that the varied orthography of the manuscripts is modernized. It is easy to understand the importance of this unique linguistic continuity for the Icelandic sense of closeness to the past.

But the sagas have also provided a literary and stylistic standard. With their tersely matter-of-fact prose style and powerfully
effective dialogue they formed perfect models for Icelandic
storytellers of later times. Not only in prose but also in poetry
has the power of the tradition given ample evidence of its continued strength. Icelandic poets still make frequent use of the
alliteration and internal rhyme which formed an essential
feature of Old Norse poetry. It is characteristic that when Mil-
ton's *Paradise Lost* and Klopstock's *Messias* were translated into
Icelandic at the beginning of the nineteenth century, the Icelandic versions of these poems were written in the *fornyrðislag*,
one of the ancient metrical forms of the Eddic poems.[2] If Icelandic authors have sometimes regarded this overwhelmingly
powerful native tradition as restrictive, as a hindrance to
literary regeneration, we can well understand their attitude. In
his short book of memoirs, *Íslendíngaspjall* (An Essay on Icelanders, 1967), Laxness has described, with his customary sharpness of emphasis, the profound extent to which the Icelandic
"School of Literature," with its strict rules, has become second
nature to his countrymen, and how "the standard set by the
Golden Age" still dominates today the literary opinions of the
public as well as of the critics. It is not to be wondered at if
"such poor wretches as myself and people like me, engaged in
the laborious work of writing books, often feel downhearted in
this country; any ordinary simpleton can prove beyond dispute
that we are worse writers of prose than the men who fashioned
Njáls saga or *Hrafnkels saga* or *Heimskringla;* and similarly,
that as poets we have declined considerably since the tenth
century, when the poet of *Völuspá* stood beneath this vast sky
of Iceland and could not spell his name."[3]

Thus even for the modern Icelandic author the great literature of the Middle Ages is to a large extent a living heritage of
which, whether consciously or unconsciously, he is always half-
critically aware. The native tradition and foreign literary trends
are continually being confronted and balanced with each other.
This process is strikingly reflected in various stages of Laxness'
development as a writer, and we shall later have reason to return
to the treatment he gives it.

II   *The Struggle for Independence*

After the fall of the Commonwealth, Iceland had greater difficulty in keeping economically and culturally apace with the other Scandinavian countries. Shipping and foreign trade, which were, of course, a condition of life for Iceland, deteriorated considerably, and the Icelanders became more isolated than ever before. From the year 1380, when Norway was united with Denmark in a personal union, Iceland was brought more and more completely under the power of the Danish crown. When the Reformation was established in Denmark, the king wished that Iceland, too, should acknowledge it. He met with stubborn resistance, however, especially from one of Iceland's two bishops, Jón Arason of Hólar (1484–1550). This warlike prelate was taken prisoner and beheaded, together with two of his sons, without legal proceedings. Jón Arason has become, through his death, something of a martyr, an Icelandic national hero. His struggle was directed not only against Protestantism but also against Danish bureaucracy and arbitrary rule. The Reformation meant in Iceland, as it did elsewhere, that the power of the king was strengthened; and when in 1660 the Danish king made his rule supreme, the Icelanders also had to accept him as their absolute ruler. The result of this was that Iceland's autonomy grew weaker and weaker. The *alþingi* was but a shadow of what it had been.

Economically, the Icelanders were especially hard pressed by the Danish trade monopoly. In accordance with contemporary custom the king gave the merchants in certain Danish towns the sole and exclusive right to trade with Iceland, and tariffs were fixed for both foreign and Icelandic products. For example, the Icelanders needed grain, wood, iron, and hemp, in exchange for which they could provide, among other things, split cod, train oil, and woolen goods. In practice, however, this could hardly be described as trade on an equal footing. The Danish merchants who had control of the shipping lines to and from Iceland gained through lack of competition an overwhelming advantage over the islanders, whom they treated as recipients of charitable maintenance.

Among those Icelanders who sought to create better conditions for their countrymen was Árni Magnússon (1663–1730), a civil

servant and professor in Copenhagen. Together with another
Icelander he made an exhaustive analysis of the situation in
Iceland, compiled a highly detailed rent roll of the Icelandic
farms, listing their resources and profits, and examined the work
of the courts, etc. But Árni Magnússon was above all a learned
collector of manuscripts who has done more than anyone else to
trace and gather into safekeeping the ancient Icelandic vellums
which are the visible result of his forefathers' literary efforts.
He left his treasure hoard of books and manuscripts to the University of Copenhagen, where they have been kept under the
name of the Arnamagnæan Collection. By a decree, however, of
the Danish Parliament, which was confirmed by the Danish
Supreme Court in 1966, these unique manuscripts are now to be
restored to their land of origin; and thus has been settled, once
and for all, a matter of long and heated dispute between Danes
and Icelanders.

In one of his works of fiction, the trilogy of novels which
began with *Íslandsklukkan* (Iceland's Bell, 1943), Laxness has
made use of many features drawn from Árni Magnússon's life
as a patriot and collector of manuscripts, and has brought to
life, with great artistry, the Icelandic world of the times in
which he lived.

In the early nineteenth century liberal movements began to
assert themselves in different parts of Europe; various oppressed
nations and minority groups raised the demand for freedom.
These ideas gave new life and energy to the Icelandic struggle
for national independence. A few young Icelanders in Copenhagen, among them Jónas Hallgrímsson (1807–45), one of Iceland's finest lyrical poets, became energetic propagandists for
the reestablishment of the *alþingi.* A forceful spokesman was
found in Jón Sigurðsson (1811–79), who for forty years was
Iceland's leading politician—"Iceland's shield and sword," as he
has been called. Thus between 1843 and 1845 the *alþingi* was
reestablished, but at first only as an advisory body. In 1854 the
last vestiges of the earlier trade monopoly were finally removed,
and the Icelanders were able to establish trade relations where
it best suited them to do so. Thus the ice was broken, both on
the political and the economic level. The hundred years which
followed tell the story of how Iceland gradually advanced towards its long-sought goal of full national autonomy.

At the thousand-year anniversary of the settlement, which was celebrated in 1874, King Christian IX visited Iceland—the first official royal visit to Iceland in the history of the country—and introduced then a new constitution, which among other things gave the *alþingi* joint legislative power with the crown and control of the country's finances. Just over twenty-five years later, in 1903, the special office of Minister for Icelandic Affairs was established in Reykjavík; and by the Union Act of 1918, finally, the independence of Iceland was fully recognized. Only the king of the two countries and the Danish administration of foreign affairs still remained as reminders of Iceland's earlier state of dependence. In 1944 the final step was taken: on June 17—the anniversary of Jón Sigurðsson's birth and now the country's National Day—Iceland was proclaimed a Republic at Þingvellir, the meeting place for the *alþingi* of the ancient Commonwealth. The country had then had a foreign head of state for well-nigh seven hundred years.

It is clear that in *Íslandsklukkan* Laxness has been inspired by political events in Iceland at the time of writing, by the exultation accompanying the birth of the new Republic—the completely independent state so eagerly desired for so long, and now a reality. In his description of a past age, with its sufferings, its spirit of resistance and the people's yearning for an indigenous culture, the novel is sustained by a profound national fervor with direct appeal to the author's Icelandic contemporaries. The work may be seen as a kind of inventory of the native Icelandic heritage, a magnificent synthesis of what is essential in the Icelandic character, as the author himself has experienced it.

III   *The Modern Writer's Background*

The political liberation of Iceland has run parallel with a corresponding development in economic and social spheres. The past fifty years or so have probably meant speedier and more drastic material changes for Iceland than for most other European countries. At the turn of the century the built-up areas or "towns" contained 13 per cent of the island's total population, which was then 78,500; and in 1945 the population of the towns had risen to 55 per cent of a total population of 130,500. In 1900 the capital city of Reykjavík had only 6,500 inhabitants; in 1965 the figure had risen to 78,000, that is, to about 40 per cent of a population of almost 194,000 people. In Iceland the essential precondition for these changes, which are so typical of the times, has been the development of the fisheries to a level of large-scale production, and the vigorous industry and trade which have grown up around them. Iceland has emerged today as a modern welfare state which is not strikingly different from the other Scandinavian countries.

Laxness himself, being more or less a contemporary in age with the present century, has lived through this revolutionary development which is also reflected, in many different ways, in his work. The novel *Brekkukotsannáll* (The Fish can Sing, 1957), gives a pleasantly humorous description of the idyllic environment of Reykjavík at the time of his childhood. In direct contrast to this stands *Atómstöðin* (The Atom Station, 1948), which is set in the same Reykjavík at the end of the Second World War: a hectic metropolis in a newly created Republic, placed only a few years earlier in the midst of international communications and drawn into events of great political importance.

In an autobiographical fragment dating from 1924, called *Heiman ek fór* (From Home I Went) and not published until much later (1952), Laxness has described his grandmother as he remembers her from the days of his childhood. He emphasizes strongly the archaic qualities of this old Icelandic woman, her links with the past and with all that is most profoundly native to Iceland and its people. It is a document of great cultural-historical interest, and merits lengthy quotation in that it throws light on how the writer has experienced the situation in which he finds himself as an Icelander and modern man of the twentieth century:

At every opportunity I point out—and always with noble pride—that I knelt at the feet of the eighteenth century to receive my upbringing. My maternal grandmother was born during that half of the nineteenth century which carries all the distinctive features of the previous century, and grew up among those members of the population who might be described as fragments broken from the rock of distant ages. My grandmother's foster-mother lived through the fires of Skaftá [the volcanic eruption of Laki in 1783, Iceland's most severe eruption in historical times], and had to lay shoe leather on the table for her family to eat. A woman who has dealt out shoe leather at meals must surely inculcate in her children rules of life quite different from those encouraged nowadays. My grandmother brought me up and taught me many rules of life which she had gleaned from her foster-mother.

My grandmother was an eighteenth-century person and did not know a thing about what went on in the nineteenth century, either in politics or science. . . . No wonder, then, that the news of twentieth-century events seemed as vague, passing fancies in her eyes, and moved her little. . . . Our telephone was now installed and was placed in a room next door to hers. But even though this strange contraption rang noisily and continually in her ear throughout the remaining years of her life, she died heartily convinced that the telephone was nothing but humbug. No notice should ever be taken of news which came from the telephone. If anyone tried to explain the telephone to her, she simply laughed at his attempts; she just could not be bothered to waste words on these fantasies, she said, and began to talk about something else.

It was from this unusual woman that the boy Halldór received his first impression of Icelandic saga and song:

But it was my grandmother who brought me up as a child, and I am proud of my good fortune in having been brought up by a woman who, of all the women I have known, was the least dependent on the fashions and spirit of the times. She sang me ancient songs before I could talk, told me stories from heathen times and sang me cradle songs from the Catholic era . . .

Her speech was pure and strong and never a note false as far as language was concerned. I have never known anything more authentically Icelandic than the language of this old woman. It was neither generally Nordic in quality like the folk tales, nor tinged with Latin influence like the writings of the Middle Ages, nor blended with Danish like the Icelandic in vogue at the time of the Reformation. It was the language of the culture, eight hundred years old, of the inland farms of Iceland, unspoilt and wonderful, imbued with the indefinable flavor of its origin, like a wild fruit.[4]

We may suspect that in the interests of gaining his artistic effect the writer has given this portrait a rather stronger element of archaism than his childhood really had. But even if this is so, the description undoubtedly tells us something of fundamental importance, not only about Laxness himself but about all Icelanders of his generation. It is sometimes said that in the twentieth century Iceland has made a direct leap from the Middle Ages into modern times. This, of course, is an immense exaggeration. Implicit in the statement, however, is the undeniable truth that the rapid development into a modern society must have seemed especially dramatic in a small, homogeneous nation with a cultural tradition as strong and ancient as that of Iceland. To the Icelander conscious of his culture and its implications, the meeting of the old and the new, of the native and the foreign, was full of problems, and will have acted as an incitement to self-examination, to a stock taking of his own national values. This situation is to a large extent reflected in Laxness' years of travel and inquiry as a young man, the period of orientation in postwar Europe, which found powerful literary expression in the novel *Vefarinn mikli frá Kasmír* (The Great Weaver from Kashmir, 1927).

CHAPTER 2

Life in Europe. The Great Weaver from Kashmir

I *From Hearth to Cloister*

HALLDÓR Guðjónsson was born in Reykjavík on April 23, 1902, the son of foreman Guðjón Helgi Helgason and his wife, Sigríður Halldórsdóttir. He was evidently christened Halldór after his maternal grandfather; and in accordance with the ancient Scandinavian system of name giving, which still exists in Iceland, he was known as Guðjónsson (Son of Guðjón) after his father. Only as a grown man did he change this patronymic for the new family name of Laxness, by which he has become known.

When Halldór was three years old, his parents moved into the country to the farm of Laxnes in the district of Mosfellssveit, just northeast of Reykjavík, and became farming people. His father died in 1919 but his mother remained on the farm until the spring of 1928, when she returned to the capital. The writer-to-be thus spent a great part of his childhood in the country. Much later, in letters and elsewhere, he has himself described the environment of his youth; the portrait of his grandmother, drawn from his childhood memories, has already been quoted. He showed rather less enthusiasm for his duties on the farm, if we may believe his own description:

I was really rather a "nice boy" at home on the farm. I was a dual character—an ordinary errand boy and milk collector in the eyes of human beings, but a far from ordinary philosopher before God. I was what people call "lazy." From my earliest childhood I have loathed physical work, and I wormed my way out of all jobs that could possibly be avoided. I was just as skillful, too, at getting others to do the jobs I was supposed to do myself. I was ill-liked by the household for my laziness and truancy, nor did my father know what to make of me; but my mother supported me when I got into trouble, and for this I am most grateful to her.

Yet the boy Halldór seems to have been conscious, at a very early stage, of his literary calling. He draws attention to "loads of scribblings," "stories and poems," which he "was constantly putting together" as early as around the age of seven:

> To tell the truth I was always awaiting some convenient opportunity to get to my books and my desk—above all, of course, the desk. At that time, if I was left to myself, I sometimes wrote the whole day through, and would turn out no less than twenty to thirty pages a day. The amount of paper I managed to use up was quite exceptional. In the intervals of this—in the course of my daily tasks—all my thoughts turned on my writing, on subjects for articles and heroes for novels. I filled many a notebook as I went about my daily work. If I had no paper with me when I was out of doors I would write things down on my handkerchief and make a fair copy when I got home . . .[1]

The traditional school system, on the other hand, with its neatly pigeonholed methods of acquiring knowledge, can hardly have seemed attractive to a spirit so precocious and impatiently active. At the end of the school year of 1918–19 he could no longer endure being fettered to his classroom desk in Reykjavík High School. In the summer of 1919, a few weeks after his father's death, he journeyed out into the world—chiefly to Copenhagen—as so many young Icelanders, eager for knowledge and experience, had done before him. By then he had already written his first book, the short novel *Barn náttúrunnar* (Child of Nature), which was published in Reykjavík in the autumn of the same year. The seventeen-year-old author appeared here under the name of Halldór frá Laxnesi, after his parents' farm. In this adolescent work the characterization and the background of ideas—the "gospel of nature" and the romantic idealization of the farmer's life—seem to have borrowed their coloring from such writers as Björnstjerne Björnson, Knut Hamsun, and Selma Lagerlöf; on one occasion the main character sits out in the field reading Selma Lagerlöf's novel *Jerusalem*. As we should expect, *Barn náttúrunnar* gives no foretaste of the mature Laxness.

With his journey abroad in 1919 Halldór began his years of travel and study in postwar Europe. This was not only, or even primarily, a quest for the "magic wand" of poetry. The significance of these early years of travel may be seen in the attempts of an intellectually and emotionally alert young man at generally finding his own way through a confused world—his struggle for a view of life. It must have been an overwhelming experience for a young Icelander to find himself suddenly face to face with life in the war-scarred cities of the Continent. Letters written to Icelandic friends give glimpses of his impressions at the time. In a letter written from Leipzig in October, 1921, he expresses the emphatic wish "to have these damned victory columns and ornamented church towers sold to the highest bidder, and use the proceeds to buy bread for the prostitutes, who shame the State by offering themselves for a few cents at every street corner; and for these disabled wretches, uglier than the devil himself, who have had their legs cut off and eyes poked out in the war, these disgusting relics of human beings who are made to line the streets, each with a beggar's moneybag and a placard saying '85% incapable of work'—a damnable disgrace not to the State, but to humanity."[2] Another aspect of postwar Germany may be glimpsed in a letter from Berlin, written in March, 1922. The writer declares himself threatened by an impending shortage of money. Yet he cannot refrain "from looking in at the Adlon in the evenings, drinking mocha coffee and eating Danish pastry for 50 marks among ambassadors, American million-heiresses and the daughters of Indian princes. It's fantastic how elegant Berlin can be, and quite extraordinary how devilishly sweet the world is on the side which is uppermost; I think of these beautiful, gorgeous women and these well-groomed and manicured diplomatic types, and repeat the expression: devilishly sweet."[3]

This repetitive and conclusive way of formulating his thoughts, this paradoxical expression of attraction and repulsion, is wholly characteristic—the alluring glitter of the world is set against the darkest kind of human misery. In 1921 and 1922 Laxness was hard at work on the manuscript of *Rauða kverið* (The Red Booklet), which has never been published. The greater part of this work is still preserved, and probably gives a reasonably accurate picture of the author's experiences

and outlook on life at the time. He has since remarked, with a
certain amount of disdain, that *Rauða kverið* was about "a
neurotic boy shaking his head at 'the transitoriness of this
world' and the like." Yet in summing up his remarks, he has
indicated the place of the work in his literary output by saying:
"The book is undoubtedly of considerable psychological interest
as a testimony to the spiritual state dominating in the author
before his conversion to Catholicism."[4]

A leading motif in *Rauða kverið* is the confrontation of a
simple life lived in the bosom of nature, the life of an Icelandic shepherd in some remote valley, with the great world,
where man has built houses fifty stories high, has built gigantic
ships, and churches with towers reaching to heaven, yes, has
achieved literally everything—"except peace and happiness"
(90). The description of the glittering misery of modern
civilization was probably inspired, in part, by Tolstoy, with
whose works Laxness had early come into contact. At the same
time, however, he was surely able to build on his extremely concrete personal impressions of postwar Europe; for both the
glitter and the misery, as we have seen, are reflected in his letters
at the time.

Rauða kverið also shows marked traces of pessimism and an
awareness of death—feelings which were partly nourished by
the ravages of Spanish influenza in Reykjavík in the autumn of
1918, and by the great eruption of Katla, the volcano, at the
same time. The epidemic and the volcanic eruption formed a
combination of events which provided overwhelming symbols
of man's precarious situation. The author describes them in
apocalyptic terms, with a passionate fervor reminiscent of some
Old Testament prophet. "At this very moment the epidemic is
raging. Death sets his mark on the door of every house. . . . Angel
of death, angel of death, what majesty and sanctity! I would
wish to fall on my knees. . . . The town has the holy atmosphere
of a churchyard" (73). "At that time the most dreadful days
began, days of horror. For our fatherland, holy Iceland, was
striking terror in the hearts of its people. . . . Fire broke loose
from beneath the earth. Mother earth herself, in whom we sought
our stronghold, was no longer to be trusted. Was it strange that
fear dwelt in the eyes of all who stared with questioning gaze at

the glowing clouds of fire in the eastern sky? The Lord shall come
with fire! say the prophecies. The first thing I thought of was
the day of judgment" (42–43).

The main character in *Rauða kverið* seems, finally, to have
reached the lowest point of personal and universal resignation.
The impressions left on the author by his varied reading support and strengthen the sentiments expressed in the work. He
refers to *Bhagavadgita,* "the holy book," as well as to Yoga and
Nirvana. Mention is also made of *maya,* "den Schleier des
Truges" (the veil of illusion) (103); the German phrase seems
to indicate the influence of Schopenhauer, who of course has
borrowed the term from Indian religious philosophy. In a work
intended to be the author's magnum opus, "the last word both
for and about human beings," "a concentration of the world's
whole experience of life" (113), we read that "Life is full of
suffering, but death is eternal silence and rest. The sooner it
comes over me, this eternal silence and rest, the better." Yet
Rauða kverið does not end with this disconsolate outlook. In the
final section of the preserved manuscript the author writes, by
way of introduction, of a decisive change: "My mind is here
called forth from the inertia of pessimism; new vistas, different
from before, and new ways, lie open before me. In this chapter
I describe how I involuntarily became aware of forces which I
had earlier thought unimportant or had overlooked, and how I
had become a new person before I realized it" (187).

The manuscript is defective in this section—several pages are
missing—and we cannot deduce from it any explicit motivation
for the awakening which the "I" of the work has experienced.
But the new forces of which the author says in the chapter's
introduction that he has become conscious, are clearly to be
found in Christianity. In a letter to his compatriot Jón
Sveinsson ("Nonni"), the Jesuit priest, Laxness explains that
Rauða kverið describes how a young man "finally discovers
prayer and its power."[5] When he wrote this, in the beginning of
February, 1923, he had been living for some time as a Catholic
convert in the monastery of St. Maurice de Clervaux in the
Grand Duchy of Luxembourg. The end of *Rauða kverið* reflects
the experiences which brought him to the monastery door.

II *Laxness the Catholic*

It was at the end of the year 1922 that Laxness was received
as a guest at the Benedictine monastery of St. Maurice de
Clervaux, with the help of the Danish writer and Catholic,
Johannes Jörgensen. It was natural that he should choose this
particular monastery, for St. Maurice was, among other things,
the center of a fellowship of prayer, established in 1910 by
Pope Pius X, to further the return of the Scandinavian and
Finnish peoples to the Catholic faith. When Halldór arrived
there he was able to meet several Scandinavians among the
young novices. On January 6, 1923, he was baptized in the
monastery church by the Bishop of Luxembourg. As was customary for converts, he chose on this occasion the name of a
saint. The name he chose was that of the Irish martyr Kilian,
which he found was well suited to the Icelandic language; and
from then on he signed his name as Halldór Kiljan Laxness.
More recently, however, he has dropped the middle name, and
now simply uses Halldór Laxness.

His sojourn in the monastery is exceptionally well described
in contemporary documents. He wrote numerous and often very
long letters to his friends, and he also kept a diary in the monastery, beginning on Ash Wednesday, February 14, 1923, and ending with an entry for the eighth Sunday after Whitsun, that is,
July 15, of the same year. The letters on the one hand and the
diary on the other are not readily comparable as sources for the
writer's inner development. The diary quite often shows signs
of spiritual turmoil, uneasiness, and depression. In the letters,
however, Laxness is ready to appear as a militant apologist in the
face of skeptical friends, and defends his standpoint with
polemical acuteness and intensity. If we compare the two
sources, we sometimes find a significant conflict between judg-
ments passed on one and the same thing.

His first letters from the monastery express feelings of relief,
liberation, and peace. "I had never really believed that such a
life as is lived here could actually exist; I had imagined, rather,
that stories about it were just an idyllic fable from the Middle
Ages. But I was to experience it for myself—to rise up from the
deepest hell of the atheists and decadents and be born again
into this world of service."[6] The personalities of the monks

made a profound impression on the young guest of the monastery. The diary and the letters bear eloquent witness to his admiration for their education, human insight, and goodness. Much space is given to the description of his "confessor, teacher, and fatherly friend," Beda Hessen, Doctor of Theology: "His experience and knowledge of human souls are renowned. When I sit before him, I can feel how he reads my every thought before I give voice to it, and understands every agitation in my mind to the very core. I have never seen a finer looking old man; the sincere, childlike smile never leaves his face; nor does the majesty, or the gentleness. I believe there can be no philosopher, ancient or modern, whose work he does not know thoroughly." [7] Yes, this man has actually "grown far beyond the stage of what we normally mean by the word 'man' —he is the personification of some higher plane of reality." [8]

Laxness earnestly sought to dedicate himself to the religious routine of the monastery and to train himself in contemplation. The diary also speaks of a diligence in prayer, which included prayers of intercession for his friends. At times the prayers can approach the heights of ecstasy, as when on February 27 he questions his ability to offer the supreme sacrifice: "I then prayed to many saints. In particular I asked St. Francis to pray that it might be granted me to attain the highest degree of humility. Prayed that God would give me strength to suffer all for His cause—even martyrdom." He evidently had plans for devoting his life entirely to the Catholic Church. Six months after his baptism he makes the following statement in a letter: "My future is now decided: within two years I start my philosophical studies in Rome, to be followed by theology and then ordination. . . . As I say, all the vanity of this world, the thing which most people believe in, has lost all its merit in my eyes. I have been divested of pride and have opened my soul to God." [9] As if to confirm his decision to turn his back on the world, Laxness on October 4, 1923, received at his own request the scapular proper to a Benedictine *oblatus sæcularis*. This, as he explains in a contemporary letter, is "a kind of monastic rank, inasmuch as an *oblatus* is in duty bound to lead a Christian life in the spirit of St. Benedict." [10]

Now Laxness, of course, never became a Catholic theologian. On the contrary, in a few years' time he was to take his leave of

God and the Church in decisive terms. Nevertheless, there is no doubt that his contact with the monks and with the discipline of the monastery left its indelible mark on the young Icelander. The lack of compromise, the strength of will, and the concentration on the spiritual life presented themselves to his view as a fascinating ideal. This period also gave him a routine of work and a knowledge of matters that would be useful to him outside the monastery walls. The runaway schoolboy was able, for example, to add considerably to his knowledge of languages—Latin, French, and English, and to some extent Italian. He was well acquainted with German from his earlier travels in Germany; and in conversation with the monks he had the chance to practice his good working knowledge of French. His reading naturally consisted to a large extent of religious and morally instructive literature. Apart from the *De imitatione Christi*—which was of great importance for his "conversion" and which he still kept constantly at his side—may be mentioned the massive *Summa theologica* of St. Thomas Aquinas, Loyola's *Exercitia spiritualia*, François de Sales' *Introduction à la vie dévote,* Pascal's *Pensées,* and Cardinal Newman's *Apologia pro vita sua.* The works of fiction which occupied his time were chiefly those of such French Catholic writers as René Bazin, Henry Bordeaux, and Paul Bourget. Another important reading experience for Laxness was the famous *Storia di Cristo* by the Italian writer Giovanni Papini.

Yet even as a guest of the monastery, Laxness devoted his main powers to his own writing. The short stories in *Nokkrar sögur* (Some Stories), his next book to appear after the short first novel *Barn náttúrunnar,* had all been written before this time. The book first came out in 1923, but apart from the twelfth story, the final one in the collection, its entire contents had been written, and in some cases also published, several years before. The stories may be seen as literary exercises, in which we can certainly distinguish one or two themes of the kind that were to return with the fullfledged writer, but which show little of his craftsmanship in style.

In the monastery Laxness chiefly concentrated his energies on writing the novel *Undir Helgahnúk* (Under the Holy Mountain). This broadly conceived work falls almost entirely outside the line represented by the clearly autobiographical manuscript of *Rauða kverið*. As a novel it has a more conventional form, modeled chiefly, it would seem, on the works of the French moralizing traditionalists such as Bordeaux. The latter's *La Peur de vivre* is mentioned by Laxness again and again in the monastery diary with an enthusiasm that is striking; thus he notes on March 4: "I also wept aloud today when I read page 199 of *La Peur de vivre* where Madame Guibert asks Paule: He is dead?—I prayed to God to give me strength to be able to write something which would be capable of capturing my readers' hearts as this description had captured mine."

Undir Helgahnúk was published in fragmentary form in 1924, and a new edition, with a short postscript by the author, appeared in Reykjavík in 1967. It deals with the development of Atli Kjartansson through the years of his childhood. This boy has many of the author's own characteristics, if we may judge from the picture which Laxness has given us of his own childhood. We find the same precocious habit of reading widely, the overwhelming experience of the reality of death, the dreams of greatness, and the sense of a mystical ascension in the Icelandic countryside. The author links Atli's visionary experience of nature with the traditional Icelandic belief in the carefree elves, who live in the rocks and are for the most part invisible to human eyes. In a dream Atli finds his way to the castle of the elves and receives from their leader a "stone of power" in exchange for his own heart. This symbolizes the harshness and ambition in his nature, and also, perhaps, the loss of his childhood faith. When he wakes up from the dream he has a small, red, heart-shaped stone in his breast pocket. It becomes his most treasured possession, the seal on his conviction that "the world is placed in his hands like a handful of clay" (163). But a young girl, a fellow confirmand of Atli's, one evening engraves the word "Jesus" on his heart of stone with her necklace ornament, a silver cross, and the stone loses its evil power. The meaning behind this symbolism is expressed on the last page of the book in the lines of a well-known Icelandic ballad:

> With elves I do not choose to live;
> To Christ my faith I'd rather give.
>
> Of my poem's paths I form a cross.
> May Holy Mary be with us.

The appearance of *Undir Helgahnúk* meant no actual "break-through" for Laxness. But even in its fragmentary form the book is incomparably his most powerful work of fiction up to that time. The portrayal of the boy Atli Kjartansson is no mean feat of characterization. We already notice several essential features of the leading character in the coming novel, *Vefarinn mikli frá Kasmír*: the tension between intellectual coldness and lyrical ecstasy, between vehement self-assertion and a feeling of powerlessness. On the whole we find in Atli Kjartansson many of the contrasts and violent oscillations which we now regard as typical of Laxness as a mature writer—even though they as yet give no evidence of the original and designedly fickle verbal skill which we notice in his later works.

As might be expected, *Undir Helgahnúk* took a certain coloring from the spiritual environment of the place where it was written, and may be said to have a tendency to instruct its readers, albeit unobtrusively. Laxness presented himself as a Catholic apologist in his booklet *Kaþólsk viðhorf* (From a Catholic Point of View), issued in 1925. The polemical edge to his remarks in this work is primarily directed against a fellow author and friend, Þórbergur Þórðarson. For the latter had included a biting attack on the Catholic Church in his *Bréf til Láru* (Letter to Laura), of 1924—a work which, with its radical view of society and its author's bold self-portrait, became an important stimulus to many, and not least to Laxness himself. Superstition and general hostility to culture were the charges against the Church which Laxness chiefly strove to refute; and he sought, with a mustering of the names of Catholic scholars and learned institutions, to prove the role of the Catholic Church as a bearer of culture through the ages.

III *Steinn Elliði—the "Modern Man"*

But the great literary document of the Catholic episode in Laxness' development is the novel *Vefarinn mikli frá Kasmír*, which was mostly written in Taormina, Sicily, in the summer of 1925, and published in Reykjavík in 1927. This great work has absorbed elements both from the earlier manuscript of *Rauða kverið* and from another autobiographical work from 1924, *Heiman ek fór* (From Home I Went), which was also left unfinished. In the new book, however, these older components have been given a more effective shape and framework, and have been fitted into a far richer literary structure. It was with *Vefarinn mikli* that Laxness made his first real "breakthrough" as a writer. The work carries great weight not only as a personal testimony, but also as a documentary of the times and an artistic achievement. So far it has not been printed in any language other than Icelandic; but an English translation, made in America in the years 1928–29, may be found in the National Library of Iceland, Reykjavík.

Vefarinn mikli contains exactly one hundred numbered sections or chapters, divided into eight "books." The idea of dividing the work into a hundred sections is perhaps inspired by Dante's *Divina Commedia,* for Laxness has chosen some verses from *Paradiso XVII* as a motto for his work. In this canto Cacciaguida enlightens Dante on the subject of his future and his exile, etc., and finally exhorts him not to suppress the truth for fear of men, even if the mighty should feel themselves wounded thereby. With this motto for his work Laxness clearly wished, partly, to draw a parallel between Dante's wanderings and his own experience of postwar Europe, and partly to ward off criticism against what might seem arrogant and shocking in *Vefarinn mikli.*

The main character, Steinn Elliði, on whom the whole novel turns, belongs to the merchant aristocracy of Reykjavík. He is the only child of an ill-matched married couple—a consumptive, highstrung woman and one of the two brother directors of Ylfingur, the powerful shipping company. The rich and gifted boy is admired and spoiled by all, and not least by his mother, who in her unhappy marriage clings hysterically to her child. He is unbalanced, and vacillates between lovableness and brutality. He is capable of participating in wild debaucheries but at the same time plays the part, before his mother, of the exemplary and virtuous son. He shows at an early age considerable artistic talents, which find expression in feverish activity—in music and writing; for the most part, however, he does not have the patience for more than short endeavors in these spheres. A strong feeling of restlessness pervades his whole character, a violent feeling of protest against the family circle with its solid middle-class respectability and plodding business mentality.

As a young man Steinn roams about in postwar Europe, desperately searching for footholds in life. He wins a certain reputation as a poet in English. In the course of time he has grown to feel alien and misunderstood among his country-men, too big for the limiting conditions of his native land. Crushed and anguished, he at last finds a haven of refuge in a Central European monastery, and decides to give his life entirely to the service of the Catholic Church. Before doing so, however, he decides to spend a last summer in Iceland. There he meets again his former love, Diljá, who has now been married for some time to Steinn's uncle Örnólfur, the mainstay of the family firm. After the death of their little son she is completely disillusioned by her marriage. She is irresistibly drawn back to Steinn and gives herself to him or, more correctly, seduces him. The book then ends with Diljá visiting Steinn at the seminary in Rome where he is going to complete his education as a Catholic theologian. She has confessed her infidelity to her husband Örnólfur, and he, in desperation, has taken his own life. She now wishes to win back Steinn and recapture him from the arms of the Church. But he rejects her: "'Poor child!' he said, and his face was as though transfigured, so that she had never seen anything more beautiful in her life. 'Man is but a delusion. Go forth and seek God, your Creator, for all save Him is a delusion'" (499).

The actual outlines of the story, the framework of fiction in which it is set, are nonetheless of relatively minor importance. The essential feature of *Vefarinn mikli* is the witches' brew of ideas presented in a *furioso* of style. With his bitterly revealing analysis the author steers his ruthless course through current expressions and ideals. Diametrically opposed attitudes are confronted with each other, driven to their extreme limits, and rejected. As far as we can judge, Laxness sees this radical skepticism, this revaluation of all values, as one of the characteristics of the time. Steinn Elliði finds himself to be a completely new kind of human being, having nothing at all in common with earlier generations. The First World War marks a landslide in man's historical development. A rather long passage in one of Steinn's letters, which is character-istic of the elements of chaos and frenzy in the book, reflects his hectic groping after a fixed point—though here it is masked, rather, as a repudiation of all fixed points:

I embody the human type which has seen the light of day in the last ten or twelve years, and which has never existed before. More precisely: I am an Icelandic Western European steeped in the spirit of the times, which have sent world history to the gallows; my thought is as free as that of a person who has fallen down from the stars in August of the year 1914 and passed his life since then at the editorial offices of the World Press, in such news agencies as KIPA and Bonne Presse, or Havas, Reuter, and Stefani. A writer who has grown up out of a continuous tradition with its roots deep down in the culture of ancient Greece has no more in common with me than Neanderthal man, for instance, or a fossilized fern from the prehistory of the earth. My thoughts play over an area which lies between the most appalling kind of expressionism and the darkest kind of pitch-black surrealism, and will never be reconcilable with the unruffled, irreproachable and simple-minded qualities of noblemen in periwigs or women in crinolines, not to mention lap-dogs and chests-of-drawers in the rococo style. It would never occur to me to quote from a book written before 1914 . . . (456).

The chief preoccupation here is the profound change which man's living conditions, and hence man himself, have undergone in the melting-pot of contemporary events. Elsewhere Laxness gives a more detailed account of "modern man's" psychical *habitus,* his special way of thinking and feeling. We get a clear picture of what lies behind the characterization in *Vefarinn mikli* from his article "Úr circus menningarinnar" (From the Circus of Civilization) of December, 1924.[11] It consists of reflections made in connection with a work on Dostoevsky which was then recently published, and had been written by a Dane, Konrad Simonsen, whom Laxness had met when they were both guests at St. Maurice de Clervaux.[12] In Laxness' article Dostoevsky is praised as the unexampled describer of modern man in all his aspects and disguises, in his "glorious misery and miserable glory," his "merciless happiness," and "laughing pain." The paradoxical phrasing is characteristic, for Laxness seizes on this very complexity and dualism in the man of the new age, qualities which he says he has pondered over since he was a child. No

human type can make a more rewarding subject for a psychological novel—an idea which the young writer here develops
in florid style:

What problem is more interesting, what riddle more curious than
this chameleon, this glittering monster, this werewolf and phantom,
this heaven-endowed ogre who defiles the holy places without
meaning any harm, and does so with a smile and for the sake of his
pleasure; he performs heinous deeds before his altars, and bows the
knee to abomination, with devout rapture and humble piety; an angel
yesterday, carried away by that which the universe worships, with
flowers in the one hand and the other raised to the stars; a man today, amiable, vain and shabby; a beast tomorrow, with his belly
filled, and dominated by a foolish lust as black as night; and a devil
the day after tomorrow, dizzy with voluptuous plans, addicted to
poison, delighting in the wish to be able to seduce and violate,
singing of the black Venus, and drunk with the impulse to destroy.
      Modern man has a hundred and fifty conceptions of life, but none
of them are his own. His own conception of life is the only one he
does not have. He has not yet realized this, but the psychologist
knows that from man's angle of approach life is a swindle, work
vanity, the doctrine of the virtues some kind of mythology, God an
esthetic consideration, and truth chimney smoke. He fights for nobody; offers no sacrifices, has no interests save golden-winged may-
flies and is a loathsome coward.

Between the active life and the intellect of this modern
man a fateful gulf has arisen. "With everything he undertakes
his consciousness is split: the one half of it acts and plays;
the other looks on, investigates, plans and works out." It
is quite clear that when he wrote *Vefarinn mikli* Laxness
was fascinated by that aspect of the dividedness and contrasts
in the life of the human soul which he so eloquently develops
in his article. In a contemporary newspaper discussion on
the subject of *Vefarinn mikli* he expressly stated that his purpose
in writing the book had been to "describe the far-ranging
variety in the life of a soul," with the "swings of a pendulum
oscillating between *angel* and *devil.*"[13] He had indeed read
of this very antithesis in the *Storia di Cristo* of Giovanni
Papini, who in one chapter opposes the beast and the angel
in human nature, "natura bestiale" versus "l'angelica."[14] Among
the literary models which contributed to the portrayal of

Steinn Elliði should be mentioned Paul Bourget's novel *Le Disciple* which Laxness read during his time in the monastery. It is a typical expression of the view of modern, irreligious man as one dominated by a coldly experimenting intellect, and stripped of spontaneity and natural sympathy. In the article just mentioned an enthusiastic opinion of *Le Disciple* is expressed in passing: "It is the most terrible and devilish work of fiction that has so far been written about modern man, but at the same time the truest and most masterly." In his depiction of Steinn Elliði Laxness has actually utilized certain concrete experiences of Robert Greslou, the young man in Bourget's novel.

IV   *God versus Woman-world*

One of the many values and concepts which are subjected to ruthless analysis in *Vefarinn mikli* is creative writing itself. Steinn's artistic nature is described with the precision of hatred by his kinsman and rival Örnólfur. Ever since his earliest childhood Steinn has been "enshrouded in the terrible beauty of falsehood" (239). The poet is "a speaking robot, a remorseless babbler of lies; his soul is a deceitful monster. Men become poets only if they are ready to enter the service of deceit, everywhere, in everything, and for always. . . ." Thus the realistic man of action gives rein to his contempt for what he calls "idle chatter, conjuring tricks, and castles in the air" (241). But elsewhere in the book Steinn himself formulates his misgivings on the subject of poetry and the poet in still more violent terms. He denies that he or anyone else writes his masterpieces to the honor of God or in the service of humanity:

All fraud! Poets have never borne the people's burdens. They hate the people. They threaten the people. They are the people's harlots. They yell at the people. They spit on the people. They flatter the people, and lie. They dress in holy apparel before the people like magicians. They shout in the face of the people like a woman in labor. They swallow fire, do somersaults and turn themselves inside out before the people—all in the hope of being able to subdue the people, able to force themselves up into the high seats so that the queens may anoint their feet with balsam and dry them with their hair. Their aim, like that of the Roman emperors, is to get themselves counted among the gods while they yet live (158–59).

Here it is the element of exhibitionism, selfishness, and amoralism in the life and work of the artist which arouses disgust in the disillusioned young poet. But Steinn has yet another accusation to throw in the face of the poets, in that he gives a gross physiological interpretation of their whole endeavor: "They are all love-sick men; they never think a thought so high that it is not a dream of conquered women and quivering wombs. The artistic nature is nothing but an *obsession du sexe*. The sexual organs are overloaded. . . . 'The simplest art form is eroticism,' says André Breton. He who grasps that sees through the whole swindle. In the future the madness of artists will be cured by a simple operation" (159).

The artist is here described as being among other things a slave to woman. On the whole, Woman plays a remarkable role in the novel about the Great Weaver. The book contains a strong element of misogyny, with impulses drawn from many sources. For example, Laxness read during his first years abroad the great work of the eccentric cultural philosopher Otto Weininger—*Geschlecht und Charakter* (1903), which with frenzied consistency advances the theory that the essence of woman is neither more nor less than sex. August Strindberg's critical view of woman and marriage also made its contribution. The young Icelandic author is, moreover, unsparing with his references to these and other authorities. And much later, in an obituary notice in 1956, he mentions that his personal acquaintance with the German painter Richard Becker gave him an important incentive for the discussion of woman in *Vefarinn mikli*. They spent much time together in Taormina in the summer of 1925, when the novel was taking shape, and Laxness says that he was stimulated in many ways by his conversations with his older friend. "One of the characteristics of his personal philosophy which influenced me very much at the time was a certain misogynist attitude in his thinking; these trains of thought have also left their mark on several chapters of my 'Weaver from Kashmir.' " [15]

Woman, of course, has for centuries often been regarded, in the Christian world, as the embodiment of temptation and sin. It is natural that such notions as this should have become actualized and intensified both for Laxness himself and for his alter ego, Steinn Elliði, in view of their time spent in monasteries. In *Vefarinn mikli* God and woman are placed in direct contrast to each other. The struggle for Steinn's soul takes place between God on the one hand, and woman, who represents the world, on the other. Woman appears as God's only really dangerous competitor for man, the incarnation of everything that man must overcome in order to accomplish his mission in life. Steinn says that he early discovered that woman appealed only to the evil side of his nature: "Every thought of mine on the subject of woman is a fleck on my soul. For the angel in my nature, nothing which is called woman exists. The man in my nature recoils with a shudder before woman as before a disgusting beggar. The beast in my nature sees in her its most desirable partner. My satanic nature enjoys woman with jubilant pleasure" (171).

Steinn sees complete sexual temperance as the only way to overcome the curbing influence of woman and to achieve the perfection of his personality. This ideal of his partly involves a violent reaction against the *cupiditas carnis* (40) by which he feels himself plagued and humiliated. Partly, however, he also sees in chastity a lever for his dreams of greatness and his lust for power. About his own aspirations he says: "God Himself has said to me that if I am sufficiently pure I can initiate a new epoch in world literature, like Dante Alighieri" (53). It is characteristic that in just this connection he should praise the Catholic Church as one based on chastity. When Steinn is drawn to the discipline of the monastic life it is obviously not the least of his hopes to win what only "the chaste and no others" can acquire: "a strong will, unfailing power of action, crystal-clear intelligence, a loving heart, strange beauty, a magnetic personality" (52–53). It is not, perhaps, with Christian humility that one first associates such an ideal. There is an obvious element of the dream of the superman here.

But this, for Steinn, is a hard-won, almost convulsive attitude. There is in reality a marked ambivalence in his attitude towards woman, a strong tension between attraction and repulsion. At home in Iceland, on the night when Diljá steals into his bed, before he gives her up for ever, the mask before his face is rent asunder. In a state of emotion which

may be called love-hate, and which almost has a taint of
sadism, he speaks to Diljá: "I left Iceland last with the
purpose of tormenting you, and came to Iceland this summer
with the purpose of tormenting you, and when I go I shall
be going in order to torment you. For you are the only
thing I love. Man's love for woman is the only truth in
life. Everything in my life is a lie, Diljá; God and the Devil,
Heaven and Hell, everything but you is a lie" (447).

If we remember that in Steinn's eyes woman represents
man's earthly existence in general, this outburst of his provides
in a nutshell the problems with which the whole work deals,
as well as the key to Laxness' own continued development.
The struggle within Steinn between God and Woman-world,
conceived as two irreconcilable principles, is balanced so pre-
cariously, that in spite of an intense mustering of the will
God's victory is every moment threatened.

V   *The Literary Background to* Vefarinn mikli

In an interview in May, 1926, just before a public reading
from *Vefarinn mikli* which had not as yet been printed, Laxness
says that in his book he has taken up "most of the more
profound problems which could be thought to cause a young
man of our times to have sleepless nights." He also explains
that the Great Weaver's web is made "with modern man's
view of life as the warp and the only true faith as the
weft." Accordingly, he stresses the character of the work
as a debate on conceptions of life, as an attempt at orientation in a contemporary age of chaos. Another equally essential
aspect of *Vefarinn mikli* emerges, however, at the end of
the interview, where it is said that the author has "lived
abroad for a whole year in order to make himself familiar
with the latest news in what he calls the technique of the
novel." [16] In his retrospective survey of this work of his
youth in the postscript to its second edition, Laxness also
points out that in *Vefarinn mikli* he had wished to test his
capacity "in as many areas as possible of what is called
fiction," and that the book is consequently "an experiment
in many kinds of form." [17] In the course of the work on
his novel he was obviously at least as absorbed with purely
artistic problems as with psychology and philosophy. Thus

he writes in a letter in March, 1926: "The fact is that I have recently discovered that my philosophy is subordinate to my art of paradox, that is to say—my art. I do not speak the truth—except to God. On the other hand I write any kind of rubbish that looks good on paper." [18] Such a statement perhaps seems lightly cynical with its emphasis on "paradox" and "art" in opposition to "philosophy" and "truth." But we must take it for what it is: a brisk and incisive formulation of his thoughts, which is something of a paradox in itself.

Part of what lay behind Laxness' wish to make *Vefarinn mikli* "a fanfare for the new trend which characterizes our time in the art of style" was his very conscious opposition to the powerful native stylistic tradition.[19] The reputation and influence of the Icelandic sagas evidently seemed oppressive to the young writer, and he rebelled against them. An opinion dating from April, 1923, is characteristic of his attitude to classical Icelandic literature during the years when the material for *Vefarinn mikli* was maturing in his mind. He had had Snorri Sturluson's *Heimskringla* sent to him at St. Maurice de Clervaux by a friend—in order to keep alive his feeling for the Icelandic language in this foreign environment. When he had finished reading it he could not refrain, in a letter to his friend, from expressing his opinion "of Snorri and these old Icelandic books in general":

And all I can say is this: Heu mihi, I have nothing to learn from them! Those old Icelandic fogeys lay the greatest stress on the very thing that modern authors lay least stress on—namely, on the drawing of contours. They are entirely occupied in gathering together a few deadly boring facts, of no concern to anybody. Descriptions of what lie behind these phenomena are so uncommon in their works that they make the same impression on one, if one stumbles upon them, as an oasis does on a person traveling in a desert.

The language of this Snorri is very likely not so bad in its way, and is good Icelandic. . . . But as I say, it moves in territories quite different from those of our language, and the man Snorri thinks with a brain quite differently constructed from that of a modern man, and is interested in events and things quite different from those which excite our interest today (he is greatly interested, for example, in whether some king gives a man a cloak or a ring).

On the whole, I do not think it is possible to learn to write
Modern Icelandic from Old Icelandic; something else is needed.[20]

The more recent models and incentives which have contributed to the contemporary coloring and style of *Vefarinn mikli*
are of a very heterogeneous nature. The very welter of literary
names and quotations from more or less contemporary writers
underlines the international and modernistic character of the
work. Some of the material of which we catch glimpses
in the book, and which must, in its time, have been a
powerful reading experience, seems nowadays to be virtually
forgotten. Among the works which Steinn Elliði quotes—and
which Laxness read in the same year that it was published—is
G. Anquetil's *Satan conduit le Bal . . . Roman pamphletaire et
philosophique des mœurs du temps* (Paris, 1925).[21] This unique
work consists, essentially, of an enormous accumulation of
quotations from various sources, especially from contemporary
newspapers and works of fiction. Its purpose is to illustrate the
moral corruption of the period after the war. The author gives a
circumstantial account of the unbounded corruption of the times
in political and economic life. Appalling atrocities in the military
action taken against the native inhabitants of the colonies are
exemplified in detail. In particular, however, the perversities of
the life of pleasure and eroticism are used as evidence for the
"decadence"—one of the key words of the book—characteristic of
the time. The picture of general decadence includes tuberculosis,
which is now mentioned in the same breath as syphilis (253),
and now coupled together with cocainism (265)—not to
mention the unprecedented spread of homosexuality after the
war (255). The book is sustained by an apocalyptic tone;
it describes a world treading its *danse macabre* on the brink
of the bottomless pit.

The frenzy in Anquetil's grasp, and his ruthlessly concrete
documentation of contemporary moral decline, appear to have
fascinated Laxness, who borrowed from Anquetil a number
of effective qualities for his own description of the utter
collapse of all values after the First World War. The picture
given of the times in *Satan conduit le Bal* must also have
generally strengthened his own feeling of disorientation and
sense of approaching disaster. The very title of the work

is of course suggestive, and is well suited to a descriptive account of an epoch in which a radical surrender to God—as in the case of Steinn Elliði—seems to offer the only alternative to annihilation.

Among the more sophisticated stylistic models for *Vefarinn mikli* should first of all be mentioned the works of August Strindberg. In an article paying tribute to that writer on the centenary of his birth Laxness has made what he calls "A personal confession to Strindberg."[22] He says here that at the age of seventeen he had already read practically every one of Strindberg's collected works. What then appealed to him most strongly were not, however, his markedly imaginative works, but the "half essayistic, half autobiographical, only partially novelistic" works:

These books, which are always dissecting society, which are often strongly critical of society, and at times are religiously lyrical to the point of mania; which are packed with a masterly kind of personal encyclopedism and have their origin in this fascinating demonic frenzy, this indescribable blending of simultaneous bursts of energy and slackening of pace in movement, reminiscent of the walk of a restless tiger—these were the books which more than all others made me besotted and beset by Strindberg, so that for many years everything I put on paper became a reflection of him — though of course with the weakness of parody.

In this connection Laxness describes *Vefarinn mikli* as "a pure Strindbergiad." This, of course, is a spirited exaggeration, but it points in the right direction. It is in this work of his "breakthrough" that his knowledge of Strindberg's works has first borne real fruit in his own. It is true that the direct references to Strindberg are not particularly striking in *Vefarinn mikli*—a book which otherwise contains such a large number of literary allusions. Strindberg and Laxness have obvious points in common—above all, perhaps, their criticism of woman and of marriage. But these are of secondary importance beside a more general and at the same time more essential similarity—the tremendous appetite for the problems of life, the inexhaustible debate, in which the arguments pile up on each other or collide with each other in a never-ending stream, and the very intensity of the discussion, the fierce pulse of the style, the rich and often shocking choice of words.

A literary name which has already been mentioned in connection with Laxness' sojourn at St. Maurice de Clervaux is that of Giovanni Papini. As a guest of the monastery Laxness studied Papini's *Storia di Cristo*. But in *Vefarinn mikli* yet another work by this same author is drawn to our attention: *Un uomo finito,* which dates from 1912. In comparison with this book the *Storia di Cristo* is just "flower-adorned verbiage" and implies "a marked retrogression" (136), Steinn Elliði believes. *Un uomo finito* must have been something of a revelation to the young Laxness. In fact, this work shows more striking similarities to *Vefarinn mikli* than does any one particular work of Strindberg's. On the last page of his book Papini explains: "This is not my biography, but the exact course of what has happened in my inner life." Laxness himself might have said something like this, even though he has replaced his individual self with the fictional figure of Steinn Elliði and sought to give his narrative the more traditional form of a novel. Papini finally describes *Un uomo finito* as his own "wild effusion in fifty chapters"; these are divided up into six larger sections, each one under its own musical time symbol. Laxness surpasses him by writing his own effusion in exactly one hundred chapters, divided into eight "books." Both he and Papini have chosen a motto from Dante for their work.

What most strikes the reader of the well-known work in which Papini comes to terms with himself is perhaps the measurelessness of his ambitions, his fantastic desire for greatness. In order to be able to accomplish something new and epoch-making for humanity, he must purify himself to moral and intellectual perfection, and transform himself into a saint and a genius. Papini, as he presents himself in these wide-embracing aspirations, is a man after Steinn Elliði's own heart. In the latter we meet the same uncompromising demand for all or nothing, the same frenzied craving for perfection. Both of them are driven to extreme lengths and pursue all doctrines to their ultimate conclusions without receding in the face of the absurd. Highly characteristic of Papini is the violent tension between the opposite extremes in his own temperament. He is a visionary and a skeptic, a lyrist and a cynic. He oscillates between devotion and rebellion, between self-assertion and penitence, is pitched between the Caliban and the Ariel in his nature. In other words, he appears as a pronounced example of the "modern man," as Laxness conceives the latter in his article "Úr circus menningarinnar."

Papini also presents a stylistic ideal of his own in brutal contrast to the harmoniously classical style represented by Goethe. He declares invective and revilement to be his favorite forms of style. He wishes that his every word should be a whistling carbine bullet, his every phrase a stream of fire. It is not hard to understand how such a plan could have had a kindling effect on a young writer who was himself just about to strike a powerful literary blow. Laxness, as we have said, had early made acquaintance with Strindberg's work and had learned to admire him. In *Un uomo finito* he encountered a similar temperament. In the case of Papini, however, this temperament is driven to a violent culmination and discharges itself in a blazing rhetoric, by the side of which even Strindberg's fiercely argumentative prose perhaps seems muffled in tone. Laxness' encounter with the work of the Italian writer has, rather, reinforced the impulses from Strindberg. Both these forerunners of his have actively contributed towards liberating Laxness' own artistic resources, towards breaking down his inhibitions and spurring him on to an uncompromising self-revelation.

As a young writer conscious of the age in which he lived, Laxness naturally lost no time in making himself familiar with the most recent movements in literature. Among them was the one initiated by André Breton's first *Manifeste du surréalisme* (1924). Among the multitude of literary names in *Vefarinn mikli* we also meet, much as we should expect, such names as Massimo Bontempelli, André Breton, Max Jacob, and Philippe Soupault; James Joyce, on the other hand, whose work Laxness does not seem to have read until later, is a name which is as yet missing. Psychoanalysis and the work of Freud, which form the basis underlying the whole movement and are cited in several passages of Breton's manifesto, are also mentioned in *Vefarinn mikli*. In a letter from St. Maurice de Clervaux in December, 1925, when the author was at his busiest putting the

final touches to his novel, he said: "I wrote the whole manuscript with a monocle before my eye in order to experience how
a man with a monocle thinks. A man with a monocle thinks
quite differently from a man with spectacles or with unaided
eyes. The funn¹est thing of all, however, is yet to come,
for in the future one will go around with a telescope ¹ ₂fore
one eye and a microscope before the other." [23] This bizarre
experiment, made with the purpose of liberating his thinking
from its accustomed tracks, seems to have been inspired by
surrealism.

Otherwise, however, Laxness' well-documented interest in
surrealism hardly seems to have left any conspicuous traces
in the organic structure of *Vefarinn mikli*. Primarily relevant
in this connection are the three chapters (59, 60, and 61)
which complete the fifth "book" of the work and follow
on directly from Steinn Elliði's attempt at suicide in Taormina.
The episodes, confused as in a dream, and all seen through
the eyes of the main character, are clearly to be interpreted
as a result of his bewildered state. They at least present
themselves as a symbol of the collapse which involves a
decisive change in his life, for the chapter immediately following
begins with Steinn arriving at the monastery in a state of
mental and physical exhaustion. The surrealistic interlude is
entirely dominated by sexual motifs, and thus tells us something essential about Steinn Elliði—in the world of his personal
problems sexuality stands in the foreground.

There is but little question, in *Vefarinn mikli*, of any psychical
automatism according with the more strict theory of surrealism.
The episodes mentioned give an impression of relatively un-
restrained and dreamlike associativeness. On the other hand,
these episodes have been inserted, with artistic calculation,
at an important juncture in the novel's sequence of events.
To that extent the writer has them under complete control
and makes rational use of them. A much later opinion of
Laxness' may be quoted as characteristic of the way he
estimates the artistic possibilities of surrealism in general.
Looking back on his encounter with the new trend as a
young man, he calls surrealism in its purest form "a kind
of *spiritus concentratus.*" It is "dangerous to take undiluted,"
but nonetheless has "become so integral a part of modern

literature, and such a vital condition for it, that it may be maintained that the writers and poets of our generation who did not learn all that could be learned from it when it began, are dead men." [24]

Laxness has himself employed surrealism in *Vefarinn mikli* as—to use his own ingenious image—a kind of *spiritus concentratus*, suitably diluted. This, moreover, is characteristic of his way of assimilating literary impressions generally. Artistically speaking, he has never committed himself to any fixed doctrine or technique. The impulses from without have purposefully been subordinated to the demands of the creative and formative impulse within himself.

When discussing a work like *Vefarinn mikli*, we naturally look first for points of connection in literary history outside Iceland. Laxness himself was very conscious of the fact that his work implied a sharp break with the native Icelandic tradition. On the other hand, it is quite clear that not even an iconoclast like this young Icelander could disclaim all interest in his literary inheritance. We could also point to new elements, portents, and incentives in contemporary Icelandic literature which were not without significance for Laxness. But whether the writer's compatriots saw in *Vefarinn mikli* a disturbing or encouraging occurrence, they were fairly unanimous in regarding this novel as epoch-making. Naturally enough, the work met with the greatest understanding and enthusiasm among Laxness' contemporaries in age. They saw in Laxness the first "postwar writer," and in Steinn Elliði the first "postwar man" ever to be presented to Icelandic readers.

CHAPTER 3

Visit to America. Social Radicalism

I   *From Iceland to the United States*

VEFARINN MIKLI FRÁ KASMÍR brought with it no resolu-
tion of life's problems—or not, at least, for its author. In a
letter written just before he began his work on the book
he had said that he wished to write a "Catholic novel." [1]
The actual outcome of the novel's events might indeed lead
us to believe that this end had been achieved, for the writer's
alter ego finally turns his back on the World and on Woman,
in order to dedicate himself to the service of God. But
this was no unraveling of the Gordian knot, it was a desperate
severance of it. The loud-voiced argumentation can by no
means smother the doubt. Many of the arguments in the
book show a rebellious and even blasphemous spirit and
seriously threaten the Christian view of life, to which Steinn
Elliði clings. The reader fancies that all the time he is
treading on volcanic ground where a slight earthquake is
all that is needed for the ground beneath his feet to collapse.
In this intellectual atmosphere the paradoxes flourish; and
we have the feeling that the one extreme can pass over
into the other at any moment.

When Laxness completed his manuscript of *Vefarinn mikli*
in the late summer of 1925 in Taormina he had already
grown away from his intense religious involvement and had
begun to direct his interests into another channel. [2] The final
and complete account of his new ideals was not to be given
for several years to come; but in any case he had had,
both before and during his time in the monastery, an inter-
mittent sympathy with socialism and a corresponding antipathy
for capitalism and middle-class self-sufficiency. For the time

52

being he sought to reconcile a radical view of society with Christianity as he interpreted it. When *Vefarinn mikli* was published in the spring of 1927 he wrote a series of articles under the prosaic title of *Raflýsing sveitanna* (The Electrification of Rural Areas).[3] There he describes, among other things, the living conditions of the Icelandic country people, in the following manner: "Oh, what measureless suffering! What measureless misfortune! So heavy a cross has been laid on the shoulders of some. But should not God comfort those who suffer from affliction, whom no human hand can cure, no human love retrieve? He who has once had his eyes opened to the extent of the irremediable misery in the world can never get rid of the thought that one ought to heal these wounds, or all of them which it lies in the power of man to heal."

But this confession, with its tender pathos, suddenly gives way to an outburst in quite another key: "Those who seek to prevent as many as possible from becoming as well off as possible ought to be shot. That fact is clear and requires no philosophy." The Christian gospel of love is here given an extremely concrete and topical application:

The best kind of Christianity in our days involves making the slave dissatisfied with his lot, and should teach him to make demands, to stir up revolution, and become a human being. . . . The best kind of Christianity which can be preached in Iceland just now should involve clearing the people away from Hornstrendur, out of the remote country districts and moorland hovels in Eastern and Northern Iceland, and bringing them into the most habitable parts of the country—cultivating the soil, laying railways, building schools and churches. . . . True Christian man! You must fight against lice, drunkenness and poverty, you must bring electricity to the farmhouses and teach people to dance and sing. What is more beautiful than Christ and his church? Nothing; that is true. But *primum vivere, deinde philosophare*, if I may show off my Latin like an old priest. . . . It is Christ's wish that people should live in comfort and happiness. He Himself will comfort those who suffer from unhealable wounds. He wishes that people should live in spacious and pleasant dwellings and that their children should be well brought up, good-natured and civil. He does not want them to go astray in snowstorms or to go down with motorboats. He wishes that they should live under good conditions and be able to afford a culture of their own.

At one point in his series of articles Laxness maintains that "a Christian way of living is a revolt against society." Society, as we see it around us, is incompatible with the principles of Christianity. For the thinking man there are only two ways open: either to flee this imperfect world and go into a monastery, or to stand his ground among his fellow mortals and rebel against prevailing conditions. As we know, the former course had once exercised a strong attraction on the writer. But now he has settled for the latter alternative, and laid radical emphasis upon it. He lashes out against the tendency of many to be content to let religion replace social improvements and become an opium of the masses. The attitude he advocates, for all the arrogance with which it is expressed, can be said to have support in the Gospels—in the parable of the Good Samaritan, for example. But his way of driving his arguments to their extreme limits is of course capable of leading him into a paradoxical situation as a Christian—a situation fraught with explosive material of a revolutionary nature.

Laxness' new interests found a kind of outward confirmation in that shortly after *Vefarinn mikli* was published he left Iceland and Europe for America, where he was to stay for about two and a half years—from the summer of 1927 to the end of 1929. It was of course no accident that he should particularly choose America. To Laxness, who once and for all had turned his course outwards, dedicating himself to the world and its people, the United States appeared as the land of great possibilities, or at least as a tempting subject for study. Modern techniques and civilization had in several respects advanced further there than anywhere else. Not the least of his reasons for being attracted to America was its status as the Mecca of cinematic art; for the young Icelander had earlier toyed with the idea of writing for the cinema himself.

After staying with compatriots for one or two months in Manitoba, Canada, where a large number of Icelanders have settled, Laxness traveled to California—mainly to San Francisco and Los Angeles; he later lived in Southern California and remained there for two years. This new period of intellectual inquiry gave him important acquaintances and experiences. He became personally acquainted with an older and well-known fellow writer, Upton Sinclair, and was influenced by his strongly critical novels about various aspects of American social life. But otherwise it was chiefly his own direct confrontation with the class antagonisms in America, with the miserable conditions facing the crowds of unemployed, which caused him to develop there on radical and socialist lines. In this vast country he also grew to an especially intense awareness of himself as an Icelander, and came to see Iceland, its people and native cultural tradition, in a new perspective. And besides, he had plenty to keep him occupied. He gave lectures on Iceland in clubs and societies of various kinds, which helped him to earn his living. He made a serious study of the film business in Hollywood itself, and wrote several scripts for the cinema. Although these were never produced as films, preparations for production seem in one case to have advanced quite far. He also had *Vefarinn mikli* translated into English, though the translation was not published. A number of poems and short stories written during these years were later published in *Kvæðakver* (Poems, 1930) and *Fótatak manna* (Steps of Men, 1933), respectively. Finally, the first drafts of what gradually developed into the great novels *Salka Valka* (1931–32) and *Sjálfstætt fólk* (Independent People, 1934–35) also saw the light of day in America. As far as fiction was concerned, this, for Laxness, was primarily a time of ripening maturity and accumulation, rather than of completed results.

II *The Book of the People*

A work of another kind stands out as the central literary document from this period of the author's life—the collection of essays entitled *Alþýðubókin* (The Book of the People, 1929). *Vefarinn mikli,* the novel of ideas, may be regarded as a summing up of his youth, with the sojourn in the monastery as its crucial experience, while *Alþýðubókin* collects and resolves the experiences of his years in America. Laxness has himself hinted, moreover, that he regarded the two books as each other's counterparts and polar opposites. The new work appears as an important milestone, especially in the light of his later development: for during the thirties and the forties, his most productive period, he adopts in all essentials the same theoretical attitude, and embraces the same view of life that he recorded in *Alþýðubókin.*

This collection of essays covers a wide range of subjects taken from both material and spiritual culture: Icelandic agriculture and hygiene; marriage, sexual morality, and the causes of crime; nationality, art, the cinema, religion, etc. What binds these diverse elements together into a whole is the fundamental socialist attitude which permeates them all in greater or lesser degree. *Alþýðubókin* may be regarded as the author's confession of loyalty to socialism—though it is socialism of a kind more fresh and enthusiastic than dogmatic. The book is a concentration of thoughts and feelings rather than a systematically constructed view of society. In the preface to the second edition, written in Reykjavík in 1945, Laxness points out that he "did not become a socialist in America from studying manuals of socialism but from watching the starving unemployed in the parks."[4] It is clear from contemporary evidence that this was no later fabrication of the author's own, for in a letter from San Francisco in April, 1928, he had written as follows: "I know that it will take me a long time to recover from having been in a position to witness how people here are trampled underfoot. There are only two alternatives to choose between here: being a reformer or a humbug. In the midst of these horrors I have learned to think as a man."[5]

The United States of the imminent depression gave Laxness a frightening object lesson in the seamy side of industrial capitalism. San Francisco's "one thousand destitute unemployed to every millionaire" (247) must have reminded him of the unfathomable gulf between rich and poor which he had already experienced at the age of nineteen in postwar Germany and described in the manuscript of *Rauða kverið.* But there is a considerable difference between his reactions to these two situations. In *Rauða kverið* grim reality is depicted in a lofty prophetic tone which has borrowed its coloring from the Bible, and the experience only contributes towards deepening still further the young writer's resignation and disgust with the world. In *Alþýðubókin* the description is direct, ruthless, and aggressive—a call to arms. Even so, this does not prevent Laxness—in spite of his attacks on the church—

from continuing to use a religious mode of expression when he lashes out against "the capitalist robbers" (247). But God and the richly overflowing world He has created for the equal profit and pleasure of all people—and not just for a privileged few—here serve to sanction the author's own indignation, and to invest his passion for social justice with a metaphysically religious motivation and sublimity.

III   *The Religious Element in* Alþýðubókin

Alþýðubókin also has some interesting things to say on the subject of Laxness' attitude to religion and Christianity. As late as the spring of 1927, he was able to explain in a controversial newspaper article on the subject of *Vefarinn mikli,* that "Among the many conceptions of life which are put forward in my book, I personally favor one alone, namely the Catholic." [6] Nevertheless, he must at that time have reached a stage far removed from the Catholic persuasion and view of life. He defends himself, with increasing determination, against the tendency of his readers to judge *Vefarinn mikli* as a purely personal testimony. He does not wish to be held responsible for any one of the many conflicting opinions which are brought forward in the novel. He wishes it to be considered as an independent and inconclusive discussion of problems, a large, single experiment with points of view. As far as we can judge, it was already becoming an embarrassment to Laxness to be known essentially as a Catholic apologist and devotee of the cloister among his countrymen; his public image no longer corresponded to his real self. Thus he seems to have felt, all the more strongly, the need to explain his position in religious matters, and the wish to free himself from his past in order to establish a more honest relationship both with himself and his public.

In *Alþýðubókin* Laxness now applies markedly relativistic points of view to religion. He writes that God is "in perpetual motion" (356) and also mentions "the three hundred and thirty-three images of Christ which have been held in readiness for the past two thousand years both in the East and above all in the West." The name of Christ has been allowed to serve as a symbol for all the illusions which the ruling classes of the Western world have needed to plant in the minds of the masses in order to subdue them. But it has

also appeared written on the flag of war "whenever the
minorities and the downtrodden believed themselves able to
muster the clans to arms." As a current example Laxness
chooses the Sacco and Vanzetti case. The two Italian an-
archists clearly had Christ as their original ideal and fought
for the coming of the only true Kingdom of Christ on earth.
Yet they were condemned to death by "the highly Christian
law courts in Massachusetts, which is acknowledged to be
one of the most Christian states in the world, Puritanism's
principal home on earth" (359–61).

The figure of Christ still has the author's sympathy, but
significantly enough he now interprets it in a context of
class antagonism: "As we know, Jesus Christ was a poor
country dweller and a fisherman on the side, who read few
books but got many ideas from simple people, and from
communing with his own soul on mountain walks; who discussed his ideas with many young men and girls of the
lower classes. But the people of fashion slew him, because
they believed him to be against their conservative class, and
the story is not a pretty one" (27). That Jesus was killed
"is in reality no more remarkable than that Sacco and Vanzetti were killed—the two cases are analogous" (358).

The section entitled "Trú" (Faith), and together with it
the whole of Alþýðubókin, concludes after a violent attack
on capitalistic culture—its resplendent glitter is compared to
"the splendor of syphilitic sores, which are more dazzling
in color than any purple" (367)—with an ecstatic confession of faith in the idea of man as the guiding star in
the struggle for the socialist society of the future:

Man is the gospel of the new culture, man as the most perfect
biological species, man as social unity, man as a life symbol and an
idea, the only true man—You. Therefore you shall not give credence
to what is said in Christian books, that when the weak man is
trodden down, then your brothers are being wronged. No, it is far
more serious than that: where the proletarian's children are sucked
to the marrow so as to benefit the bloodhounds of capitalism—in that
situation you yourself are being trampled down into the mire—you,
the only man, the highest manifestation of life, You . . . (368).

This is in striking contrast to the message of *Vefarinn mikli,* to the Christian view of life, in which God is seen as the highest idea. Laxness himself was undoubtedly conscious of the contrast and did his best to give it an effective form. The metaphysically religious aspect of man's existence seems no longer to interest him. This, however, in no way means that he denies it, only that he resolutely leaves the question open. Earlier he had wished to efface his own individual self before the face of God. Now he wishes, ecstatically, to enter the fellowship of men. It is true that the message of *Alþýðubókin* is expressed in terms of rationalism, in the manner of a socialist program and polemical work. The author reveals himself here as an educator of the people on a socialist basis. He talks about the people's daily needs, about housing, clothes, and hygiene—including toothbrushes and lavatories. He wishes to make the ordinary people of Iceland, the farmer and the fisherman, participants in the material standards which he came to know in America. Nevertheless, the mystical strain in his nature remains unchanged. He now dismisses as a fruitless game with words all discussion of what lies beyond our faculty of knowledge, all disputes about the ultimate causes of existence. "Yet—if faith were to show itself to be a subjective and relative gift, and not an objective and infallible truth, then I beg leave to recommend myself as one of the most fervent of the faithful." When the writer listens to Bach's Mass in B Minor, he feels himself convinced that "our worship of the inexpressible" possesses no higher language than that of music (366). And when as a young shepherd boy he once "saw for the first time the eastern mountains when looking down from Blásteinsbringur," this became for him a kind of "initiation": "I do not know for certain what happened, but I came home a much nobler and more sublime being, and now had higher thoughts about the world than before." At times, when he gazes at Icelandic mountains in the spring, especially after a long period of absence in foreign cities, he can feel "as though I were now standing before my soul's uttermost revelation." This is a matter apart. "But in the world of reality, in the dwellings of men, lies our

field of activity; and this we must forget least of all, however lyrically enthusiastic we may be when we look at the
mountains" (133).

The tension between these two poles, the contrast between
man as a social being and as an individual *sub specie aeter-
nitatis,* and the rapid alternations of rationalism and mysticism,
of the cold and the hot, and of irony and pathos, were
later to characterize Laxness' art as a novelist to an unusual
degree.

IV *Jónas Hallgrímsson and the Icelandic Soul*

In a letter to his fiancée Laxness wrote from San Francisco
in March, 1928: "I feel that if I do not start to 'pull
myself together' from now on I shall be just a rootless
piece of wreckage for the rest of my life. It is insane
to tear oneself away from the culture of one's own country
and people and to roam about among foreigners for years
on end. In that way one will not be of full value anywhere—will be neither whole nor half, and will nowhere
accomplish anything positive. . . . Nothing has taught me
better to appreciate Iceland—the land and the people—than
my stay in the million-peopled cities of the United States
and my experience of the spirit prevailing there. . . . I
have lived through a number of instructive adventures here,
which have taught me to judge of my own worth in relation to my nationality. I am an Icelander, the complete
Icelander—that is what I have managed to learn in the
course of the past months." [7]

Laxness has here indicated what is perhaps the most important insight that his years in America gave him. Beside
the fundamental idea of socialism, the strong sense of Icelandic individuality is also the sustaining element in *Alþýðubókin.* The two elements are entwined together in characteristic fashion and in their very union give the work its individual character. Most beautiful of all perhaps is his interpretation of the destiny shared by individual and nation in
his essay on the naturalist and poet Jónas Hallgrímsson
(1807–45). Although his literary output is small, the work
of Jónas Hallgrímsson contains some of the pearls of Icelandic poetry—nature poems and lyrics, written in the first

person, and characterized by a wonderful clarity, sincerity and simplicity, as natural as the drawing of breath.

For Laxness, Jónas Hallgrímsson had early stood out as an incarnation of what is most profoundly and mysteriously Icelandic. The tradition of the saga literature, with its harsh objectivity and cold impersonality, found in Jónas Hallgrímsson its lyrical complement. In his poetry the Icelandic landscape laid aside its guise of ruggedness and coldness and came to meet man with warmth and trembling life. Laxness sees the life and work of this poet as "an uninterrupted song about Icelandic destiny": "In him are refracted all the rays of our being. When I say, then, that he is our best poet, I mean that he is our most Icelandic poet." Every "unadulterated Icelandic soul" is a fragment of Jónas Hallgrímsson—but for this very reason it is extremely difficult to give an idea of his individuality to people of another nation, particularly as "the style expressing the life of the Icelandic soul" is very much "of an origin different from that of general European culture." The words in his poems might perhaps be rendered, to some extent, in another language, "but the unmistakably Icelandic flavor, the secret of our very nationality, cannot be explained to foreign people; the glimmering fire of its origin cannot be analyzed" (79–81).

Laxness' interpretation of the concept of nationality—and particularly Icelandic nationality—is based on intense personal experience. But we also find certain general traces, in *Alþýðubókin* as a whole, of the influence of Oswald Spengler, who is curiously enough by far the most frequently quoted authority in Laxness' socialist "manifesto." At one point he describes Spengler's "theory of historical patterns" as "perhaps an even newer and better" key to historical reality than Marx's economic interpretation of history (146). What fascinated the young Laxness in *Der Untergang des Abendlandes*—and he says that he began to read the great work "with genuine zeal" in the years 1927–28—was clearly the encyclopedic learning together with the bold analogies and the powerful cultural syntheses, which are presented in an evocative and rhetorical style.[8] For Spengler regards cultures as organisms, which are permanently linked to the same place of growth, and in which the stages of budding, flowering, and withering follow each other in a relentless rhythm. Our own Western culture, the "Faustian" culture, has now reached its final stage; its creative period is past, in art as in other spheres.

Laxness appears to have been attracted by this pessimistic vision of Spengler's. But paradoxically enough, it only serves to form the background, in Laxness' case, for an enraptured faith in the future of Iceland. He points out that from the cultural point of view the passage of time in Iceland differs strongly from the way time has passed in the rest of Europe. And just now he thinks he can perceive, throughout the whole nation, a seething life which bears witness to unexpended powers, to a rising culture. His conviction is expressed lyrically, in the manner of a prophecy:

The decline of the West does not concern Iceland. The nation with the oldest highly developed language in Europe, and the oldest continuous history, is now awakening as the youngest civilized nation in our part of the world. . . . The people slept among the mountains which teemed with elves and supernatural beings, and in this virgin landscape, where every valley is a memory from our history, every desolate scene a symbol of our most secret perceptions— there we rise up today as newborn people, gifted with the pristine freshness of the child of nature, with the language of the gods on our lips and the morning sky above us blazing with prophecies and signs (69–70).

It is interesting to note that the passionate fervor which Laxness exhibits—not only as a writer on society but also as a national writer—so often finds expression in a manner reminiscent of religious linguistic usage. We have our Old Testament in the Icelandic sagas and our Song of Songs in the Edda, he maintains (37). He compares Jónas Hallgrímsson with St. Francis and finally asks whether the former should not be counted among the number of the saints (97–98). For the poet's countrymen, who may be called the initiated, the reading of his work thus becomes something of a national cult, a non-Christian sacrament. We even get the impression that there is more religious feeling in *Alþýðubókin*, Laxness' socialist "manifesto," than in *Vefarinn mikli*, the "Catholic" novel. One of the reasons for this, perhaps, is that the new book is sustained by a jubilant sense of deliverance and certainty of belief, while the great weaver's desperate struggle to conquer faith led primarily to the tightening of his problem in a Gordian knot.

V   *The Socialist as Literary Critic*

Laxness' ideological reorientation also involved a reconsideration of his view of literature and its purpose. The first chapter of *Alþýðubókin* is entitled "Bækur" (Books), but begins, curiously enough, with a warning *against* books. For the truth lies "not in books, not even in good books, but in people of good heart"; "I have made the acquaintance of many people who have attached great importance to book learning, and they have most often been rather inhuman in their way of thinking and somewhat inwardly conceited, but poor in the culture of the heart which my grandmother possessed and which expressed itself in playful good humor, in sturdy perseverance, in an unwillingness to interfere with the religious beliefs of others, in equanimity in distress, in courtesy towards the needy, in consideration for travelers, in a dislike of fooling, and in kindness to animals" (9).

Laxness gives a controversial review of contemporary literature and casts his critical eye in two directions: mainly at the fashionably superficial and artistically worthless novels which are currently turned out, but in some measure also at novels of a more unconventional and exclusive nature. In both cases he finds that the authors have little or no fruitful contact with ordinary people and their problems. The lack of such contact has wreaked its vengeance on the very gift of storytelling. He declares that most bourgeois novelists, especially in America and England, are totally devoid of the ability to tell a story, since they are dominated by "the vanity of capitalism," by the habit of "cringing before those who wish to choke man's aspiration towards development" and by "a cynical attitude towards the defenseless class of people who bring forth the good things of the earth for the benefit of thieves and murderers" (13).

We have earlier caught a hint of Laxness' view that the best storytellers are to be found not among professional writers

but among the ordinary people. This thought is perhaps especially likely to suggest itself in Iceland, where poetry and
the art of narrative seem to have had a deeper anchorage
among the people than almost anywhere else. But neither,
according to Laxness, is art as such, nor the specifically
literary element in literature, really relevant here. Everything depends on the author's cast of mind, on his wish
to share with others some remarkable experience, some burning
conviction. "What was said in ancient times holds good
today: Though I speak with the tongues of men and of
angels, and have not charity, I am become as sounding
brass or a tinkling cymbal" (16). Laxness again resorts
to biblical images, as he often does when discussing matters
of such deep concern to him. He himself had complained,
in a very full letter written at the end of his stay in America,
that he had lost his literary gift, though he consoled himself
with the fact that he had what was more important—"a
view of life."[9] By "literary gift" he surely meant just that
element of pure fiction or professional artistry which in *Alþýðubókin* he disparagingly contrasts with the all-important view
of life.

The view of life, then, which Laxness for his own part
had chosen, was socialism—the spirit of which he associated
less with theories and rigorous systems than with his old
grandmother and her simple humanity, and with his own
"childlike sense of justice" (179). This partly meant that
he was resolutely committing himself to the cause of the
anonymous multitude—to the cause of poor, unschooled, and
simple people. These were the kind of people he wished
to reach with his new message: "I have been talking to
poor country women as they went about their work, crofters
who have a small vegetable plot, young men who earn their
living on trawlers, day laborers who never get onto the parish
council and penniless girls working on the fish—humble and
simple people like myself." More than from "famous books"
and "so-called far-famed geniuses" has he learned from people
"who live in little houses and have suffered tribulations of
many kinds on land and sea in order to get themselves
some rye bread and a potful of fish" (42-43).

It is of course quite natural that a socialist "manifesto" like *Alþýðubókin* should dissociate itself not only from everything that carries a hint of Art for Art's sake, but also from exclusively esthetic points of view in general. If you have something on your mind which you want to communicate to the public, you should acquire "the knowledge necessary for saying the thing plainly instead of wrapping it in some disguise" (13), Laxness writes in the essay on books. When he says that Knut Hamsun practices "the writing of novels as a profession" (14), nothing favorable is meant by this remark. Inherent in all art is "insincerity, pretence, and falsehood"—especially when it is at its best! Not even when Laxness is discussing the poetry of the revered Jónas Hallgrímsson, does he forget to remind his readers that "all form contains in itself a certain element of pretence" (90)— which reveals how strongly conscious he was of this dilemma. His criticism of the element of illusion and pretence in art does not lose its sting in being directed in the highest degree against himself. The situation is not, of course, unique to Laxness. After all, such a conflict may easily become acute in every writer with serious aims; a Swedish example is August Strindberg during his "utilitarian" period in the eighties. Laxness himself had already experienced it. When he now treats rhetoric and the brilliant style disparagingly in *Alþýðubókin,* his criticism may be said to strike indirectly at, for example, *Vefarinn mikli.* The adoption of this self-critical attitude implies a kind of asceticism and training in humility on the part of a young writer who undoubtedly possessed unusual gifts of artistic expression, together with a fair amount of authorial arrogance.

In studying Laxness' years in America we catch several glimpses of his resolve to return before long to Iceland, "to shelve all this stuff about novels" and throw himself into "the struggle for the people's welfare," as he expresses himself in a letter written in April, 1928.[10] This corresponds entirely with the strong distaste he showed for his novel writing during his time in the monastery, although the direct opposite of this activity was then, in his view, a life dedicated to God and the Catholic Church.[11] We should not, perhaps, take his word too literally in either of the two

cases. He hardly did so himself; and indeed, his artistic
impulse must have been far too irresistible, his faith in his
future as a writer far too strong, for him to do so. But
the conflict, though latent, is there, and constitutes one of
the artistically enriching tensions in his nature.

When a writer's work is to a large extent characterized
by a definite view of life or of society, this view is usually
regarded as more or less primary: his work becomes the
medium in which the author gives shape to his conviction.
This is to look at the matter rather too schematically. The
opposite may also be true: a writer may find his way to
a certain view because it is well suited to serve as a catalyst
for his profoundest qualities and aims as an artist. If we
keep this latter point of view in prominence, it may perhaps help us to deal more easily with the problem of *Tendenz-
literatur*, of literature written "with a purpose." It will then
become clearer that the purpose in itself does not need to
work against art. The two elements can, in fact, support
each other; and the creative power of the imagination can
force them to work together in a higher harmony.

We are left with the strong impression that artistic resources were released within Laxness by the ideological decision he made after the completion of *Vefarinn mikli*. Like
Steinn Elliði he had searched for God with an egocentric
and fanatical desire for perfection. This had led him into
a "blind alley" as a writer. It is as if his resolve to concentrate on the world and ordinary people had supplied him
with unsuspected powers as an objective literary creator. In
his great novels of the thirties, which deal in turn with
the fisher girl Salka Valka, with the small farmer Bjartur
í Sumarhúsum, and with Ólafur Kárason, the parish pauper
and folk poet, he develops a masterly strength as an epic
writer. This is the more striking in that *Vefarinn mikli*, the
novel of his "breakthrough," hardly points forward to a literary
output of just that kind. The novel is a hectic discussion
of ideas from beginning to end, and although it is certainly a remarkable work in its way, the delineation of its
characters is somewhat neglected, and the epic pattern blurred.
The new dynamic quality in Laxness' art is undoubtedly
linked with the fact that after his cosmopolitan years of

wandering, his period of restless searching, he found his proper role as a portrayer of the Icelandic people. The certainty of this must have filled him with exultation and strength. And in the socialist view of society, in the socialist dream of a new state for the people, he found nourishment for his own visions. It became the myth which gave wings to his imaginative work, and which gave it passionate vehemence, dramatic intensity, and a sweeping perspective.

CHAPTER 4

Salka Valka

I Return to Iceland

LAXNESS' first literary work after his return to Iceland from America was a book of poems, *Kvæðakver* (Poems, 1930), his only collection of poems to date.[1] Their style is highly experimental. In the foreword the poet refers to his poems as being among other things "efforts in the technique of the lyric, researches into the elasticity of the lyrical style." Traces of surrealistic influence show themselves in the fitful flow of the associations, in the occasionally bizarre imagery. The break with traditional Icelandic poetry, with its form and choice of subjects, is as sharp as it could possibly be. These poems must in their way have seemed as shocking as *Vefarinn mikli frá Kasmír*—even though they were certainly not taken as seriously, either by the author or his readers. Yet the little volume of poems gives interesting insights into Laxness' personal development. He reveals a profound satisfaction with having now left bewilderment and division behind him, with having refound his native country. "Henceforth my past is reduced to ashes and my future is the song of the northern hemisphere. . . . My smile is as sweet as *brennivín* [aquavit] in a bottle. I drink a toast of friendship with thee, my beloved people." In using the singular form, "thee," the poet lays aside formalities in addressing his nation, his countrymen. It signifies that he feels at home among them and is making their cause his own.

The particular poem which perhaps tells us most about Laxness' view of Iceland and its people at the actual time of his return from America is the final one in the collec-

tion; it is moreover the only one which was written as
late as 1930: "Alþingiskantata. Til saungs eftir 1930" (The
alþingi Cantata. To be sung after 1930). In that year, from
June 26—28, the thousand-year anniversary of the Icelandic
alþingi was celebrated at Þingvellir in the presence of the
King and Queen. The poets of Iceland tuned their harps
in preparation for competing together in the composition
of a festival cantata. Laxness' own "cantata" comes as a shower of
cold water over all their swelling national rhetoric. With
a strain of harshness he exchanges the symbols inherited
from literary tradition for the economic realities of the day.
He taunts the poets with the fact that nowhere in their
songs do they mention agriculture and dairies, or the stalwart
toilers of the sea who haul in from its depths a "thousand
million cod." This latter phrase is clearly a direct allusion
to the considerable talk, then current, of Iceland's thousand
years. "But few or none may speak the name of man,"
exclaims Laxness resentfully. The reality of Iceland's contemporary situation is wrapped in a mist of lofty phrases
by poets and by speakers on festive occasions. Beyond all
the oratory at Þingvellir, where "potentates on speaking plat-
forms" pay tribute to the glorious history of the nation,
he evokes instead the picture of a "penniless people, which
for a thousand years has chewed its bread, weeping the
pauper's tears of hunger, bleeding, torn and tormented by
the black art of the exploiter."

In itself this picture could easily correspond to the traditional Icelandic view of the nation's history. For an Icelander,
the memory of the economic exploitation of times gone by
is closely associated with the trade monopoly of the Danish
crown. But in Laxness' choice of words we find something
quite new: class antagonism, viewed in the spirit of Marxism,
has entered his field of vision. He is thinking of his own
times rather than of the past. The ordinary people's conditions are regulated in our society by the same laws now,
under home government, as had applied before, under foreign
rule. In Laxness' next novel, Salka Valka, Arnaldur, the socialist,
is made to express himself with more direct relevance to
the situation; as far as we can judge he reproduces the
author's own opinion: "But what was it that happened in

1874, when our finances were separated from those of Denmark? All that really happened was this: the exploitation of the people was brought into our own country. The robbers simply changed their nationality" (II, 257).

II *The World of Óseyri*

The novel *Salka Valka,* named after its main character, did not receive this title until the second edition of the work appeared in 1951. It was originally published in two parts under the titles *Þú vínviður hreini* (O Thou Pure Vine, 1931) and *Fuglinn í fjörunni* (The Bird on the Beach, 1932). The story may be outlined as follows. On her way southwards to Reykjavík on board the mail boat, Sigurlína Jónsdóttir, the unmarried mother of the little girl Salvör Valgerður (known as Salka Valka), gets left behind with her at the fishing village of Óseyri við Axlarfjörð (Óseyri on the Axlarfjord), since they cannot afford to continue their journey. This is a chance incident, a freak of fate, as everything in her life seems to be. As soon as she arrives in Óseyri, Sigurlína lands up with the local Salvation Army. The hymns about the Pure Vine and the Glory of the Lord sound from then on as a jarring accompaniment to her life, which reveals itself as an uninterrupted testimony to human helplessness. She falls into the hands of Steinþór Steinsson, a wild and brutish fisherman and sailor, who is an amoral personification of the magnificently rugged landscape itself.

Steinþór takes Sigurlína and Salka Valka home to stay with him at his aunt's cottage. In reality it is not Sigurlína but her young daughter whom he desires, with the ruthlessness of an elemental force. He makes an attempt at raping the girl, who desperately defends herself and calls out to people in the neighborhood. Steinþór escapes in the confusion and lives for a time abroad. When he reappears in Óseyri he has given up drinking and seeks to reestablish his earlier relations with Sigurlína and Salka Valka. Sigurlína bears witness, before the Salvation Army, to his improved ways, and a "hallelujah wedding"—her forthcoming marriage to Steinþór— is announced. But on the actual day of the wedding Steinþór has disappeared; once again he has fled the country. On the evening of the same day Sigurlína does not return from

milking the cow, and the next morning—on Easter Sunday,
the day of the Resurrection—her swollen corpse is found
on the shore, with wet sand in its mouth.

Thus the first part of the work ends. The author himself
has stated that its events are supposed to take place in
the years 1910–14, in the period just before the First World
War. When the second part begins a good ten years have
passed, and we are now in the middle of the twenties. The
life of Salka Valka, living on her own as an orphan in Óseyri,
now reveals itself as a struggle both for and against that
which her mother had represented. The girl defends herself
against the fate of falling a victim, like her mother, to carnal
desire. She hates Steinþór, not only because of her personal
experiences of him, but equally because she sees in him
the seducer and destroyer of her mother. When she is
the only one of the village girls to dress in trousers like
a man, her doing so is an act of self-assertion and a declaration of her own freedom. But perhaps it is also due to
a fear of her own sex and of the dangers it may involve.
Salka Valka can be said to be fighting for her mother's cause
when she instinctively takes the part of all oppressed beings,
and more and more consciously strives towards a clear understanding of her own life and the lives of her equals in
society. In the incipient social struggle in Óseyri she joins
the opponents of the merchant's power.

Up to now the merchant Jóhann Bogesen has served
as Óseyri's Divine Providence in human form. It is he who
buys up the fish and through him people are given work
in preparing it for sale. The payment is made in the form
of credit given at his own shop, where in exchange for
deductions made on their wages accounts people can provide
themselves with the bare necessities of life. But this society,
run on patriarchal lines, is invaded by the thoughts of a
new age; people no longer regard the merchant's power as
a kind of natural law which cannot possibly be changed.
Unions aimed against Bogesen are formed. First comes the
fishermen's trade union, which breaks his monopoly on the
fish and gives the small traders a chance to compete. The
result of this, however, is that the real proletarians—those
who have no share in a boat and live solely by their work

in preparing the fish—have to pay with reduced wages and still worse living conditions for Bogesen's diminished profits. The answer to this, in turn, is a fish workers' trade union: and the first strike in Óseyri begins.

Salka Valka plays an active part in this development. She does so at the side of her childhood friend Arnaldur Björnsson, who has now become a socialist agitator and organizer. They have a love affair, and in the light summer evenings indulge in daydreams of a socialist state of the future which will give all people a share of the earth's treasures and the riches that life has to offer. But when Bogesen has gone bankrupt and absconded to Denmark, Steinþór Steinsson remains instead as the victor in Óseyri, as the figurehead of the village: "I am the saltfish and the place itself. There is no power in existence over me" (II, 345). There has been no social revolution to speak of. Arnaldur has to leave Óseyri with his task unaccomplished. At the same time he leaves Salka Valka; their short love story is at an end. It is then autumn. The lively tern has made its departure and so has the "hot-spirited, downy" eider duck; all that remain are the "birds of winter," the "indifferent, broadwinged seagulls" (II, 362).

III *Steinþór Steinsson*

In *Vefarinn mikli frá Kasmír* the world-roving Steinn Elliði had once confessed his homesickness for Iceland in the following words: "And July wraps my mountains in majesty and peace, wraps them in sunshine haze and in dream, and the evenings begin to grow dark, and the cry of swans is heard by the lakes of the highland moors, and up from the hot springs of my country rise white mists which steal to and fro through the valleys of my land. . . . What chastity! What divine majesty! It is my innermost desire to be able to walk here again, to be able to hover like a strange bird over Icelandic mountains on the silent nights of high summer after I am dead . . ." (200-201).

It is an egocentric dream, a longing for the Icelandic countryside—the countryside unsullied by the dirt and struggle of human life. In *Salka Valka,* on the other hand, the writer has placed himself in the midst of a God-forsaken Icelandic

fishing village where the people are engaged in a daily struggle
for existence in a barren and seldom attractive natural setting.
At Óseyri "there never seemed to be any fine weather, for
the Creator was continually experimenting with His heaven."
Altogether it seemed as if His favorite weather in this place
was "the rain, together with every kind of stench it brought
with it, the smells of sea and seaweed, of fish, fish heads,
fish guts and train oil, of tar, dung, and offal" (I, 86–87).
The entire life of the people is inextricably bound up with
the fjord itself, with its wind and continual rain, with its
smell of sea and fish, of fish offal and oil. It consists "entirely in fish and of fish, and the people are some sort
of variant which the Lord makes out of fish, adding, perhaps, a few bad potatoes and a tiny portion of oatmeal;
on the whole it can be said that everything is of fish, the
illegitimate children too" (I, 160).

What is stressed above all in the author's comments is
nature's indifference to the fate of these people. "No one
understands the heart, least of all the bleak mountains which
rule like heathen gods over this narrow strip of shore by
the ice-cold sea-green fjord and are enveloped in mists or
whirling storms. The sullen sea winds blow into the fishermen's wretched cottages in the middle of the night and do not
care in the least if frail breasts are perhaps sleeping there."
In the darkness of the night Salka Valka hears her sick little
brother's "piercing cries, full of wordless despair and pain,
blending with the roar of the sea, the whining of the storm
and her own feeling of helpless littleness." And the writer
observes: "What infinite burdens God lays upon this fish,
to which he has deigned to grant human life on the salt
sea shore beneath the stony faces of the mountains!" (I, 175–
76).

Steinþór Steinsson has been made to embody the village
of Óseyri in a manner almost overemphatic. He is a brutal
figure who is nonetheless able to suffuse his existence with
a certain kind of primitive poetry. When he first meets Sigurlína,
he greets her with the following tirade: "I am the sea which
breaks against this coast, I am the wind which plays around
these peaks, I am the ebb and the flow which rule upon
this shore—come into my strong and faithless arms, my

beloved, and I shall fulfill all your hopes and drown all
your sorrows" (I, 19–20). And indeed, it is in this very
light that Sigurlína sees the man as together with her little
Salka she trudges after him on her way to the humble
cottage, where her destiny will gradually complete its course:
"And as the woman noticed the uncurbed, ruthless strength
in his walk and movements, there came a moment when
she perceived, as in a kind of mirage, how closely the stature
of the man was akin to that of the country, how completely the beat of the country's pulse accorded with the
man's, and the customs of the country with the customs of the
man, so that she was no longer able to distinguish the
one from the other; instead, heaven, earth, and sea, along
with the man Steinþór Steinsson, ran together into a single,
consummate, and menacing unity" (I, 69).

All ethical standards and all sense of social responsibility
are totally foreign to Steinþór. His only guiding principle
is his own ego, with its greedy appetite for life. Of course
he cares nothing for religious sentiments and ideas; he cares
just as little for Sigurlína's Salvationist raptures as for the
Rural Dean's more worldly admonitions. The Dean's gentle
reminder that every honest person must assume responsibility
for his own deeds before God and men, is parried by Steinþór
with the following words: "You know with whom you have
to deal, you old priest. I was born here in Óseyri, on
this coast, in just the same way as the roar in the sea
wind. Will you perhaps ask the sea wind to assume responsibility for you? What am I? A wind that comes. A wind that
goes. The breath in my nostrils is the breath which blows
across this coast. The same is true of the blood in my
veins: a wave that rises, a wave that falls" (I, 271).

Eyjólfur, the blind old man who functions as a kind of
philosophizer in Þú vínviður hreini, at one point says: "But
I'll tell you one thing, Steinþór, you who possess most of
the necessary and unnecessary qualities that can be contained
in the breast of a tiny human creature living by the sea,
that there will never be any order in this town, until you
and people like you have become people with a sense of
responsibility towards themselves and the community in which
they live" (I, 261). It often seems as if the writer himself

has imagined Steinþór as an incarnation of the soul of the fishing village: a raw, amoral life force, which must be tamed and must submit to the laws of social coexistence, before one can speak of humanity. Hence a kind of grandeur and rugged lyricism plays around this otherwise repellent figure. Steinþór is given, at times, some measure of the dimensions of saga or myth. He himself is said to visualize his existence "in primitive, almost mythological symbols" (I, 131).

At the same time, however, the author may rather abruptly deprive the reader of this illusion about Steinþór and give a quite sober account of the man's character and behavior. His incessant talk of owning Óseyri in heart, blood, and lungs, and his stories of his remarkable exploits as a sailor abroad are then exposed as "drunken talk" and bragging. What most emerges in his fantasies, when they are critically judged, is "the delusion of grandeur characteristic of the wanderer, who exaggerates his nationality abroad, and his experience and worldly wisdom when he has come home." Among people of other nations on foreign seas he has been, as an Icelander, too alone to be able to adapt himself to different customs and ways of thinking; the isolation has brought about "a kind of fermentation in his primitive nature" (I, 130–31).

The portrait of Steinþór thus illustrates the writer's twofold vision; it shows a combination of attraction and repulsion, of empathy and cold observation. It may thus seem difficult, both for writer and reader, to retain a harmonious impression of a character such as Steinþór. His unbridled personality extends across violent contrasts; he combines "the child and the ruffian in a manner almost touching; he is as arrogant in crime as in virtue" (II, 341). He is at once a realistically drawn character and something of a symbol. It rather seems as if Steinþór, with his primitive nature, were displayed to greater advantage in the first part of the work where the role of fate is more marked, and where nature and the lives of the people are presented in simpler and grander outlines. He hardly shines to the same extent as the calculating climber and successful fish merchant in the second part of the book. The new and more complicated period with which it deals does not provide the same reverberation for his flamboyant self-assertion.

IV *Sigurlína Jónsdóttir*

Laxness generally works with strong contrasts; and in this respect his characterization is no exception. Steinþór has a female counterpart and polar opposite in Sigurlína. The primitive streak in both of them is strongly emphasized. But while the man may be said to embody brutal strength and activity, the woman's nature may be marked down as harmlessly submissive and passive. While Steinþór shapes his life according to his own primitive nature, Sigurlína is carried unresistingly along by the wayward vicissitudes of fortune. In *Þú vínviður hreini* Sigurlína is to some extent the main character. We follow her through the course of several years, from her arrival in Óseyri to her suicide by drowning one Easter. Her way runs through "Love" towards "Death," as the two parts of the work are entitled. Her story, a pathetic and harrowing one, is unfolded in a unified and well-planned sequence of events.

The people of Óseyri do not welcome too warmly strangers who they fear may become a burden on the community. And Sigurlína represents with her whole being the outcasts of the world, the stepchildren of life. "Never has so unimportant a woman stepped ashore at so unimportant a village" (I, 13–14). Everything that could possibly go wrong for her seems to do so; and at times the author's comments underline this fact as though in passing. When mother and daughter first set foot in Óseyri on a winter evening, we read that "The snow was driving straight at their faces, as it always does with such people" (I, 14).

On that very same evening Sigurlína finds herself at a meeting of the Salvation Army. In her helplessness and forlornness she falls an easy prey to the tide of suggestion which surges forth from the Salvationists' vivid testimonies and, above all, from their sweetly compelling hymns and music. The Salvation Army appears as an oasis amid hard reality. But for this poor woman religion turns out to be little more than an anesthetic—a means of warding off the overwhelming demands of life. When Steinþór has fled at the last moment from their solemnly announced "hallelujah

wedding," Sigurlína's Salvationist sisters come to comfort and
edify her with the hymn about God's overflowing love:

> The Lord's rich love for high and low.
> It surges forth, it surges on.
> That stream will never cease to flow;
> It surges forth, it surges on.

But this exultant song no longer finds any response in
Sigurlína. The stunning and final blow has made her quite
apathetic. The reader sees the hymn about God's endlessly
flowing love as bitterly ironic. He also, perhaps, associates
its ecstatically compelling flow with the relentless consistency
of Sigurlína's destiny. By a strange and dreamlike transference
of ideas—which as an intentionally artistic stroke surely betrays the influence of psychoanalysis and surrealism—the words
of the hymn about streaming love are associated with the
incessant Easter rain. "What enormous quantities of water
there are in the sky:

> That wondrous wave which never fails,
> It surges forth, it surges on" (I, 298).

The gush of religious emotion is harshly confronted with
brutal reality. The impression left is a complex one: comedy
stiffens in a desperate grimace. Thus Laxness has used the
Salvationist hymn to crystallize the emotional possibilities of
the situation. Its banal rhythms have a powerful effect of
pathos as an accompaniment to the final act in Sigurlína's
drama.

Characteristic of what is vague and confused in this woman's
nature is the fact that she cannot properly distinguish between
her impression of Steinþór and her new religious experience.
When she first encounters the fiery glow in his eyes she
fancies that she has gazed into them before; they are linked
with "some forgotten secret" in her past: "they reminded
her of an outbreak of fire by which she had been fascinated
as a child just when she was learning about the agony
and death of Jesus; that fire had perhaps smoldered in
the hidden corners of her mind ever since" (I, 65). On

a later occasion, when going to bed, she makes a long, impassioned prayer to the Lord, "in which Jesus Christ, Steinþór Steinsson, and the Holy Spirit were muddled together in a supernatural manner" (I, 153). The fire in the earlier example was probably conceived by the author as a sexual symbol; for the burning flame also has that function in one of Salka Valka's dreams of anguish (I, 178–79).

The juxtaposition of Steinþór and the suffering Christ indicates the strain of masochism in Sigurlína: she seems to submit to her brutal lover's contempt and ill treatment with a pain that is filled with pleasure. The blending of religious and erotic associations also characterizes another image in the night-time scene just mentioned: Sigurlína turns down her lamp but leaves a small flame burning in it "like the wise virgin, who awaits her bridegroom." The effect of this biblical comparison is bitterly ironic—not only because Steinþór is as unlike Jesus as he could possibly be, but also because Sigurlína herself is anything but a prudent virgin.

The whole of Sigurlína's life and character is markedly lacking in foresight, purposefulness, and responsibility. When Salka Valka, with "the mercilessness and unforgivingness of youth" calls her mother to account because she "must always be kissing and fondling every fellow" who looks at her, Sigurlína replies by making a virtue of her own weakness. God rules over her life and heart: "He has created me with a woman's nature and I can do nothing about it. When I have a child I do so against my own reasoning and my own will; I simply bow down to the will of God and have my child without grumbling" (I, 213–14). Sigurlína's situation is made the more unbearable by the fact that she must live to discover that it is not herself but Salka Valka whom Steinþór desires. It is chiefly, perhaps, her awareness of this which finally and hopelessly entangles the threads in the web of her life, and drives her to death.

The futility of such a life as Sigurlína's is strikingly summed up in Salka Valka's conversation with the Rural Dean on the day that her mother's corpse has been found. "For form's sake," says the clergyman, a funeral address should be given, if only for "two to three crowns" (I, 309). Sigurlína Jónsdóttir was born according to the church registers, and died according to the death certificate. But what more can be said about her? The daughter recalls that the dead woman was very fond of a hymn, and quotes "O Thou Pure Vine" to the Rural Dean. But this, it appears, is one of those Salvation Army hymns which consist, "to say the least of it," of "blasphemy and empty drivel" (I, 311); it is therefore best to keep quiet about such hymns where Christianity is concerned. All that is finally left for the record is Sigurlína Jónsdóttir: born, died.

Least of all, however, do we find any cynicism in the author's description of Sigurlína, or any malicious delight in the misery of life. For all her helplessness and humiliation this woman also has human dignity, as is movingly shown by her feelings for little Sigurlinni, the fruit of her relationship with Steinþór. She has watched over the sick child until death delivered him from his torments, and "Such holy and melancholy expanses had opened in her soul on the nights when she watched the involuntary tremors in this innocent body which God had called forth from her sin and given a suffering which reminded one of His only begotten son "(I, 222). Her love for the little boy finds pathetic expression, too, in the final picture we are given of Sigurlína. Lying dead on the seashore, she is holding in one hand a well-made pair of little boy's shoes—"she had taken them with her out into eternity in case she should meet her son there wearing no shoes" (I, 304).

For the writer, the figure of the drowned woman represents a single question, without speech and without hope. One of her eyes was "watery blue and stared uncomprehendingly straight up to heaven as if its questioning gaze had frozen for ever in the hallelujah of the Easter night"; it "looked towards heaven, asking, asking, without sleep and without redemption—just open" (I, 304–305). The question which the author reads in this unmoving eye—the question of human suffering on earth—is placed before us again and again, directly or indirectly. The same suffering, in one of its apparently inexhaustible variations, is manifested in the portrayal of Salka Valka's woman friend Sveinbjörg, who dies after severe and long-lasting torments, leaving a delicate husband who cannot provide for the children. She is no irrational

being like the infant Sigurlinni; nor is her character vague
and loose like Sigurlína's. She thinks her situation over, she
passionately seeks the truth—this woman "on her cheap deathbed, where her children had been conceived and born" (II,
29). She tells Salka Valka that the Rural Dean had exhorted
her to remember Gethsemane. "What is hanging on a cross
for twenty-four hours to a man who has no child?" Sveinbjörg had rejoined, "and knowing, moreover, that one is dying
for a good cause, yes, even saving the whole world and
then going straight into the finest place in the kingdom of
heaven." She herself will shortly be dead after years of pain
and suffering: "and I am dying for nothing at all, and
there is no kingdom of heaven prepared for me, for I know
that the children will continue to cry after I am dead and
learn bad words and beg for milk which is not there" (II,
30–31).

In the presence of Sveinbjörg's suffering Salka Valka often
broods on "why God and people have so much against
the individual" (II, 170). And when she enters the house,
where her friend has just breathed her last and where the
grandmother is rocking a baby, the author cannot suppress
the following comment: "In this house and at this moment
life and death met in all their solemn shabbiness, in their
all-devouring, all-embracing scorn; houses as interesting as
this can be found even in a little village" (II, 171–72).
Such reflections serve to underline the wider implication of
the human destinies with which the book deals. It is as
if these pictures of destitution and suffering were expanding
into a general pessimistic view of the world. We have the
strong impression that the author sees Sigurlína or Sveinbjörg
not just as particular cases, but that in them he has also
wished to give a concentrated picture of every human being's
situation—so helpless is Sigurlína, in the final analysis, and
so exposed to the cruel play of unassailable and incomprehensible powers. The statement "It is so hard to be a human
being" (I, 80) is quite consistent with her life and character.

In a letter from St. Maurice de Clervaux, written in February,
1926, while he was working on *Vefarinn mikli frá Kasmír*,
Laxness said that basically he was nothing but "a colossal
juggler who knows only one thing, and operates on the

basis of the single certainty that *l'homme est un grand rien.*" [2]
A few years later—in *Alþýðubókin*—he was to take the
opposite view, and pay tribute to man in terms of almost
infinite admiration as "the highest manifestation of life." There
seems to be—and probably is—a great gulf fixed between
these two declarations, for in the course of the years which
separate them the author had subjected his standpoint to
thorough reconsideration. Yet we should be careful not to
interpret the pessimistic strain in *Salka Valka* as a kind of
relapse into earlier points of view. What he is talking about
in *Alþýðubókin* is not the individual but "man as the most
perfect biological species, man as social unity, man as a
life symbol and an idea." In *Alþýðubókin* he embraces this
idea with studied optimism and faith in the future, and
we may venture to maintain, in spite of everything, that
he also does so in *Salka Valka*. The resigned and bitter comments we have quoted from the novel refer, on the other
hand, to man as a private being—to the individual in the
metaphysical sense. This twofold vision, which is typical of
Laxness, shows itself as clearly as we could wish within
the novel itself, and especially in Salka Valka's conversations
with Arnaldur.

V   Salka Valka and Arnaldur

Salka Valka is of course the dominating figure of the book,
and perhaps the most living portrait of a woman that Laxness
has ever created. The portrait stands out in sharp relief,
and is seen most fully in her relations with the three other
main characters—her mother, Steinþór, and Arnaldur.

When they arrive in Óseyri, Sigurlína is faint and ashen-
gray with seasickness, while little Salka's body is seething
with the "unruly energy of life" (I, 10). This is symptomatic
of the contrast between mother and daughter. Sigurlína is
weakness, helplessness, and submissiveness personified; Salka
embodies the opposite qualities. As a poor, illegitimate child in
strange surroundings she has to undergo a harsh term of trial
and early acquires a bitter kind of worldly wisdom. Her mother
allows herself to be borne away on the rhythms of the Salvationist hymns, for as long as they can sustain her. Her daughter
looks reality straight in the face; at the age of thirteen she says

to a woman neighbor: "Mother also believes that there is a God
who creates us, just as it says in the Bible. That may have been
so in earlier times and in some country quite different from this
one. But that has nothing to do with me. I am just an ordinary
illegitimate child born in Northern Iceland" (I, 184).

Salka Valka's relationship with her mother is given a special
element of tragedy, in that through no fault of her own
she becomes in Sigurlína's eyes a favored rival for Steinþór's
attentions. The girl has certainly not tried to encourage him—
whatever her jealous mother may believe, or pretend to believe. Nevertheless, Salka Valka can hardly be said to have
an entirely easy conscience in this respect. For in spite of
her fear and disgust Steinþór exercises upon her a mysterious
power of attraction. Her nature, with its profound affinity
to the surrounding landscape, is akin to his. At one point
we read that in the "strong and primitive features of her
face" are "all the qualities of the saltness which is and
remains in the sea as long as it beats against the coast,"
and that in her eyes and mouth are "all the paganism and
simplicity imaginable in a country which originally was intended for gray-spotted seals and the indifferent, broad-winged
seagulls" (II, 280). Alone with Steinþór, in the presence
of "the fever-heated rhythm of his speech and the thrilling
passion in his breath," she can feel "as if the surf itself
had forced its way into their salt veins" (I, 286–87).

If Steinþór represents primitive nature, and the life force
which in itself is amoral, Arnaldur represents culture, and
the struggle fought in the service of an ideal. Characteristically
enough, it is Arnaldur who teaches Salka Valka to read when
she is a little girl, just as he later imparts to her his views
on society. On one occasion she tells him what he has
meant to her and to the whole of the little village: "Before
you came, Arnaldur, I was asleep, like literally everything
in this place. Then you came and woke me up. But since
the time that I awoke to you, I have been just a part
of you and nothing in myself" (II, 331).

On the other hand, Salka Valka with her manifestly earth-
bound existence is the sure foundation, the one absolute
foothold in life for Arnaldur, the uneasy dreamer. When
they meet as grownup people, he says that he has admired

her since they were small children. "There was no face in the world that could be compared with hers for sincerity of expression. All duplicity was foreign, and probably incomprehensible, to it" (II, 260). Arnaldur himself exemplifies modern man's rootlessness, division, and uneasiness, and his tendency—or compulsion—to see things from several different points of view at the same time. He appears in much the same light as the modern man described by Laxness in *Vefarinn mikli frá Kasmír* and in articles dealing with that novel's world of ideas. "I am like the pros and cons of the world. But you, Salka Valka, you *are*" (II, 149), says Arnaldur, thus pertinently summing up the difference between himself and her.

We may, if we so wish, see the reunion of Arnaldur and Salka Valka as symbolizing the new relationship between the writer himself and his native country. Like Arnaldur, he returned from abroad, full of "the pros and cons of the world." In *Alþýðubókin* the young author had come forward as the educator of his people, as the prophet of modern civilization in all its aspects. Arnaldur teaching Salka Valka to brush her teeth and not to stick the table knife in her mouth is very much in the spirit of *Alþýðubókin*. But his influence on her way of living and thinking is not limited to trivial details of this kind. When Arnaldur returns to Óseyri as a grown man, he comes, like Laxness in *Alþýðubókin*, bearing the message of socialism; he has the exultation and the passionate zeal of the social reformer. And Salka Valka joins his side. Arnaldur's dream of a new world can, just as much as Steinþór's animal nature, exercise a strange fascination upon her.

Yet Salka Valka, with her warmly spontaneous reactions to the hardships of those around her, can grow skeptical of the abstract element in Arnaldur's idealism; she often sees this idealism as something coldly foreign to the immediate needs of the individual. After the death of her friend, Salka Valka takes Sveinbjörg's four children into her home, and Arnaldur asks her why she bothers herself with them. Salka answers shyly that she can almost see herself mirrored in these motherless children. But Arnaldur does not accept that form of human love: "It is nothing but bourgeois sentimentality

and hypocrisy to help individual people. As Upton Sinclair
says, it is like sprinkling a few drops of water into Hell.
All that really matters is entirety, the people as a unity,
the idea of society. And nothing can save this entirety but
a revolution against the yoke of capitalism" (II, 192). In
an interview given shortly after the publication of *Fuglinn
í fjörunni* Laxness denied the value of all kinds of charity
and reform work, save the kind which involves a radical
reshaping of society[3]; and Arnaldur's talk of entirety is virtually
a quotation from the final passage in *Alþýðubókin*: "man as
social unity, man as a life symbol and an idea, the only true man."

Salka Valka is even tempted to pit Steinþór against Arnaldur's
reasoning, which sometimes seems inhumanly theoretical:
"Steinþór is worth much more than you. He is a human
being, like me, wherever he may roam and travel. You
are just a theory, and a false theory at that. Is it possible
that you could ever have human feelings for any individual
soul?" Heaven preserve him from that, replies Arnaldur:
"I am inseparably bound to the multitude, I am like the
bird . . ." (II, 194), he explains. A little later, however,
he admits that it is "difficult to be a human being—most
difficult of all, though, to break oneself of the habit of
thinking and feeling as an individual . . ." (II, 198). It
is clear, too, that socialism for Arnaldur is a hard-won and
firmly held conviction. In any case it cannot be described
as a simple or easily acquired collectivism. Paradoxically enough
it is Arnaldur, the consistent and militant socialist, who gives
clearest expression to the idea of human solitude in *Salka
Valka*. There are just a few moments, he believes, which
decide man's fate as an individual: conception, birth, and
death. On none of these decisive points can his lot be altered
by any power, "neither God nor the multitude, not even
a trade union, not even the revolution": "When all is said
and done, man is alone, absolutely alone, and he feels it,
when his dying hour approaches, when he knows that he
must die his death—alone" (II, 322–23).

Arnaldur's social Utopianism may be seen as a passionate
attempt to conquer man's incurable sense of solitude, and
to blunt the sharpness of death. In a corresponding manner
the hero of *Vefarinn mikli frá Kasmír*, Steinn Elliði—a young

man who has certain similarities to Arnaldur Björnsson—had desperately sought a supra-individual sense of communion in Catholic theology. We notice in both cases the radicalism of the solution chosen. Both Steinn Elliði's attitude and Arnaldur's are marked by fanaticism and lack of compromise because both men know that they are fighting for their lives. Their different ideals represent, for them, the only means of deliverance from desperation and from disgust with the world.

However, the problem of solitude is not confined to Arnaldur's comments in his conversations with Salka Valka. The girl is herself desperately conscious of what it means to be an individual, a particular person. As a little girl she wakes up in her bed at night to find that her mother is no longer by her side; Sigurlína has gone to Steinþór, has "stolen away from her in the darkness of the night, in order to live her own life" (I, 84). In her relationship with her mother Salka Valka has to learn that "two souls can be so distant from each other even though they have once lived in the same body": "When all is said and done, it seems as if every human being has his own aim in life and that all human love is nothing but nursery tales" (I, 297).

The short love story of Salka Valka and Arnaldur also unfolds itself in a context of solitude; their affair is not first and foremost political, even though it is so called. The girl feels uncertain of Arnaldur's love and asks him if he can ever speak the truth about his feelings. He replies with an argument in which we recognize the author's own views on the love between man and woman, expressed in *Alþýðubókin*. "The mutability of life is the truth. Man *is* that moment in which he lives and changes." Arnaldur knows only what is true just now: he loves Salka Valka "at this moment"; he can say no more (II, 321–23).

The love between them becomes pathetic and tragic, because in reality it is only a transitory meeting between two solitary lives. "Their love had been like a trail in the dew of spring" (II, 355). At their final farewell on board the coastal steamer Salka discerns in Arnaldur's face the helpless pain—"the same that had once dwelt in the face of her little brother, who died—the pain of life": "Perhaps they had never loved each other more than at this moment. One moment" (II, 361).

Here we have only been able to give some of the more important aspects of Salka Valka's personality and destiny in life. The limitations necessary in a study such as this should not be allowed to conceal the fact that the portrayal of her character is richly abundant in small touches of detail. The author has depicted with great subtlety her change in puberty from a cheeky young lass into a young woman. Her love affair with Arnaldur does not, in spite of everything, only involve the ideals of socialism and the idea of human solitude. The episode also gives many amusing, touching, or poignant examples of Salka Valka's female intuition, jealousy, tenderness, and self-sacrificial spirit. In her own way she seems as complex to Arnaldur as he does to her. On one occasion, when she opposes him at a political meeting, she is described as follows: "She looked very dreamy but nevertheless seemed quite at one with reality: there was also something in her manner which suggested looseness, and yet one felt that a woman more chaste, or more unacquainted with all that is called coquetry, could hardly be imagined" (II, 125). But if the ambivalence in Arnaldur's nature has a dialectic-intellectual strain, it seems in Salka Valka to be irrational and charmingly unconscious.

In *Vefarinn mikli frá Kasmír* woman had for the most part been negatively judged as a serious obstacle on man's road towards perfection. Now, in the figure of Salka Valka, woman is positively valued as an incarnation of uncorrupted life itself. We might perhaps believe that in *Salka Valka* we are faced with a literary "worship of life," or a cult of what is femininely instinctive and vegetative in life. Yet if there really is such an element here, then its character can hardly be described as sensuous—and this is in harmony with the rugged coastal landscape of Iceland, which is intended for the "indifferent, broad-winged seagulls"; it is counterbalanced, too, by the intellectual and satirical streak in Salka Valka's creator.

VI   *The Satirical Element in* Salka Valka

As is usually the case in Laxness' novels, the satire in
Salka Valka strikes first and foremost at social conditions and
political life. An Icelandic reader could easily recognize in
the novel a good deal of topical material taken from the
contemporary history of Iceland. In his description of the
political struggle for the souls of Óseyri the writer has by
no means cut himself off from reality—we can assure ourselves of this by studying Icelandic newspapers of the time—
though he has, of course, exaggerated the dimensions of
some peculiarities. By a kind of quick-change technique he
can transform some bizarre episode, drawn from reality, into
a burlesque tale.

In the seventeenth chapter of *Þú vínviður hreini* Laxness
has skillfully solved the problem of conveying to the reader,
in a natural context, the main outlines of Óseyri's history.
The grand old man of the village, Jóhann Bogesen the
merchant, has had a party arranged in a fish warehouse
for the benefit of the widows and children of recently drowned
fishermen. On this occasion Bogesen gives, in a speech, a
survey of Óseyri's development over the past thirty-six years,
since he first came there; and the speech provides, at the same
time, a vivid portrait of the man himself.

The growing opposition to the Bogesen regime takes the
form not so much of a class-conscious struggle as of a
blind, instinctive search for an existence worthy of human
beings. It also develops in an atmosphere of indecision and
reversion; the people waver in their faith in a new social
system. Jóhann Bogesen was at all events something to hold
on to; and to rise up against him is like denying the very
foundation of their existence. When he was away from Óseyri,
"it was as if all ideas had run wild in people's minds,
so that they no longer had any idea what to do." When
he came back, and when people saw once again "his broad
back somewhere in the distance," the slander and agitation
against him somehow lost all their power (II, 238). Among
the villagers everything is taken very literally and personally.
It is no use for an agitator in this politically primitive environment to paint the merchant as one who exploits the working

class in the most general sense. He must be able to point
to something tangible, such as the fact that Bogesen has
prevented this or that person from repairing a cottage. Symbolic
of the back-and-forth sequence of political events is the artificial
leg from Germany which Jóhann Bogesen donates to Beinteinn
í Króknum. When the fickle-minded Beinteinn conducts himself well, the leg remains safely upon him. When he shows
himself untrustworthy in the eyes of his benefactor, the latter
sends someone to unscrew the leg. The leg is finally returned to Germany, still not paid for.

The writer also allows himself a spirited frolic with the
confused forms assumed by the workers' struggle. In Óseyri
people see the strike as introducing an element of festivity
into an otherwise monotonous existence: "It really seemed
to be a strike of the most glorious kind: daily progress
in Bolshevism and universal revolution, a red flag, incessant
meetings, especially among the younger people; fine oratory,
singing and flirting. The fathers of families rowed out in
shabby little skiffs and hauled in small fish for boiling, 'since
the village store was determined to starve people,' and divided
the catch among themselves according to the theories of
Marx and Lenin" (II, 162). Good-natured irony of this
kind frequently protrudes its cloven hoof.

A distinction is made between object and person. Arnaldur,
the only truly conscious representative of socialist theory,
is far from being an idealized figure as a person. Jóhann
Bogesen, the employer and merchant, on the other hand,
is no blackly painted extortioner; he is a good-naturedly cunning
patriarch. The writer follows him with a humorous glint
in the eye when Bogesen visits, in fatherly fashion, his drying
grounds and stock of fish, sporting his gold-mounted cane—
a gift presented to him on his fiftieth birthday by the Women's
Union of Óseyri: "In the sunshine he would often poke
the cane at some fish or other on the drying ground, like
a king addressing a single private soldier among ten thousand
at a military parade" (II, 42).

Yet, when all is considered, the bantering political caricature hardly goes deeper than the surface layer of the work;
it forms a playful arabesque around the destinies of its characters. This is not to say that it could safely have been

dispensed with. On the contrary, as yet another example
of the author's twofold vision it lends relief to his bitter insight
into the living conditions of man. And indeed, Icelandic
readers and critics gave particular attention to the more or
less political elements in the novel. Naturally enough, the
criticism varied considerably according to the reviewer's political
persuasion. The reviewer in *Morgunblaðið*, the leading organ
of the Conservative Party, found that in this novel Laxness
was the first Icelandic writer to have "created a picture—
large, rich in characters, evocative and uncommonly alive—
of the living conditions and culture of the poor, of their
life and state of health in an Icelandic coastal community."
But a distinct reservation goes with the critic's praise. Since
the author has made "the representatives of the upper classes
in the village such a collection of idiots, human scum, or
villains, the novel loses its universality as an impartial, truth-
ful, and serious description of an Icelandic fishing village." [4]

In the opposite political camp, the noted socialist Einar
Olgeirsson gave, from a strictly Marxist angle, a speedy analysis
of Laxness' character and work, in an article with the characteristic title of *Skáld á leið til sósíalismans* (Writers *en route* to
Socialism). The author of *Fuglinn í fjörunni* is said there to
adopt, as a socialist, an attitude similar to that of the pure idealist,
before the labor movement was yet amalgamated with socialism;
he scourges the middle-class community in the manner of the old
Utopianists. "For Laxness himself socialism and the labor movement are two separate things"—hence the vacillating attitude in
the novel. Consequently, his picture of the labor movement becomes to some extent a caricature—naturally enough, for Laxness
"caricatures everything middle-class—and that labor movement
which he describes is, indeed, essentially middle-class, and limited
to the struggle for better conditions within the framework
of the middle-class community." The writer finally points
out, however, with good reason, that it would be "unjust
to throw 'the blame' for this vacillating attitude in the 'political'
love story onto Halldór's artistic nature. The Icelandic labor
movement really has its share in the blame." [5] In this there
seems to lie an admission that when all is considered the
author has given, also on the point criticized, a tolerably
accurate picture of what Icelandic society was really like.

VII   *Literary and Other Impulses*

For his description in *Salka Valka* of Icelandic community
life Laxness obtained his purely literary impulses from foreign
rather than Icelandic literature. The works of Strindberg—
among them such a manysided satire as *Röda rummet* (The
Red Room)—formed part of his early and intense experiences
in the world of the intellect. He was able to get additional
models for a satirical and caricatural picture of society from
such writers as Dickens and Mark Twain, both of whom
are several times mentioned in *Alþýðubókin*.

But Óseyri perhaps reminds us above all of Knut Hamsun.
This may seem strange, considering that Halldór Laxness,
at the early age of nineteen, had reacted violently against
the view of humanity characteristic of that author.[6] But
the article in which he attacked his older fellow writer testifies
at the same time to the strong impression made on the
young Icelander by Hamsun's art. The ethical basis—or the
absence of an ethical basis—in Hamsun's work is criticized,
but his esthetic merits draw an acknowledgment from his
follower. It would not be surprising, either, if the Norwegian
writer had become of renewed topical interest to Laxness,
when the latter was embarking on the task of creating a
panoramic description of an Icelandic fishing community. Hamsun had partly drawn his epic material from corresponding
environments in his native country. It may seem an irony
of fate that the story of Óseyri should especially remind
us of *Konerne ved Vandposten* (The Women at the Water-
pump, 1920), the novel which had done most to cause
the nineteen-year-old writer's violent denunciation of Hamsun's
fictional world!

We should hasten to add, however, that a comparison
of the two works must chiefly reveal their fundamental dissimilarity. What aroused Laxness' disgust with *Konerne ved
Vandposten* in 1921 was neither the setting nor the subject
matter of the book, but its spirit. In itself there is nothing
wrong with writing about "the waifs and strays of society"
or even with writing "a long story about a eunuch and
a harlot, who are husband and wife, as Hamsun does."
What is unfortunate is simply the fact that the author finds

"baseness and meanness" everywhere; his contempt for mankind
prevents him from discerning "the nobility and beauty of
life."

It is true that the people in *Konerne ved Vandposten* are
dominated by narrowly private interests; they spy on each
other and spin petty intrigues. Laxness places his characters
in a large social pattern. Their actions are made to express
ideal concepts and powerful social forces, and to some extent,
also, ungovernable elemental powers. This will already be
clear after our hasty inspection of the leading characters
in his story: Salka Valka, Sigurlína, Steinþór, and Arnaldur.

In the article just quoted Laxness pits Maxim Gorky against
Knut Hamsun. Gorky, the proletarian writer, "looks into
people's destinies, however contemptible they may seem to
be, until he has acquired sympathy with them." He strikes
"the most sacred and sensitive chords in the reader's heart,"
in that he extracts human dignity from even the most humiliat-
ing of human destinies. It is highly probable that Gorky has
played a part in contributing to the spirit and mood of
the pictures which Laxness himself has drawn from the life
of ordinary Icelandic people. Laxness, of course, may also
have been influenced in various ways by Dickens: partly
by his social satire, partly by his passion for social justice,
and especially, perhaps, by his capacity for allowing grotesque
comedy and pathos to work together in one and the same
situation—as in the famous scene where Oliver Twist asks Mr.
Bumble for some more gruel.

Charlie Chaplin is another artist who should not be forgotten
here. His films had captivated Laxness for approximately
the same reasons as Gorky's work: their main theme, he
found, was sympathy and fellow feeling, a "living participation
in the conditions of social outcasts and a love directed towards
the weak man's cause."[7] At least one of Laxness' short
stories from the American period seems to show distinct
traces of Chaplin's influence.[8] And when he had just begun
his work on *Fuglinn í fjörunni* he wrote in a letter from
Leipzig in April, 1931: "I have now seen City Lights *three
times.* . . . I believe it is one of the most solid works
of art I have ever seen. It is exceedingly strongly built
and its execution is, quite simply, divine."[9] The passage

testifies to the fact that Laxness has not only seen but actually studied Chaplin's art. It is very difficult, however, to give concrete examples of how Laxness in his own work has benefited from his experience of Chaplin—partly because it is a problem in itself to make a direct comparison between two art forms as different from each other as the film and the prose epic, and partly because Laxness' mature writing surges forth with so much breadth and depth that the influxes from various sources are quite imperceptibly absorbed by the main flow. Where Chaplin was concerned, Laxness was surely affected most deeply by what he called "the melancholy sense of life" in his films. But Chaplin's way of expressing this sense of life through bold contrasting effects, with a blending of pathos and comedy, with a smile smiled through tears, must also have found an echo in the writer's own temperament.

CHAPTER 5

Independent People

I "The Life of the Independent Man"

WITH *Salka Valka* Laxness' interests as a writer had become firmly rooted in the soil of his native country. In one work after another during the thirties he adopts typically Icelandic subjects and gives them broad epic form. The book dealing with the fishing community of Óseyri was followed by the story of the Icelandic small farmer—the novel *Sjálfstætt fólk* (Independent People) which was published in two parts, in 1934 and 1935. Like *Salka Valka* this great work also goes back to a draft dating from the American period.[1]

The main character is a certain Guðbjartur Jónsson (Bjartur), who after toiling for eighteen years as a farmhand in the service of Jón hreppstjóri á Útirauðsmýri, (Bailiff Jón of Útirauðsmýri) has managed to scrape together enough money to buy his own little farm. From his employer he buys a patch of ground on the very edge of the Icelandic wilderness, where the remains of an old sheepfold, called Veturhús (Winterhouses) can still be found. As if to conjure the future into a favorable direction the new owner rechristens the place Sumarhús (Summerhouses). On his land he raises a dwelling place of turf and wood, as the Icelandic farmer has done for a thousand years, and moves in as a newly married man with his wife Rósa, a dog, a horse, and twenty-five ewes. Now he is Bjartur í Sumarhúsum (Bjartur of Summerhouses), a yeoman farmer, an independent man in his country, the king of his own small realm.

Yet his life as an independent farmer, the life he has so passionately desired, begins with a tragedy. The marriage between him and Rósa has chiefly been arranged by the

wife of the Bailiff, and not without ulterior motives. For
Rósa who, like Bjartur, has been in service at Útirauðsmýri,
is pregnant at the time of the wedding, and the father of
her child is the Bailiff's son. Bjartur becomes aware of the
situation and pretends that he wishes to have nothing to
do with the expected child. As Rósa's time approaches, he
leaves her alone at home in order to go out by himself into
the wilds and search for a lost sheep. After appalling hardships on the highland moor he returns one evening in midwinter
to his snow-covered cottage and is welcomed only by the
howling of his dog. Upstairs in the loft he stumbles over
something huddled on the floor—his wife, who is lying there
dead in her own congealed blood. But in her bed lies the
dog, shielding with the warmth of her body a new-born
girl child who shows feeble signs of life.

Bjartur is not the man to let himself be broken down
by a misfortune such as this. The spiritual shepherd of
the parish, The Reverend Guðmundur, who is respected by
Bjartur for his magnificent rams, provides him then and
there with a new wife, along with her old mother, to help
on the farm. With his family Bjartur endures a brutally
hard struggle for his existence as an independent man.
In that struggle he himself renounces and relentlessly forces
his family to renounce even the barest necessities of life.

But even a man of his tough disposition has a tender
spot, a romantic weakness. These softer feelings are bound
up with the little girl, who came into the world in such
dramatic circumstances. She is not, it is true, his own daughter,
but he nonetheless feels a special tenderness for this tiny
creature, to whom he gives the name of Ásta Sóllilja. But
the trust existing between them is brought to a tragic end.
One winter, by which time his second wife has also died,
Bjartur sets off for the coastal village to work as a day
laborer for the subsistence of his family. In the meantime
Ásta Sóllilja, who is not yet confirmed, is to keep house
for her three half-brothers and their old grandmother. But
from the village Bjartur sends up to Sumarhús a young
man to instruct the children—particularly Ásta Sóllilja, who
must be prepared for confirmation. As ill luck would have
it, the teacher, who on top of everything else is a consump-

tive, cannot one night resist the temptation to take the innocent girl to his bed. When the teacher has left and Bjartur has returned to his family it comes to light with the approach of spring that Ásta Sóllilja is expecting a child. Bjartur experiences a feeling of cruel betrayal and brutally drives her from his home. By way of farewell he gives her a box on the ears: " 'Take that,' he said, 'for the shame which you have brought upon my land, the soil which I have bought. But there is not a drop of my family's blood in you, and so much the better; I ask you, therefore, to give birth to your bastards in the houses of those who are more closely related to them than I.' " For Ásta Sóllilja this blow was "like some sort of confirmation; now she was free, and this was her confirmation" (II, 175–76). She goes off in the direction of Fjörður, the village on the coast, in search of the loved one of her dreams.

But Bjartur struggles on, more and more alone. His eldest son has been mysteriously lost in a whirling snowstorm, and his youngest son is now in the care of a relative in America; only the middle one, Guðmundur, remains. But the First World War—known to many "by no other name than the Blessed War"—brings good times for Bjartur and for other Icelandic farmers. Even the poor farmers now begin to see a little money and to live a more endurable life. "People began to grow things on a larger scale than before, people increased their livestock, people actually sent their children to school, and on some farms four china dogs of the larger sort had appeared. . . ." In times of such affluence it may be difficult to keep a cool head: "It could not be denied that many farms were bought for more than they were worth; on some of them too many extensions were built, and a number of children came home from their schools both speedily and excessively educated." Others, however, took the matter calmly, "did not change their way of living or buy china dogs . . . but quietly steered their course towards higher goals" (II, 194–95). One of these is Bjartur í Sumarhúsum. But his time of grace does not last long. He is generously urged to borrow money so that he may add new buildings to his farm. Then one fine day, when the prices of his products have fallen again, nothing is left with which to pay the interest and the installments on the loans. The bank cuts off his credit, Sumarhús is put up for auction, and is bought back at an absurdly low price by the Bailiff, who intends to start a fox-breeding farm there.

One day soon afterwards Bjartur finds himself down in Fjörður with his son. There is an atmosphere of unrest in the place—a strike among the harbor construction workers is going on, and there is talk of police reinforcements being sent from Reykjavík. In the evening father and son fall in with a group of young strikers, and Bjartur is actually tempted to share their bread, even though he knows that it is stolen. He deeply regrets having done so; he felt "that he had sustained the greatest defeat in his life; he was so ashamed, even, that the blood rose to his cheeks; time and again he had been within an ace of rising from his bed and spewing up the bread of humiliation out through the door" (II, 335).

Early next morning he walks aimlessly around in the village; the independent man has tamed his pride to the extent that now, after many years, he is prepared to visit Ásta Sóllilja. He finds her in an indescribably wretched hovel where she is living with her two children, deserted by her lover and stricken with consumption, which is in a highly advanced state. It seems to her as if she has been dead and recalled to life by this meeting: " 'Father,' she repeated simply, and did not take her eyes from his face; she remained standing there as if rooted to the spot. 'No, I cannot believe that you have come' " (II, 341). In the evening of the same day Ásta Sóllilja walks with her children alongside the brook which runs through the farm at Sumarhús, her old home, and gazes wonderingly at the ugly new building; the whole of the new farmstead calls to mind "the ruin of some building which had been riddled with bullets in the war": "It was the palace which he had built in the hope that she would come." All she misses now is the old cottage with its gentle outlines, where she had experienced her most sacred pain, her most treasured hopes. In her thoughts she recapitulates her short life, which "had been laid in ruins before it began, like the house and independence of Guðbjartur Jónsson." Even so, she felt that evening as if "she was not too old to see the future once again in a dream; in a new dream. To hope is to live" (II, 343–44).

Bjartur has been able to take over his mother-in-law's abandoned farm, Urðarsel, and has built it up again with turf and wood. The book ends with a description of how he finally moves from Sumarhús to the new farm. At the head of the little procession goes the old horse Blesi (Blaze), the same as when Bjartur long ago moved into Sumarhús. But the journey is too much for Ásta Sóllilja. She falls down and coughs up blood in the grass, and Bjartur has to take her in his arms and carry her. He asks her to hold her arms tightly round his neck and she whispers: " 'Now I am with you again.' And he answered: 'Hold your arms tightly round my neck, my flower.' 'Yes,' she whispered. 'Always— as long as I live. Your only flower, the flower of your life. And I shan't die quite yet—not straight away.' Then they went on."

II   *The Social Slant in* Sjálfstætt fólk

Sjálfstætt fólk readily invites comparison with an earlier and famous Scandinavian novel about farmers and settlers— Knut Hamsun's *Markens Gröde* (*The Growth of the Soil,* 1918); it was primarily for that work that Hamsun was awarded the Nobel Prize two years later. Laxness himself has commented in a few words on the supposed similarity of the two works. He finds it correct to juxtapose them in so far as he in his own book poses the same questions as Hamsun does in *Markens Gröde.* Yet his own answers to these questions are directly opposed to those of Hamsun: "I do not wish to claim that all the social—or other— conclusions in *Sjálfstætt fólk* are the right ones, but my certainty that Hamsun's social conclusions in *Markens Gröde* were on the whole erroneous had its part to play in the origin of my book. These two books, like thousands of other books, have in common the fact that they deal with farmers and their problems; but the keynote of the one book is clearly opposed to that of the other." [2]

We can indeed find a number of striking similarities between *Markens Gröde* and *Sjálfstætt fólk* in certain episodes and details. It is essential to realize, however, that in Laxness' work such episodes and details have received a quite different

character and been fitted into a new total view of the subject.
On the first pages of both these novels the settler appears
as a wanderer coming to survey his land. Hamsun's Isak
ends up in secure possession of his world, a well-to-do man;
he could without irony be called the king of his little realm.
Bjartur, on the other hand, finally has to leave everything
which, through thirty years of slavery, first as a farm boy
and then as an "independent" man, he has worked to acquire; he has to move off in order to begin anew. Isak's
story develops into an idyll, while Bjartur's departure from
Sumarhús is veiled in tragedy. There is above all in Laxness'
work a social slant which is not to be found in *Markens
Gröde*. It is true that Hamsun bitterly criticizes industrial
capitalism, which he contrasts with the life of the farmer—the
life lived according to nature's laws. But otherwise, Isak
and his little world are described as being virtually independent
of society. The mining of copper on his land results in
much commotion and an influx of money. But it is an
episode which passes, and afterwards people manage just
as well as before. In *Sjálfstætt fólk* economic policy and trade
conditions are made to shape the course of the farmer's
life both perceptibly and irrevocably. The fixing of prices
on agricultural products, the trade boom during the First
World War, the liberally granted or actually forced bank
loans, the fall in prices and the bankruptcies—all these things
are realities which make their presence thoroughly felt, even
in the remote moorland farm of Sumarhús. Near the end
of the book, when Bjartur happens to fall in with a group
of strikers down in the coastal village, he hears tell of the
poor farmers of Russia who had tired of their masters and
plunderers and joined forces with their comrades, the workers
in the towns, in order to create "a new society in which
no one can profit from other people's work" (II, 333).

The reference to the Russian Revolution is no accident.
During his time in America Laxness had already talked of
visiting the Soviet Union—"the only one of the great civilized
countries which I have yet to spend some time in," as
he wrote in a letter from San Francisco in March, 1928.[3]
He went to Russia in the autumn of 1932 and stayed there
in October and the greater part of November. He recorded

his impressions of the visit in the short work *Í Austurvegi* (Going East, 1933), an eyewitness account which deals essentially with agriculture in the Soviet Union. As a farmer's son Laxness has always been greatly interested in the work and living conditions of the Icelandic farmers, and has made frequent critical contributions to the subject. At this particular time the subject must have engaged his interests more than usual—partly because a severe agricultural crisis, following in the wake of the great world depression, was prevailing in Iceland; and partly because he was then fully occupied in writing his novel about farmers. It is significant that the very word "crisis" occurs in the projected title of a handwritten manuscript dating from 1933: *Bók kreppunnar, sagan um frelsi Þorleifs Jónatanssonar og heimsstyrjöld hans* (The Book of Crisis, the Story of Þorleifur Jónatansson's Freedom and his World War). On the same title page we also find a highly illuminating note, written as a memorandum for the continued work: "Sharpen the contrasts between the small and large-scale farmer. Show how the large-scale farmer exploits the small farmer in his service both politically and economically, and dubs himself a knight at his expense with promises and flattering gifts—such as roads, a telephone, and building loans—until the large-scale farmer has become a bank manager in Reykjavík and a Cabinet Minister, while the small farmer has become completely impoverished, has to leave his farm and joins up with the crowd of unemployed in the towns." [4]

This declaration should be placed side by side with the author's impressions of his visit to the Soviet Union in the autumn of 1932. The postscript to the second edition of *Sjálfstætt fólk* in 1952 provides, inter alia, a few glimpses of this decisive phase in the story of the work's origin. It says that the draft written in Los Angeles in the summer of 1929 was very incomplete. The writer had early become aware of his inadequate knowledge of the subject, and it was not until three years later that he considered he had laid the proper basis for a continued work. The journey to Russia, where collective farming was just then making its name, seems to have provided him with a new grasp of the task before him: "In the Soviet people's realistic view of the matter, where no lyrical faddists got an opportunity to confuse the onlooker's view, I soon noticed a few dominant features, and among them was the simple but clarifying method of grouping farmers according to class: large-scale farmers, middle-type farmers, and small farmers. This classification, which is afterwards found to be the most obvious one of all, actually opened the whole problem to me, and enabled me to handle it, fully and clearly, on a social basis." [5]

With the guidance of this comment we may easily notice that in *Sjálfstætt fólk* Laxness has attempted a social differentiation of his farmer types, in accordance with the knowledge he had acquired on his visit to the Soviet Union. Certain of Lenin's ideas, which are reproduced in *Í Austurvegi*, are clearly discernible in *Sjálfstætt fólk*. Thus Jón á Útirauðsmýri, the Bailiff, obviously represents the Icelandic version of the Kulak or "rural capitalist" (Icel. *landburgeis, sveitaburgeis*). Much as we should expect, his son Ingólfur rises within the farmers' party to the status of member of Parliament, bank manager in the capital, and Cabinet Minister, just as the author had indicated in the memorandum, quoted above, for his work on the novel. Between this country-dwelling upper class and the out-and-out poor farmers, the proletarians of the soil, like Bjartur, Laxness places a man like the "mountain king," the typical "middle-type farmer" (Icel. *miðlungsbóndi*). In the travel book we find a quotation from Stalin: "The middle-type farmer, that is, the man who waits and sees. He waits to see who will triumph; he waits and waits, and only when we have gained the upper hand and freed ourselves from the bourgeoisie and the landowners, will he begin to incline in our direction. He is, after all, a middle-type farmer" (57-58). This reminds us strongly of Laxness' characterization of the "mountain king," who is always cautious and vacillating: "the mountain king who had not, it is true, become a large-scale farmer yet, although he had wormed his way onto the parish council, but was a middle-type farmer, who for more than a year had been in agony of mind because of the merchant and the cooperative society, for when two strong parties are disputing, it is important to have the patience to wait and see" (II, 45).

The task of taking up the challenge offered by Hamsun's famous novel about farmers, and of doing so on the basis of his new points of departure, must surely have seemed tempting and pressing to Laxness. By virtue of his experiences and radical views he had found that the social outlook in *Markens Gröde* —or rather, perhaps, its lack of any real view of society—showed an escapist and perhaps dangerously reactionary tendency. In the years when *Sjálfstætt fólk* was written the Blut-und-Boden ideology of National Socialism had already had time to place in an ambiguous light even the essentially harmless concept of Rousseauism, and the romantic tendency to idealize the farmer's life. In July, 1934—before Laxness had seriously set to work on the second volume of his novel—he published a short article about farmers, in which he described himself as an "Icelandic farmer's son and a member of the Icelandic Agricultural Society"; it is an ironic "Þakkarávarp" (Speech of Thanks) addressed to a German Commissioner for Agriculture who on leaving Iceland after an official visit had had published a turgidly phrased message of greeting to the Icelandic farmers.[6] The idea of romanticizing the Icelandic farmer's life must surely have appealed to Laxness less than ever once he had encountered its German equivalent as expressed by an envoy of the Third Reich.

III   *"The Cosmopolitan of the Whole Earth"*

Sjálfstætt fólk confronts the reader with the question of how it can happen that a man like Bjartur, with his cunning, his strength of will, his physical endurance and toughness and the endless anxiety he suffers on behalf of man and beast, must nonetheless see himself defeated in the struggle for his own and his family's livelihood. The author gives a kind of answer to the question when he comments on Bjartur's departure from Sumarhús; the passage is a beautiful expression of his humane passion for social justice:

Once again they had broken down a poor farmer's farm; they are the same from century to century, and that is because the poor farmer always remains the same, from century to century. A war abroad may strengthen his backbone for a few years, but the help it brings is merely illusory; a delusion; through all centuries the poor farmer never escapes from his state of crisis; he continues to exist in misery as long as man is not man's safeguard, but man's worst enemy. The life of the poor farmer, the life of the independent man, is of its very nature a flight from other men who seek to kill him. From one night lodging to another one still worse. A poor farmer's family moves to a new home, four generations out of those thirty which have kept up the continuance of life and death in this country for a thousand years—but for whom? Not, at least, for themselves and their children. They resembled nothing so much as fugitives in a ravaged land, where long-lasting wars have raged, or outlaws without sanctuary—but in whose country? Not, at least, in their own country. In foreign books there is a legend about a man who became perfect through sowing in his enemy's field for one night. The story of Bjartur í Sumarhúsum is the story of the man who sowed in his enemy's field all his life, day and night. Such is the story of the most independent man in this country (II, 345-46).

In the eyes of their describer, the activities of Bjartur and his like are hopeless as a solution to the practical problems of life. Their independence, which they uphold with tooth and claw, is an illusion and a deception, both a self-deception and a deception on the part of the landowners; we ought, indeed, to imagine ironic quotation marks on either side of the book's title—*Sjálfstætt fólk* (Independent People). For his own part Bjartur cannot, or will not, revise his opinions. But he leaves his son behind among the strikers in the coastal village, where the exploited workers who have begun to grow aware of the mechanism of society glimpse a solution to the problem in the idea of joining forces and working together in the struggle for a better existence.

But once it has been pointed out and established that this social attitude is adopted in the book, we see at once how inadequate it is as an expression of the work's individual character. Considering the great extent to which socially critical viewpoints contributed towards the origin of *Sjálfstætt fólk*, it is surprising indeed that this social slant does not thrust itself more directly forward in the finished work. The chief reason for this is probably that the social motif has expanded to mythical proportions of universal applicability. The first chapter of *Sjálfstætt fólk* relates the ancient legend of Kólumkilli, a powerful raiser of spirits and sorcerer of Irish origin, and his woman worshiper, the housewife Gunnvör, who murdered people in order to drink their blood and suck their marrow. After being exposed and broken to death this woman walked again on her farm and haunted the place as a ghost to such a degree that it lay

deserted for many a long year. It is, however, the very place
which under the name of Sumarhús becomes Guðbjartur Jónsson's property. Thus his life on the moor is laid from the beginning beneath the spell of supernatural and terrifying powers—
even though he refuses to acknowledge them to the very last.
Kólumkilli becomes a symbol of what has been inimical to man
from time immemorial. His shadowy figure melts imperceptibly
together with the invisible enemies in society who are constantly
depriving Bjartur of the fruit of his work—these "they," who
"are the same, from century to century," according to the passage
quoted above. These latter seem in their way as irrational, and
as unapproachable for the purposes of honest combat, as Kólumkilli himself, for it is impossible to wrestle with a bank.

Thus the present is linked together with the distant past in
such a way as to provide a powerful perspective through the
centuries. Despite the fact that we have the First World War
as a landmark in the chronology of the narrative, the story
of Bjartur leaves an impression of bewildering timelessness. According to the Marxist pattern, and perhaps in accordance with
the writer's earlier intentions, the poor farmer, who is forced
to leave his farm, ought surely to have been made to join up
with "the crowd of unemployed in the towns." But the final
scene in *Sjálfstætt fólk* shows the aging Bjartur, still unbroken,
leaving Sumarhús to start life all over again in a new dwelling
place. As a character in the book he has grown away from
the pattern and acts according to his own inherent logic.

There is, however, no reason for trying to challenge the author's view that his radical and politically social outlook has
helped him, in a decisive way, to give artistic form to his material. A political conviction or belief does not, of course, constitute any guarantee of esthetic qualities in an imaginative work.
But it looks as if Laxness' own view of society has contributed
towards giving steadiness and dramatic stature to *Sjálfstætt fólk*
—qualities which are noticeably lacking in the draft of the novel
dating from 1929. But as we have hinted, this theoretical basis
never reveals itself in a crude or obtrusive form. It lies embedded
in the narrative's mass of teeming life and individual human
destinies, and plays the part of an invisibly supporting structure.
This is one of the reasons why Laxness' social outlook—to say
nothing of his Marxist or socialist view of society—here seems

so universally applicable, so little bound to a definite political situation, such as the agricultural crisis at the beginning of the thirties. Commenting later on his work, Laxness has emphasized very strongly that "the small farmer is a classic, international type, except in the Soviet Union and in those countries which have advanced far in socialism":

. . . Bjartur í Sumarhúsum is understood in all countries of the world: he is the cosmopolitan of Iceland, because he is the cosmopolitan of the whole earth. And it is not only in the sparsely populated areas of the countryside that this type of man belongs; he has his parallel and surprisingly exact equivalent in every man who, with a similar financial position and a corresponding way of thinking, fights for his own and his family's life in the cities of the world. I recall that shortly after *Sjálfstætt fólk* came out in the United States, [in New York, 1946] I was visited by a gifted American who, to judge from his manner, was a city dweller. He said that he had interrupted his journey at the airport here, in order to talk to me about Bjartur í Sumarhúsum; he told me, among other things, something which might seem strange to many, although nothing could seem less surprising to me: that in the very city of New York there were millions of people who in all essential respects lived more or less exactly as Bjartur í Sumarhúsum and his family did—not only under the same economic conditions, but with the same moral principles and way of thinking.[7]

IV   *"Father" and "Daughter"*

In *Sjálfstætt fólk* there are many individualized characters who deserve closer study as fictional creations. Here, however, we must concentrate on three characters who, to a higher degree than others, have been made to crystallize the narrative's deepest meaning and pathos: Bjartur, Ásta Sóllilja, and Bjartur's youngest son, Nonni.

Bjartur himself has been given some measure of the Icelandic sagas' dimensions, of their heroes' superhuman toughness and strength of will. It is not just for amusement's sake that he takes comfort from the story of Grettir Ásmundarson—Grettir the Strong—who lived as an outlaw among the Icelandic mountains for nineteen years; his own situation is basically not very different from Grettir's.[8] In his characterization of the book's leading figure Laxness for the first time makes use, in a truly masterly way, of his country's ancient poetic tradition. Loudly singing *rímur* (rhymed ballads) about the exploits of ancient warriors, Bjartur forces himself onward, dead tired, against the snowstorm on the highland moor.[9] In his own old-fashioned Icelandic poetry, with its intricate rules, he binds his own thoughts and experiences in rigorous bonds. It is one of his ways of molding and mastering his existence, of raising himself above it; it is the triumph of his spirit over matter.

This adventure on the heath shows the writer's art from yet another angle. We are given here an excellent example of his capacity for allowing the landscape itself to play a living part in the description. Bjartur's fantastic ride on a wild bull reindeer over the ice-cold and rapidly flowing glacier river has, for all its palpability, an element of saga and myth about it. "There came moments, both then and later, when it seemed to Bjartur as if it were the fiend Kólumkilli himself, and no other, who had shown himself here" (I, 149). In the storm on the highland moor the man fights for his life in single combat with the monsters of the land, the enemies of man. The severity of the landscape is in harmony with the *rímur* which he sings about the legendary warriors of ancient times, and with his own indomitable will.

Bjartur dominates the narrative and gives it its fundamental tone. But here as elsewhere Laxness works with strong contrasts and tensions. In Ásta Sóllilja he has created a contrast and complement to her hard-hearted father. If a snowstorm on the heath seems the natural setting for Bjartur's struggle for existence, the author surrounds Ásta Sóllilja with the most ethereal shades of feeling, with the most spiritual kind of lyricism, which the Icelandic countryside can inspire. The young girl is to be allowed, for the first time, to accompany Bjartur to the market town and "get to know the world from her own experience" (I, 310). The night before the journey is midsummer night, when those who bathe in the dew may have a wish, and Ásta Sóllilja steals out alone:

A dell by the river. Two inexperienced feet. Hither leads her curving track in the dewy grass. For a while the birds are silent. She sits on the bank and listens. Then she takes off her worn-out, everyday rags beneath this sky which actually manages to veil in oblivion

the midwinter darkness of a whole life—a midsummer sky. Young
goddess of the sunlit night, perfect in her youthful nakedness. There
is nothing more beautiful in life than the night before what is yet to
come, and its dew. She makes her wish, half-grown and slender in
the half-grown, dew-besprinkled grass. Body and soul are one and
this unity is perfectly pure in its wish (I, 311–12).

If Bjartur embodies man's indomitable qualities, then Ásta
Sóllilja represents man's defenselessness in the face of life. Her
very birth in the snow-covered hovel, where she is being kept
alive by the warm body of a mangy dog, gives a pathetic picture of man's situation in life. "It is terrible how weak humankind can be when one sees it as it really is" (I, 178), says
Bjartur, when he looks at the newborn child. Coming straight
from his fantastic adventure on the highland moor, he touches
the girl's face, "with his strong and grimy hand which had fought
against the monsters of the country: 'She shall be called Ásta
Sóllilja'" (I, 179). He is proud that the poor little creature has
no one in the world but him, and is determined that the same
fate shall befall them both.

In Ásta Sóllilja's eyes this father of hers is safety itself, her
stronghold in life. She can lean against his chest and feel that
he is the strongest thing that exists: "There was one lovely
place on his neck, between the neckband and the root of the
beard, and when her mouth is hot and trembling with weeping,
she pines for this place; and finds it. Thus life's misfortunes
vanish, perhaps all at once—just a moment in the dusk, and
they are gone" (I, 272). A faint element of eroticism gradually
becomes apparent in the way she looks at her father—who is
not, of course, her real father—and clings to him. The innocent
girl cannot separate the shy dreams of love awakening within
her from her feelings for him. On his side Bjartur shows that
he, in a corresponding way, is attracted towards Ásta Sóllilja.
But he is on guard against his feelings and fearful of the girl's
constant need for tender affection and security. This can be
seen most clearly in Chapter 32, in the description of their journey
to the market town. In the bunk which they share at the simple
hostel Ásta Sóllilja feels her father's warm, strong hand touching
her body. A tremor goes through her and she clasps him with
both hands, "with an iron-hard grasp, in a transport of this

impersonal, demanding kind of selfishness, which in an instant
had made her forgetful of everything. This was the world's long-
awaited joy—" (I, 335–36). Then Bjartur violently pushes
the girl away from him, gets up, dresses, and walks out into
the darkness. For Ásta Sóllilja, who sees no harm in what has
happened, who has merely believed herself to be seeking a sweet
safety in him, this experience is in the nature of a shock. It
will "cast an indelible shadow on her awakening youth, and
add the final load to the burden of harshness and cruelty, which
already was her lot" (I, 336). After her father has left her
to herself in the bed she thinks that her life is wasted, and
that she is alone in the world.

This episode on the visit to the town gives a darker and
more bittersweet character to the relationship between Ásta Sóllilja and Bjartur. Indeed, their mutual trust is precipitately and
tragically shattered. And when in spite of everything they are
finally reunited, it is too late for them to continue their life
together. Bjartur with the dying Ásta Sóllilja in his arms reminds
us of a similar situation in one of the great dramas of world
literature: King Lear with Cordelia dead in his arms. In both
cases the pathos of the story is capable of rising to a breaking
point, because it is so thoroughly steeped in the writer's total
vision of the tragedy of human life. When all is taken into
account it is hard to say whether, from the point of view of
its creator, *Sjálfstætt fólk* may be thought to end happily or
unhappily. For in his eyes man's personal triumph in life is
seldom more, perhaps, than a fleeting moment of close contact
between human beings, or a glimpse of tenderness in the shadow
of death. "There is nothing so merciless as human life" (I,
367), he writes. Bjartur is a man who seems to have made
this insight his own and is ready to take its consequences, and
when his middle son Guðmundur, the last child left at home,
is on the point of leaving him, he reflects: "Let those who wish
to go, go; it is probably best that way. Strongest is he who
stands alone. A man is born alone. A man dies alone. Why,
then, should he not live alone? To stand alone, is not that the
perfection of life, its aim?" (II, 218).

But it takes a man like Bjartur to sustain so tough a philosophy
of life, a philosophy so free from illusion—"the man who had
fought with his bare hands against the monsters of the land"

(I, 335) on the very night that Ásta Sóllilja was born. More
applicable to the weak and ordinary human type is another saying
in the book: "The human soul needs a little consolation each
day if it is to live" (II, 78). This opinion is given on the
very subject of Ásta Sóllilja, with the characteristic addition:
"but there seems to be no consolation." The element of tragedy
in the relationship between her and Bjartur is due in considerable
measure to the infinite distance which separates them both. They
stand there before each other, and before life, without understanding this—"each one with his own soul, he strong, she weak.
Yes, there certainly was, quite definitely, an unbridgeable sea
between them; his life was far too complex to be able to har-
monize with her simple life of few words, or for his strength
to go with her tender sensitivity" (II, 68).

Basically, the author's opinion is surely that human beings
in general are strangers in life and strangers to each other. All
that has happened here is that the situation has been artistically
and symbolically intensified in the description of Bjartur and
Ásta Sóllilja. Thus the author is also able to give expression
to their bitter experience in a sentence of universal relevance;
it is said of the girl, who is listening to her father's words,
that "She looks at him with beating heart and knows that he
is talking about serious things, even though she has difficulty
in understanding him; two human beings have such difficulty
in understanding each other—there is nothing so sad as two
human beings" (II, 70).

However, Ásta Sóllilja does not simply function in the novel
as a contrast to Bjartur. It is above all her own character which
appears as a bewildering interplay of contradictions. Laxness
often presents one or another of his characters as a paradoxical
and tension-filled complex of opposing elements. In his earlier
work this is true of Steinn Elliði and Arnaldur Björnsson, for
example, and also, in her own way, of Salka Valka. And we
are given this portrait of Ásta Sóllilja, with her bitter experience
of life, when her brother Guðmundur sees her again for the
first time after her departure from Sumarhús: "In the whole
of her manner and appearance there was something at once
strong and weak, attractive and repellent; one had to notice
her—there was no sign of dullness in her face, never a moment
of dumb stupidity in the glance of her eye, and no movement

without personal expression; all her expressions had their opposites, showing humiliation and exaltation at the same time, and
her life was a single uninterrupted and impassioned torment,
so that one had to wish to be good to her; and to push her
away; and to come back to her again because one had not
understood her—and perhaps not oneself either" (II, 223).

Man's difficulty in bringing into harmony his contrasting qualities and conflicting impulses must have been an experience deeply
felt by the creator of Ásta Sóllilja. In her pathetic defenselessness in the face of the riddle posed by life and by her own
nature, she appears to be a true expression of the author's view
of humanity. We might perhaps call her the victim of her open
trust in life, of her dreams for the future. Bjartur, on the other
hand, clings persistently to his own unalterable will. He will
not allow himself to be carried off course by any irrational "streams"; he regards feelings as air, and tears are in his
view just another kind of wetness, like some sort of rain leaking
through the roof. His armor seems to be without chinks. But
for this very reason his character takes on the proportions of
something inhuman or superhuman.

When her half-brother Guðmundur visits Ásta Sóllilja in the
coastal village, she is depicted not merely as a symbol of defenseless humankind itself, with its hopelessly contradictory nature.
She stands there "clad in rags, clad, perhaps, in the shame of
a whole people, of a people innocent for a thousand years, with
a decayed tooth and an illegitimate child" (II, 223). It seems
as if the author here wishes to present her as something of
a national, proletarian symbol. The social slant also plays its
part, perhaps, in one of the very last comments on her destiny.
As she walks with her children in the evening alongside the
brook running through the farm at Sumarhús, for one last time,
she is described as follows: "She was like unprotected nature,
which withers in the storm, because it receives no shelter—neither
from God nor from people; people do not give each other shelter;
and God?—we shall find out about that when at last we have
died of consumption" (II, 344).

Such words can, of course—and probably do—imply an indictment of the prevailing social order; immediately after this,
for example, Bjartur is characterized as a victim of forces in
society which are unjust and inimical to man. But fundamentally,

the drama shared by him and Ásta Sóllilja seems to belong
to that kind of destiny which—to concur with Arnaldur in *Salka
Valka*—"not even a trade union, not even the revolution" can
change. And Ásta Sóllilja receives no more shelter from God
than from people, we are told. It may be asked whether this
indictment of the divine order is not of a more primary nature
than the indictment of the social order. The harrowing and primary experience of man's forlornness and defenselessness in life
has increased the writer's sensitivity to what he regards as social
injustice and human tyranny—both of which it is possible to
remove. Pessimism on the metaphysical level has found its complement on the social and political level in a consciously developed optimism and faith in the future.

Against the background of such a darkly conceived view of
life, even the most simple kind of comfort for the soul, even
the most fleeting moments of sincerely felt human companion-
ship, will be suffused with an exceptional splendor. Thus it is
that little Nonni on a day in early spring can bring the news
that there is a blossoming dandelion by the cottage wall. The
mother and her children go out together to look at this "little
flower of eternity"; "They touched it with the extreme tips of
their fingers in reverential silence, like members of the faithful
who are allowed to touch the bones of some saint in the presence
of the Pope, in order to be saved; it was as if they wished
to say: you are not alone, we also exist, we also are trying
to exist. Light shone over that day. All the anxiety of winter
had vanished in a single day. The brightness of the day was
as boundless in the soul as in the vault of heaven; it was one
of the happy days of life and they remembered this day all
their lives" (I, 399).

Another example of how the single moment may hold a saving
and heartening experience of eternity is given in the presenta-
tion of Ásta Sóllilja. As a young girl she sees the goodness
and gentleness in a stranger's eyes: "It is in this that the soul
longs to rest; from eternity to eternity. And she saw it for the
first time in his eyes, and perhaps never afterwards; she stood
face to face with it and understood it. And that was how it was"
(I, 376).

To pause once again before the final scene of the work: Bjartur has suffered defeat in his lifelong, unrelenting struggle for

independence; in his arms he carries Ásta Sóllilja, who is dying
—perhaps chiefly through his own doing. Viewed from without
the situation may seem merely depressing or meaningless, but
for Bjartur and Ásta Sóllilja it must, in spite of all, mean a
rare and happy glimpse of eternity such as two people may
experience when able to meet each other in a state of mutual
understanding, free from turbid reservations. Thus the final reaction of the reader or spectator here, as in the case of Lear
with Cordelia dead in his arms, is not a feeling of oppression
and despair, but a sense of human richness and greatness.

V *Little Nonni*

Laxness has undoubtedly put much of himself into Bjartur
and Ásta Sóllilja, however distant from both of them he may
seem to be. As a writer and an interpreter of human life he
must have possessed Ásta Sóllilja's open and trembling sensitivity.
But in his work as an artist he has also shown a good deal
of the strength of will and fixity of purpose characteristic of
a man like Bjartur. Perhaps, however, we meet the author most
directly and completely in little Nonni, Bjartur's youngest son.
For if nothing else Laxness has, as far as we can judge, made
use of his childhood memories of his own grandmother in describing the child Nonni and his grandmother at Sumarhús.[10]

Nonni is an imaginative person, an artist-to-be, who gives form
to life in accordance with his dreams and visions. In the remarkable chapter called "Winter Morning" the world of fairy tale
blossoms forth. In the early, awakening day the household uten-
sils change their form in the boy's imagination and become people: the blackened pot is none other than the Bailiff; the ladle,
which plays "a role of great importance in the pot," is the
Bailiff's wife, and so on (I, 225–26). Laxness here shows himself as a teller of fairy tales and a maker of myths in the sense
that Hans Christian Andersen was. It is also striking how often
the animals—sheep, dogs, horses, cows, and birds—are personified, and not only in the children's imagination. Little Nonni
has a healthy respect for "The Reverend Guðmundur the ram
and his brother" (I, 228), who sometimes fight down in the
byre the whole night through. When the cow on the farm has
calved, everybody—except Bjartur—participates sincerely in her

joy, and looks at "the recent mother and her son, keeping a respectful distance" (I, 364).

In the beautiful days of spring, when Nonni is allowed to go with his mother out into the field to tend the cow, Búkolla, the countryside seems mysterious and holy in its peace. The rocks and hillocks are peopled with elves friendly to man, who come to life in his mother's fairy stories. For the boy, his awareness of his mother and the experience of this animated nature both run together into a wondrous unity, in which he as a grown man fancies he perceives the meaning of life, the reconciliation between earth and heaven, between time and eternity. The evening before Nonni is to leave Sumarhús forever in order to go to America, the singing of birds is heard from the marshes—or perhaps "bird song from the marshes echoing in his soul, and unwilling to fall silent for the brief space of this tranquil night in spring": "It was a sound which was never afterwards to desert his soul, however far and wide he traveled and however grand were the halls in which he later trod—the marsh with its Icelandic birds, one short night in spring" (II, 156–57). The long, strange story of the redshank may seem rather uneventful, "just going hee, hee, hee for a thousand years." But one fine day, in a distant continent, perhaps, it will be discovered to have been "more beautiful and more sweet than most other stories," simply "the most remarkable story in the world," and then one will dream of being able to "wander about on the marshes at night, on the night before Ascension Day, after one is dead, and hear this incredible story; nay, this story and absolutely no other" (II, 154).

A rather similar wish had been placed in the mouth of the widely traveled Steinn Elliði, the author's alter ego in *Vefarinn mikli frá Kasmír:* his innermost longing is that after his death he should "be able to hover like a strange bird over Icelandic mountains on the silent nights of high summer." We are obviously faced here with something that belongs to the world of Laxness' deepest experience. On one occasion he praises his countryman Jónas Hallgrímsson, for the reason that in his poetry Jónas has recreated with brilliant spontaneity the simple, fundamental experiences of nature which have left their mark on the Icelandic sense of life. These "happy, ancient memories" are free from "heavy, dramatic strains": they have a delight "which nei-

ther revolutions nor world wars can wipe out." Laxness himself,
in his own writing, has given them a sincerity and intensity
which is virtually unsurpassed. The Icelandic countryside as he
describes it is raised at times to a wholly spiritual plane, and
is handled with a "visionary gleam" and trancelike sublimity
reminiscent of religious feeling.

Little Nonni is said to have "so strange an instrument in
his breast." He does not yet know how to play upon it but
merely fingers at its strings in wonder and reverence. But in
his breast there trembles "a poetic melancholy and a mysterious
feeling of sorrow" (II, 143). It is his dead mother's sighs which
have "planted sorrow in his breast, that sorrow which was afterwards to follow him through his whole life and color his every
song" (II, 158). Nonni early becomes familiar with "that death
from which no one returns." As a seven-year-old boy he has
seen his father carry away on his back a baby of the family
in a box, to have it buried by the Bailiff and the local clergyman. The next day he talks about this with his mother. When
he realizes that not only really small children die, but that
all shall die, and he himself shall die, a string breaks within
him—"one of these fine strings of childhood, which break before
one has realized that they sound, and this string never sounds
again" (I, 224).

In his early novel *Undir Helgahnúk* the author had described
how death became a terrible reality for the boy Atli Kjartansson.
The latter shares noticeable features with his creator and on
essential points reflects his psychical *habitus* and experiences.
But Laxness also gives intense expression to his fear of death
in autobiographical documents dating from the years of his youth,
such as the manuscript of *Rauða kverið* and the monastery diary.
In the case of Atli this harrowing experience seems to have
increased his tendency towards self-assertion and caused him
to tie himself up in a frantic desire to become a famous man,
and thus defy mortal decay and blunt the sharpness of death.

His early contact with death has surely also given expansive
force to little Nonni's longing, and has fanned the flame of his
efforts to deaden, by means of creative activity, the metaphysical
perception of void. But he has nothing of Atli's ruthless self-
centeredness. The experience of death and human suffering has
not made him hard-hearted; on the contrary, it makes him feel

the more deeply, and with all the more compassion, for his fellow mortals. One day Ásta Sóllilja is lying out in the grass and crying bitterly as a result of her first painful experience of love. Her little brother, who his dead mother has prophesied will become a singer and sing for the whole world, comes to her and timidly listens to her moaning: "It was the first time that he looked into the labyrinth of the human soul. He was very far from understanding it. But what was more, he suffered with her. Much, much later he relived this memory in song; both in his own most beautiful song and in the world's most beautiful song. For the understanding of the soul's defenselessness, of the conflict between the two poles, is not the fountainhead of the highest kind of song. Compassion is the source of the highest song. Compassion for Ásta Sóllilja on earth" (II, 150–51). With these words the author widens the situation into one of universal applicability. The figure of Ásta Sóllilja becomes a symbol of what is eternally and helplessly human, of that which calls so irresistibly for our sympathy, because in it we recognize ourselves. Thus the author can also speak of the "magic power of poetry, which shows us the human condition so truthfully and with so much sympathy and so much love of what is good, that we ourselves become better people, and understand the life of man better than before, and wish and hope that what is good may always triumph in human life" (I, 346). He must have seen as an ideal the ability to communicate something of this magic power in his own poetic language.

VI   *"The Heath of Life"*

"This moorland valley contained all the turns and changes of mood which characterize life" (II, 154), as we read on one occasion of Sumarhús and its surroundings. And when the middle son wishes to go out into the world and travel to America Bjartur can answer him: "World? What is that? This is the world, the world is here; Sumarhús, my farm—that is the world" (II, 214). A similar thought is formulated at one point in *Salka Valka*, in the following words: "It is so difficult to realize that the world is just here, in Óseyri við Axlarfjörð" (II, 70). On the whole, the author has laid great stress on giving the sequence of events in *Sjálfstætt fólk* a significance for humanity in gen-

eral. Among many examples two or three must suffice to illustrate here how this process of expansion may present itself
in the novel. From the first twitches around little Nonni's eyes
in the early winter morning, to the time when he has raised
his eyelids completely, not only hour after hour goes by—"no,
age after age passes by through the immeasurable expanses of
the morning, world after world, like the visions of a blind person, reality after reality; they pass by, and no longer exist—the
light of day begins" (I, 223). The joy of the brook running
through the farm is "eternally new, every spring, for a thousand
years." And when Nonni sits at its brink he is the boy who
"listens for a thousand years": "The boy and eternity, two friends,
with the sky over the land, cloudless and never ending. Yes"
(I, 287). When Bjartur finally moves off from Sumarhús with
his family they look like "travelers on a long journey, leaving
a poor night lodging on a heath. *It was the heath of life*" (II,
345).

The wish to derive a symbolic or universally applicable meaning from that which is particular and special characterizes virtually all literature to a greater or lesser degree. But in the case of
Laxness it is quite often unusually pronounced, and goes together
with his whole individuality as a novelist. Despite the fact that
his work teems with unique and living individuals, it is hardly
to psychological realism and individualization that he is chiefly
adjusted. In a letter written as early as February, 1926, from
St. Maurice de Clervaux, where he was completing *Vefarinn mikli
frá Kasmír,* he says that he is always getting "further and further
away from the 'psychological novel'"—and here he is probably
thinking, in the first place, of certain French analysts of the
psyche, such as Bourget.[11] The psychological novel has taught
him a good deal, he admits, and has been a necessary stage
in his development. But, on the other hand, nothing is "so limited
and massively positivistic as it; it acts as a hindrance to all
strong wing beats."

Laxness' own novels seem to express, first and foremost, a
vision of man's condition in life. The different figures in the
epic sequence of events—such as Bjartur, Ásta Sóllilja, and Nonni
—give rhythm and dynamic qualities to this vision. This does
not mean that they were supposed to surrender their individual
character and freedom of movement. But perhaps we may notice

at times, in the characterization, a certain tension between the demands of psychological realism—or of realism in general—and the desire to rise with "strong wing beats" to the bird's-eye view which the vision offers.

CHAPTER 6

World Light

I Ólafur Kárason

WITH *Salka Valka* and *Sjálfstætt fólk* Laxness had become indisputably the leading novelist in Icelandic, and was also well on the way to becoming internationally known. But he did not rest on his laurels, for during the following years the four volumes of his novel about Ólafur Kárason, the parish pauper and folk poet, appeared in rapid succession. These were *Ljós heimsins* (The Light of the World, 1937), *Höll sumarlandsins* (The Palace of the Summerland, 1938), *Hús skáldsins* (The House of the Poet, 1939) and *Fegurð himinsins* (The Beauty of the Skies, 1940). Later, in the second edition, *Heimsljós* (World Light) became the collective title of the whole work; and the first part was renamed *Kraftbirtíngarhljómur guðdómsins* (The Revelation of the Deity).[1]

Ljós heimsins describes the life of the boy Ólafur Kárason as a parish dependant, living on the farm of Fótur undir Fótar-fæti (Foot under Foot's Foot). The book begins with the following words: "He stands together with an oyster catcher and a purple sandpiper on the strip of shore below the farm and watches how the waves are sucked in and out. Perhaps he is playing truant from work. He is a parish child, which means that the life in his breast is a separate world, a different blood, without kinship with the others; he is not a part of anything, he stands outside, and is often surrounded by a void; it is a long time now since he began to yearn for some inexplicable consolation" (I, 5). But no such consolation is afforded him on this farm. The mistress of the household, the widow Kamarilla, her daughter Magnína and sons Nasi and Júst, the housemaid Karítas and her daughter Jana, the servant girl—none of them have

any understanding of the lonely boy's need for affection and
loving care. They are in the habit of imposing upon him heavier
burdens of work than his frail body can stand. He awakes in
agony to every new day with its "fetching of water, bad weather,
hunger, shivers of tiredness, exhaustion, slave-driving, curses,
blows, kicks, and the birch." The whole of his childhood is
"one long ordeal, as in the folk tales where people fought with
giants, dragons, and devils" (I, 21).

The brothers Nasi and Júst, who run the farm, are constantly quarreling about how the work is to be conducted, and
their disagreement often discharges itself in blows directed
against the defenseless Ólafur. After a more than usually harsh
bout of ill treatment he has to lie in bed for a long time and is
only able to follow the succession of the days and seasons in
a patch of the sky seen through a narrow little window, in
the passing of a streak of sunshine over the sloping ceiling of
his room. But in this situation, with its appalling poverty of
incident, his own inner world and his dreams as a poet begin
to blossom forth. The boy has early had an inclination towards
poetry and suspects that in books may be found the consolation
which he so passionately desires. His fondness for books, however, meets with no more encouragement at Fótur undir
Fótarfæti than do his own small attempts at following in the
footsteps of the poets: "On the sly he would scratch with a stick
on the grass-free patches of earth and in the snow, but he had
been forbidden to do it and told that he was signing himself
away to the devil. So he had to write in his soul. The mistress
of the house, Kamarilla, hated literature" (I, 10). If his attempts at writing get discovered, they are scorned and condemned by the rulers of the household as dirt and blasphemy.

But Ólafur is in possession of an unassailable certainty, an
indestructible joy. For in a rapturous state of ecstasy he has
perceived a miraculous revelation of the deity, the sound of
a wonderful Voice (hence the title *Kraftbirtíngarhljómur guðdómsins*—The Sonic Revelation of the Deity). In a vision he has
actually experienced the presence of his admired master Sigurður
Breiðfjörð (1798-1846), the long dead Icelandic folk poet, who
stepped down from the little ray of sunlight on the sloping
ceiling, "as from a celestial chariot of gold," laid his gentle hand

on the boy's tormented brow and said: "You are the light of the world" (I, 99).

Ljós heimsins ends with Ólafur being taken away from Fótur undir Fótarfæti on a horse-drawn litter by the light-hearted jack-of-all-trades Reimar the poet; their destination is the little coastal village of Sviðinsvík. Despite the fact that young Ólafur is, or has at least believed himself to be, a conglomerate of various mortal afflictions, he becomes wondrously cured in the unreality of the summer night at the farm of Kambar, by a laying-on of hands performed by the mysterious girl Þórunn. A new person now, "buoyant and hopeful, like Iceland's first man at the beginning of time" (I, 236), he is ferried across the fjord to Sviðinsvík, which glitters like a fairy world in the golden glow of the evening.

The title *Höll sumarlandsins* (The Palace of the Summerland) alludes to a large warehouse building with towers and countless windowpanes, most of which are broken. Here the homeless Ólafur Kárason, after a short stay in the combined poorhouse and lunatic asylum of the village, has been provided with a summer lodging among the rats and wild cats. His benefactor is Director Pétur Pálsson (known as "Three Horses") the man with most influence in the village. With this richly caricatured figure at the center, Laxness gives us a gaily satirical account of economic and social conditions in Sviðinsvík. Pétur Pálsson's cool business methods and despotic ways are naively masked by idealistic interests, which partly express themselves in his zealous habit of singing hymns in private, and in the foundation of a Society for Psychical Research. A description of one of the meetings of this Society turns out to be a hilarious satire on the spiritualist séances which were at the height of their popularity in Iceland during the twenties and thirties.

In his spiritual aspirations Pétur Pálsson can use a promising poet like Ólafur and seeks by means of threats and charitable gifts, applied in suitable doses, to win him over for his own purposes. But there are also other forces working on the young man's susceptible mind. There is his opposite, the strong-willed and austere Örn Úlfar (it is to be noted that the words forming his name mean respectively "eagle" and "wolf") who pits his own demand for social justice against his friend's vague longing for beauty: "He who does not, on every day of his life, fight to his last gasp against those representatives of iniquity, against those living symbols of ugliness who govern Sviðinsvík, blasphemes if he lets the name of beauty pass his lips" (II. 198).

By way of escaping pressure from those who wish to involve him in the controversial problems of the community, Ólafur finds refuge and warmth in the company of certain women. He has a short and happy love affair with a cheerful and spontaneous girl named Vegmey Hansdóttir (Meya á Brekkunni—"Meya on the Slope"). This is an earthy experience of such fullness that ·it may seem a threat to the poet's idealistic longing. Of quite another kind is the young man's relationship with Hólmfríður á loftinu ("Hólmfríður in the Loft"), a married woman who quietly and naturally attends to his needs as a homeless person, and who also, as a fellow poet, imparts to him some measure of her seriousness and bitter worldly wisdom.

The summer ends in disaster for Ólafur. His beloved Vegmey becomes pregnant, marries a fisherman-farmer for financial support and goes away. Ólafur's place of abode, the castle of wood, is one night burned to the ground. Hólmfríður, together with her husband, is driven out of Sviðinsvík because she has let it be known to Pétur Pálsson that she has undesirable opinions. For similar reasons Ólafur falls into serious disfavor with the same potentate. He now makes a tragicomic attempt at taking his own life; he takes a powerful sleeping draught, lies down on the sandy beach at the water's edge and waits for the rising tide to drown him. But when the waves actually reach Ólafur, who is chilled to the marrow, he swiftly jumps to his feet.

In *Hús skáldsins* the setting is still Sviðinsvík, but several years have passed. Ólafur now lives together with a considerably older woman, Jarþrúður, who is known as the Epileptic. He had met her once during his time as a parish dependant at Fótur undir Fótarfæti. They had found each other through a common feeling of being outcasts in life, and Ólafur had started a religion-tinged correspondence with her. Jarþrúður had sought to find in him the resurrected Hallgrímur Pétursson (1614-74), Iceland's great hymn writer, and decided to devote her life to Ólafur, whom she sees as her protégé. After his unsuccessful attempt at suicide she comes over the mountains on foot from her home district and takes him under her wing. The passive Ólafur lets this happen, even though after his summer with

Vegmey he has become quite estranged from Jarþrúður. Pétur Pálsson allows the betrothed couple to take up their quarters in a cabin on the mountain slope—for after having lost the director's favor for a time, Ólafur has been reinstated, and dubbed the poet of the village after Reimar. The latter had, in a satirical elegy, shown himself opposed to the Soul and been driven away by the director with the verdict that he "was a filthy poet, coarse of mouth and dirty in his thoughts; he infected the character of the young and destroyed the Icelandic language as well as the reputation of Sviðinsvík" (III, 26).

The social tension in Sviðinsvík has increased, and Pétur Pálsson is feverishly active with new schemes for counteracting the seething discontent among the wage earners, and their more and more conscious unity. Among other things he wishes to put an end to the use of snuff and *brennivín* and replace these well-tried stimulants with vitamins and codliver oil, to the end that the people in Sviðinsvík may be able to "keep their auras pure." At the very time when he is engaged in espionage on behalf of some fish-poaching foreign trawlers, his idealism soars to more spiritual heights than ever before: "The main thing is to have ideals, together with a burning, seething faith in life, my friend. Oh that I had wings, old fellow. Present-day ethics do not only demand a healthy life, but also a holy life as in ancient times—maturity of soul, and light. We must keep our auras pure, as Skarphéðinn Njálsson was saying to me at a séance in the capital a little while ago" (III, 68).

As always, Ólafur is particularly careful to keep well out of the disputes going on in the community; his chief desire is to be left in peace with his poetic dreams. But the poet has a house, as well as a "fiancée" and a little daughter; this binds him to people, whether he likes it or not, though he mostly allows Jarþrúður to look after the three of them. Being cautious by nature, Ólafur has avoided legalizing his cohabitation with Jarþrúður, even though she has continually implored him to do so; he has clearly wished to keep the door to freedom partly open. A new woman also enters his life, the daring and vigorous Jórunn, who has an indomitable faith in the future. She urges him to break his bonds, to step down from "this detestable cross." But sympathy binds him to his betrothed more strongly than anything else. It would have been different if she had been

young, beautiful and rich, had had a family and friends: "But
she has nothing, nothing. She is humankind in all its nakedness:
sick, defenseless, without a friend, without anybody to be fond
of her or put a nail between her teeth when she has her attacks. God, people, and nature have taken everything from her—"
(III, 177).

Nevertheless, when their little daughter has finally died of
consumption, Ólafur decides to separate from his betrothed. One
day he accompanies her on the way back to the place she once
came from and turns back, drunk with the sense of freedom,
to Sviðinsvík, where Jórunn is expecting him for the night. The
lovers spend the night together, and at dawn Ólafur goes off
to set fire to the wretched hovel where for six years of his
life he has "never been himself, never said a true word, always kept quiet about his inner life as if it were a crime."
But when he steps over the threshold into the house his glance
falls on a black huddle on the floor. It is Jarþrúður, who has
returned during the night and now beseeches him in God's name
not to cast her out. And the poet realizes that his flight from
his own compassionate feelings has been doomed to failure from
the beginning: "My poor Jarþrúður, how could it ever enter
my head that I, a poet, could forsake those who are in distress?" But now he wishes to go away with her from Sviðinsvík
and leave everything behind: "Everything. All his dreams. All
his poetry. All his hope. All his life. Everything." As he sits
at the table staring out into the morning light, he is depicted
as follows: "Like nothing so much as one who seems dead,
he perceived without seeing and hearing, knew without arguing
and thinking; this was cowardice or compassion, whatever it
is called: he did not break his vows to life in the fatal hour;
or rather: he did break them. He was a true man" (III, 230–
34).

In the final part of the tetralogy, *Fegurð himinsins*, Ólafur
lives in the remote village of Bervík, where Jarþrúður has managed to get him a position as a schoolteacher. The surroundings here are as unsympathetic, and the daily life as taxing to
the poet as in Sviðinsvík. He escapes more and more into his
poetic dreams, his longing for a beauty passing all understanding.
But he cannot avoid entanglement with things of this world. As
a man who yields weakly to his impulses, he cannot resist,

in the heat of the moment, a girl who is one of his confirmation pupils, the willing and well-developed "giant-maiden," Jasína Gottfreðlína. The offense comes to light, Ólafur is sentenced to a term of imprisonment in Reykjavík and thus has to make the only journey of any length in his life.

Naturally it is nothing but a relief to him, at first, to be able to hide in the humanely run prison, in the company of petty thieves, illicit distillers of spirits, counterfeiters, and the pride of the house—the murderer. But gradually his mood becomes strangely melancholic; the anguish of his heart seems to be overcoming his faith in the sun. Finally he has to keep to his bed and fancies himself assailed by the same unendurable pains that he suffered in his childhood beneath the sloping ceiling of Fótur undir Fótarfæti. In this extreme darkness, "with benumbed heart, in the midst of that eternal death which hovers over the smallest life of the world," he once again goes through the experience of being visited by his celestial friend, Sigurður Breiðfjörð, in his golden chariot. Suddenly a name is flung "onto the heaven of the soul, in blazing letters: Her name is Bera." Ólafur's thoughts dwell upon "the saving words" in this vision and upon "this name, this key to the future, this unknown happiness, this life" (IV, 193–94).

One day in high summer the poet again stands outside the prison door, a free man. On the voyage home round the coast he meets a young woman, and calls her Bera after his revelation. Their love is half real, half unreal, bathed in the light of the Icelandic summer night. And the place where it finds fulfillment—in a little coastal village, where the boat stops for a few hours—is set in natural surroundings of a spiritual beauty: "Wide flat meadows with the smell of hay from the ricks; the evening star and the crescent moon were reflected in the sedge marshes and rushy tarns or glittered in the calm flow of the river; and these simple jewels of heaven reigned supreme over the country; but up from the tarns rose white, thin veils of mist and spread themselves slowly out over the damp ground. In such a light as this the Soul was born" (IV, 245).

Bera goes ashore at one of the coastal villages, and they have to part. Ólafur asks to be allowed to think of her. "Not in the darkness," she says, "but when the sun shines. Think of me when there is much sunlight about you" (IV, 248). They have found out that their homes are on either side of the very same glacier, the glacier which, for the poet, is associated with his dream of a supraterrestrial beauty. Ólafur writes to Bera, and his old friend Reimar, the poet and postman, delivers their letters. But then her letters stop coming, and one day Reimar visits his fellow poet to inform him that the girl he has called Bera is dead. But Ólafur no longer allows himself to be deceived: "The beauty of the heaven cannot die. It will rule over me for ever and ever" (IV, 257). One morning he gets up very early, before sunrise, and sets out walking on his final journey: "He proceeds inland towards the glacier, to meet the dawn, from hillock to hillock, in deep, new-fallen snow, without heeding the stormy weather which may pursue him. As a child he had stood on the shore at Ljósavík and seen how the coastal wave was sucked in and out, but now he was going away from the sea. Think of me when there is much sunlight about you. Soon the sun of the day of resurrection will shine on the paths of light where she awaits her poet. And beauty alone shall reign" (IV, 263).

II *"What Is Human Is International"*

Thus, in words which express a mystical certainty of belief, the story of Ólafur Kárason the poet comes to an end. This résumé, with its occasional quotations, will have given at least some idea of the scope and stylistic art of this work, which is regarded by many as the culminating achievement of Laxness' literary career. In it we find a rich abundance of symbolically concentrated characterization alternating between, on the one hand, gay humor and biting satire, and on the other incurable melancholy and trembling pathos. And the undulating movement of the narrative, with its sudden turns and changes, is accompanied by a personal style in which the Icelandic language has gained a more flexible fullness of expression than perhaps ever before.

For all its varying components, the work is far from giving an impression of looseness and disunity. The component elements are held together in a purposeful and well-balanced structure, which is already partly hinted at in the different titles of the work's four parts. While both the second and the third book, *Höll sumarlandsins* (The Palace of the Summerland) and *Hús*

skáldsins (The House of the Poet), are essentially devoted to
the society which surrounds the poet, the introductory and final
books, *Ljós heimsins* (The Light of the World) and *Fegurð
himinsins* (The Beauty of the Skies) are concentrated on his
own inner world, on the dreams and visions which dominate
his life from beginning to end.

This time, in fact, Laxness has had unusually diverse materials
to fuse together in the crucible of the imagination. At the
same time, the conditions for following the process of artistic
assimilation are in this case particularly favorable. For the description of Ólafur Kárason's destiny is based on a real and
well documented life history. Among the manuscripts at the National Library of Iceland, Reykjavík, is an exercise book eighty
pages long, with the title: "Magnús Hjaltason's life history. Written by himself. Begun at Suðureyri in Súgandafjörður, January
12, 1914." Also to be found there, however, and most important
of all, are his diaries, which Magnús kept for a quarter of a
century from October 22, 1892, when he was nineteen years
old, until his death in 1916. In about twenty large notebooks—
in a fair copy based on rough drafts—he has conscientiously
recorded the events of his life in an elegant hand, and given
abundant examples of his work as a poet. In all, this amounts
to well-nigh four thousand pages. This poor and ailing folk poet
shows in several passages that he was conscious of creating a
historical document of cultural interest. Under the most difficult
conditions—which already seem unbelievably primitive after half
a century—he shows an affecting preoccupation with his books
and papers. He is conscious of his responsibility to truth and
to posterity. In the prefatory note to the autobiographical account
just mentioned he says that he has always wished to "take care
that the truth should be allowed to come first." And with his
work he hopes to win "some gratitude from people of later
times."

This, then, is the folk poet—a rather inconspicuous person
during his lifetime—whose flesh and blood have been borrowed
by the Ólafur Kárason of fiction. With his own contribution he has
provided a younger compatriot and greater writer with subject
matter and inspiration, and has thus gained a monument more
lasting than that which he was able to create for himself. It is not
only the main outlines of Magnús Hjaltason's life history which

reappear in the story of Ólafur Kárason. Laxness has also been able to take up many episodes, details and exchanges of dialogue, either directly or with only very little revision. In Magnús' work, for example, we find the remarkable expression *kraftbirtíngar-hljómur guðdómsins*, "the sonic revelation of the deity"; and much of Ólafur Kárason's innermost character may already be found in this writer, who really existed. Amid all his distress Magnús somehow seems exceedingly unruffled and unassailable. This feature is particularly striking in his uncompromisingly fact-ual account of his fateful offense against the girl who corresponds to Jasína Gottfreðlína, the "giant-maiden" of the novel; what is more, he even composes a *ríma* of seventy-six stanzas about his experience with the law.

In spite of the fact that Magnús seems to show extremely little similarity to the heroes and skalds of the Icelandic sagas, the spirit and stylistic ideals of the latter have in many re-spects left their mark on his own literary efforts, and among books he rated *Njáls saga* the highest. With his faithful recording of facts, and of all the phases of his life, he has, as it were, transferred his subjective experience to an objective plane and freed himself from the oppressive reality of his own life. It is in this persevering articulation that his strength lies, for there he is a person different from the unsuccessful, snubbed, and despised breadwinner of everyday life.

Corresponding statements may be made of Ólafur Kárason. In *Hús skáldsins,* on the subject of his stories about Strange People, we read:

It never happened that he was partial in his narrative; he never passed moral judgment on deeds or those who did them—any more than Snorri Sturluson did when he told of the exploits of kings and gods. It never happened in the stories written by this man, who himself was incapable of harming the tiniest creature, that any offense taken at so-called evil deeds made itself manifest; he would tell a story only for the reason that something seemed to him worth telling. Nor did he ever use high-flown expressions about so-called good deeds or edifying ways of thinking. . . . He who wrote the books was a man quite different from the humble devotee of general average behavior who was seen in the daytime to be quite prepared to bend to the will of anyone he met (III, 75-76).

In Ólafur Kárason we find an inner independence which is also fairly clearly perceptible in Magnús Hjaltason. Ólafur's final walk from the coast towards the glacier and his death—which have no counterparts in the story of his prototype—may, if we like, be regarded as a last means of defending this independence against overwhelming and unendurable reality.

While Magnús Hjaltason's diaries must have been fascinating material for Laxness to work with, it is nonetheless wisest not to emphasize too strongly the numerous points which fiction and reality have in common. All these elements have provided Laxness with hints and glimpses, and footholds for the literary imagination. But without a powerful vision of his own he would never have been able to fuse them into a new and great work of art; many of them, in any case, are displayed to much greater advantage in the framework he provides. To a large extent, and perhaps for the most part, the diaries make rather colorless reading; and the many poems are seldom more inspired than those of any Icelandic rustic poet of average quality. Laxness has freed Magnús Hjaltason's destiny from its national limitations; he has broadened its scope, and given it universality; from the house of the poet he has opened a view over the world.[2]

Like most writers, Magnús Hjaltason, too, was anxious for the chance to see his works in print. One day in April, 1896, he went to see an editor in Ísafjörður, to hear the man's opinion of his poems. In the eleventh chapter of *Fegurð himinsins* Laxness has turned this episode into a kind of blackmail scene. For the editor in the book seeks to persuade Ólafur to portray him and his political party in a favorable light, with a threat that otherwise things may go badly for a certain poet. This element is quite lacking in the corresponding passage in the diary. On the whole, social and political satire has no place whatever in Magnús Hjaltason's authentic life history. The most he does is to make a few bitter reflections on merchants, who "fleece the public to its very skin" (December 31, 1900), or priests who show a debtor no mercy, even though they are constantly preaching leniency and charity (May 7, 1902).

Thus the social slant in the novel about Ólafur Kárason must be attributed to the author himself. And here Laxness has drawn copiously from his personal experience of Iceland as it was in the thirties. Like *Salka Valka* and *Sjálfstætt fólk, Heimsljós*

also teems with elements drawn from the contemporary history
of Iceland. In the years just before the Second World War—in
the face of the Fascist and Nazi threat—many of Europe's intellectuals, as is well known, became increasingly left-wing. Laxness himself played an active part in the debate then current
in Iceland; on the basis of his socialist standpoint he entered
the field on the side of the radical labor movement. Indeed,
in more conservative Icelandic circles his writings were judged
as a threat to national and conservative ideals. Director Pétur
Pálsson's opinion of Reimar the poet, quoted above—"a filthy
poet," who "infected the character of the young and destroyed
the Icelandic language as well as the reputation of Sviðinsvík"—
shows just the kind of accusation that was made against Laxness.
But the writer had an answer ready. By branding such accusa-
tions as an echo of the Nazi cultural leaders' talk of "entartete
Kunst" he placed his adversaries in a suspicious light as the faithful followers of the most extreme kind of reactionary attitude. His
deft handling of the controversy is typical of his way of seeing
Icelandic society in a larger, international perspective, and of
placing Iceland in the midst of the world.

The elements of social satire in the novel thus really belong
to the thirties, while Magnús Hjaltason's life ran its course about
one generation earlier. The fusing together of these two periods
may seem a hazardous undertaking; for it would surely be difficult to avoid offending against verisimilitude in a manner fatal to
the element of artistic suggestion. But in this respect Laxness
has been greatly helped by the very structure of Icelandic society,
by its sometimes paradoxical points of contact between old and
new. The contrast between ancient and modern is hardly more
striking in his literary work than in Magnús Hjaltason's diaries.
Thanks, perhaps, to a certain distancing or chiaroscuro effect,
he has actually made the world of the novel seem more homogeneous than that of reality.

There are distinct episodes in *Heimsljós* where the inspiration derived from the author's own times perhaps shows
itself especially clearly. On a grotesque excursion from the village
Ólafur Kárason is made to work as a groom for Pétur Pálsson
and the latter's greatly admired business associate from the capital, Júel J. Júel (known as the "Stationist"), director of the
shipping company Grímur Loðinkinni. In the course of their

discussion these ruling personages, who have had quite a few drinks, happen to let fall a few remarks on the subject of human worth. The sentimental Pétur betrays a certain weakness for human beings. Grímur Loðinkinni, Ltd., on the other hand, will not tolerate any such drivel. For Júel the only things of value are fish, fish roe and liver, fish offal and train oil. "Even dung has a good deal of value. It is only people who are worth nothing. . . . Grímur Loðinkinni will not have any of this damn socialism."

When Júel has let fly this dreadful tirade, his glance falls once more on Ólafur, upon whom he has been keeping a watchful eye throughout the whole trip. The Stationist's "instinctive rage" against the poet flares up again, he flings himself at the boy, sits astride him and tries to force brandy into him from a bottle: "Poets should be given a drink to make them get crazy, . . and if they won't drink, then they'll have to starve—they'll be trampled down into the muck with boots." But in this situation of extreme humiliation, when people seek to deprive him of all human dignity, when he really is made to feel "the boot of the upper-class man on his face," Ólafur remains, in spite of everything, unassailable: "He thought of his poems: the fact remained that he possessed such things of value as the Stationist's hands would never be able to touch. He thought of those thousands of poets before him whom the Stationists of the world had trampled into the dirt with their boots. Time will go by and the graves become covered with grass. But long after the Stationists have sunk and vanished in a black night, wrapped in the contempt of centuries, the songs of the poets will still resound from the lips of living and loving people" (II, 236–37).

In the face of a description such as this it is worth bearing in mind that it was written in the years 1937–38, that is, in the heyday of Nazism, when the bearers of spiritual culture were literally trampled down by boots in various parts of Europe. In Júel J. Júel—"Grímur Loðinkinni, Ltd., two stations in Northern Iceland, five trawlers" (II, 221)—we catch a whiff of international capitalism. He embodies the Fascist mentality in a coldly conscious form. His agent, Pétur Pálsson Three Horses, with his picturesquely Icelandic individuality, is a more harmless type, who is perhaps more comical than frightening.

The director is a bully, to be sure, but only within national
and domestic limits. His hypocrisy is partly unconscious. In his
craftiness and false idealism there is something disarmingly naive,
and he is not lacking in a certain spontaneous benevolence towards his dependants in Sviðinsvík. Ólafur's tormentors on the
farm of Fótur undir Fótarfæti, the brothers Nasi and Júst, represent a primitive hostility to all spiritual life, a contempt and
perhaps fear of the wretched parish child's own hidden world,
which is so alien to them.

From the very beginning Laxness himself was well aware of
the topical significance of his work. Some six months after the
first part of the tetralogy had come out, he was asked by an
Icelandic interviewer if it would be possible to give a penetrating
analysis of the poet and his problems within the framework
imposed on Ólafur Kárason's world by time and space. Laxness
answered: "The parish pauper's Icelandic environment is just
a pretext, an opportune setting for a description of the poet's
position in the struggle of the present time. If the reader tires
of imagining Iceland as the stage and Icelandic people as the
actors he may imagine that the scene is an English country
seat or a Chinese ivory tower—that Nasi is called Lord Ponsonby
and Júst is called Chang-Pei-Fu. What is human is international.
I place the poet in the everyday life of Iceland because that
is the everyday life I know best. But the story could have taken
place in any country in the world." [3]

Later—in a foreword primarily intended for the German edition of the work and dated Kassel, September 28, 1955—the
author stressed, very strongly and surely far too onesidedly, that
his novel was "in certain respects a projection of the Hitler
regime," and that its setting was "in many ways a microscopic
equivalent of the National Socialist Thousand-year Reich, a Third
Reich seen through an inverted telescope, or, if we like, a Third
Reich resolved into aliquot parts." In this Reich the poets had
only two alternatives: either "to get into conflict with the remarkable 'heroic race' and chamber of horrors which dominated
the state and receive their remuneration in the form of torture,
hanging, or death in the gas chamber; or to choose what was
called inner emigration—a term current at the time." This reminds us in a far-off way of the poet Ólafur Kárason's village
of Sviðinsvík, "a humorless, microcosmic thousand-year state

where it costs a thrashing to express one's opinion with the unutterably revolting word: 'indeed.' " [4]

It is thus clear that in his description of the poet Ólafur Kárason's position in society Laxness has made full use of elements both old and new: of the Icelandic tradition as well as his own experiences as a writer in the Europe of the nineteen-thirties. This living contact with contemporary problems is perhaps not the least important of the factors contributing to the universality of his fiction—the universal appeal of a setting and dramatis personae which are characteristically and inimitably Icelandic.

III *"This Must Be the Realm of Myth"*

While working on his novel tetralogy Laxness made a second visit to the Soviet Union and recorded his impressions in a long eyewitness account entitled *Gerska æfintýrið* (The Russian Adventure, 1938). Certain of his reflections here throw light on his artistic principles and working methods as a writer of fiction. Part of the book is taken up with an interesting discussion of things Russian and things Icelandic. Laxness maintains that individualized characters are more firmly rooted in the art of Russia than in that of most other countries, and continues:

> The exaggeration of personal peculiarities has its El Dorado in semi-civilized countries. Among us Icelanders—who in a great many respects are at the same stage of civilization as the Russians—exaggerated personal peculiarities are very usual; and they have gained with us, just as much as with the Russians, a lasting place in art, or at least in literature. In countries where civilization is very widely and comparatively evenly spread—not infrequently at the expense of culture itself—people become like each other, and exaggerated peculiarities become rare, so that the public involuntarily regards such types as insane, and recoils before them with a shudder. Civilization does not have room for the screaming, fanatical emphasis which the individual in a less civilized society lays on his own personality, on his words and actions.

Scandinavian literature "outside Iceland (and Finland)"— apart from the works of the Norwegian Hamsun, who has "learned more than anyone else from the Russians"—is poor in "types," he claims. Life has become "too civilized, too smooth

and polished, too psychological, too lacking in contrasts." Apart
from such types as alcoholics and other poor wretches, the *petite
bourgeoisie* is "the constantly recurring distinctive feature of life
and art in such highly civilized countries as Sweden and Denmark, for example." What do they have to compare with the vast
gallery of characters in Russian literature? asks Laxness, and
gives a number of examples from the great narrative art of
Russia, from Pushkin to Gorky (175–76).

   In the years leading up to *Vefarinn mikli frá Kasmír* Dostoevsky's characterization had made an overwhelming impression on
the young Icelander. Tolstoy and Gorky, too, formed part of his
early reading in literature. But then he seems to have been im-
pressed throughout by their conceptions of life and of humanity,
and by their ethical messages, rather than by their specifically
artistic qualities. Now, during his stay in Soviet Russia, another
Russian storyteller, Gogol, entered the foreground of his interests;
he experienced *Dead Souls* in a dramatized version as a joyful
reunion which brought to life again the "unforgettable characters"
of the novel: "A writer who has happened to read Gogol in
his childhood will never recover from the experience afterwards.
For even if *Dead Souls* is carried off for a while in the stream
of time, its author—this preposterous fellow who has quite certainly made a more difficult art form of the novel than anyone
else—will visit you again when you least expect it. When all
the analytic, psychological chitchat has subsided, one is visited
again by the wholeness, by the synthesis" (179).

   It is hardly a coincidence that Laxness should make this statement at the very time when he was busily engaged in writing
Höll sumarlandsins; the manuscript of the future book is frequently mentioned in *Gerska ævintýrið*. With its fantastic realism,
whereby certain characters may suddenly give the impression
of having risen from the world of the folk tale, the story of
Ólafur Kárason seems to show an affinity with Gogol's narrative
art. It is conceivable that his renewed and more direct contact
with Russian prose fiction has contributed towards making this
element more conscious in Laxness' case, and brought it
to speedier maturity. Besides Gogol, Gorky, for example, may
have influenced Laxness in the same way. Certain of Gorky's

characters have the same kind of exaggerated reality, and the same troll-like proportions characteristic of folk-tale figures, that we find in Pétur Pálsson Three Horses.

But perhaps we should not insist too strongly on any one or more of these predecessors as having provided Laxness with literary impulses. He himself refers to classical Russian story-telling in its entirety as a treasure house of unique types. In this connection he might have quoted an observation made by Dostoevsky in *The Idiot,* to the effect that authors often select social types for their descriptions—"types rarely met with in their entirety, but these types are nevertheless more real than real life itself"; "in real life typical characters are 'watered down', so to speak." [5] It is a writer's policy which Laxness might have formulated himself, however much he may otherwise differ from Dostoevsky in his artistry and view of life.

Laxness must have been exceptionally well prepared for these literary impulses, for they surely corresponded to his own propensities, and especially, perhaps, to the view of the Icelandic character at which he had arrived. In the early summer of 1936 he traveled in the very parts of northwestern Iceland where Magnús Hjaltason had lived; and this was clearly a direct preparation for his great novel. In his diary of this rambling trip Laxness wrote down, among other things, the following observation:

The Icelander has a distinct and dramatic grandness of stature, which has its origin both in his magnificent country and in his fantastic struggle for life. In the destiny of the most insignificant person there is always something grand and overdimensioned; a man who is so insignificant that nobody pays him any attention may easily have a close affinity with awful natural forces and dangers, having grown up with the most incredible poverty as companion. Thus the life of the people does indeed constitute an inexhaustible subject for fiction, wherever one may be; life is everywhere equally magnificent, remarkable, and extraordinary.

Sad stories, which exceed all reasonable bounds, are usual; so are comic stories, which border on the insane. [6]

The author goes on to give some concrete examples of such stories, several of which were later worked into the novel about Ólafur Kárason. We notice that Laxness already mentions here an "overdimensioning," or exaggeration, which borders on the

incredible or insane. His point of view here is just the same
as when in *Gerska æfintýrið* he compares the life of the Russian
people with that of the Icelanders.

In his tetralogy of novels Laxness has undoubtedly applied
exaggeration as an artistic principle more boldly and consistently
than before. It is illuminating to compare the director in
Sviðinsvík with his counterpart in Óseyri. Jóhann Bogesen is
a realistic figure all through. Pétur Pálsson, on the other hand,
is ruthlessly stylized. The unquestionably realistic features of this
latter figure have been specially selected and overexposed, and
have thus acquired fantastic dimensions. This difference between
two dominating and comparable characters is symptomatic of
the two works.

There is an amusing episode in *Þú vínviður hreini* where the
schoolteacher gives Salka Valka, who has never received any
school education, her first test in general knowledge. In *Fegurð
himinsins* we find a parallel situation in which Ólafur Kárason
questions his girl pupil Jasína Gottfreðlína. In both cases vigor-
ously spontaneous young girls are confronted with the world of
conventional education. The encounters is full of comedy in either
case; primitive and homegrown opinion is well able to hold its
own against schoolteaching. But while Salka Valka remains an
ordinary lass who simply has not had time to learn to read,
Jasína Gottfreðlína is a "wild daughter of the headlands" with
"gigantic jaws." Standing in the poet's cottage with her stockings
slipping down around her legs, she has about her "an atmosphere
of horsemeat, fulmar, and fish roe." She seems "charged with
an impersonal strength derived from earth and sea, a strength
utterly irreconcilable with every conception of the soul." This
girl with the "horselike glance" in her eyes seems to embody the
primary human state which lies beyond all Christianity, morality,
custom, and teaching (IV, 45–48).

We have already quoted the opinion of Ólafur Kárason's life
as a parish dependant—"one long ordeal, as in the folk tales,
where people fought with giants, dragons, and devils" (I, 21).
Even if the author had not expressly made the comparison himself, the reader could hardly have helped thinking of the folk-tale
"genre" in this context. The whole setting and group of characters
on the farm carry our thoughts in this direction. The two evil
brothers Nasi and Júst—portrayed as they are, with a few strokes

of the pen, as contrasts and complements to each other—have
much of the stylization typical of the folk tale; and their obese
sister, Magnína, the stay-at-home daughter of the house, stands
with one foot at least in the world of the folk tale. The same
can be said of a number of characters in Sviðinsvík, like the
old miser Jón the snuff-cutter, the wealthiest man in the community, who for decade after decade has sat alone in his tarred
cottage and "cut snuff for God and just about anybody from
six o'clock in the morning to eleven o'clock at night" (III, 169)—
a grotesque and dismal illustration of a sterile and inhuman
ideology of work.

Yet it is not just the more or less negative elements in this
narrative which bear the mark of a symbolic intensification and
exaggeration of this kind. Characteristic of Laxness' fondness
for antithesis is the very fact that he also condenses the positive
experiences and at the same time raises them to a level of mystical
unreality. In the midst of his hopeless struggle as a child against
"giants, dragons, and devils" Ólafur can experience visions of
supraterrestrial goodness and beauty. The sonic revelation of
the deity surrounds and fills him in such a way that he himself
merges into the sounding flow. Nature, the Icelandic countryside
itself, plays an essential part in these ecstasies. In the latter
days of his life Ólafur's thoughts often turn to the infinitely
white glacier and the lonely little farm close to it. He thought
when he first discovered the place that the people's life there
must draw its character from this closeness to the mighty dome
of ice: "The glacier was within easy reach beyond the wooded
ridge, and its nearness was like the nearness of a perfectly pure,
Divine being—consummately beautiful and without all mercy. It
seemed to the poet as if those who lived in the neighborhood
of so perfectly white an enchantment could not be of merely
human nature. This must be the realm of myth" (IV, 9).

The few inhabitants of this place seem under the spell of
a unique enchantment about which, however, there is nothing
alarming or diabolical. On the contrary, these people are found
to have perfect peace of mind and humility, with a quiet reverence towards life in its simplest manifestations—all of which is a
reflection of their living together with this divine nature. The
people there have no part in the clamor, ferocity, and ugliness
of life; the gleam from the ethereally white glacier falls on their

humble deeds. Pure-hearted humanity and the poorest kind of
everyday existence have here acquired the quality of legend,
and have been raised to a level of mystical dignity. Among
these people the unworldly poet feels at home; and they regard
him as one of their own.

IV   The Poet and His Compassion

Heimsljós may be read, not least of all, as a memorial
to the Icelandic folk poet through the ages. Ólafur Kárason is
himself such a poet. He seeks comfort and moral strength in
Sigurður Breiðfjörð, "the greatest of all poor folk poets in Iceland" (IV, 199). When Ólafur has been released from the prison
in Reykjavík on a day in high summer, he visits the cemetery
and after a long search finds Sigurður Breiðfjörð's humble
tombstone, on which is carved a five-stringed harp. The
real Magnús Hjaltason in fact paid the same tribute of veneration
to the master in a corresponding situation, according to a note
in the diary on May 11, 1912. In words charged with pathos
Laxness now pays his tribute both to the indispensable cultural
value and to the national and spiritual power represented by
the work of the Icelandic folk poet, whose spirit

. . . has lived among the Icelandic people for a thousand
years in the smell of smoke from the lonely cottage; in a fisherman's
poor hovel close to Snæfellsjökull; on a shark fishing boat off the
north coast when all the seamarks were lost in the midwinter darkness
of the Arctic Ocean; in the rags of the tramp who slumbers at the
side of the mountain sheep among the willows of the moors; in the
fetters of the convict at Bremerholm; this spirit was the quick in the
life of the people through its whole history, the spirit which has
made this poor island country in the western sea a great nation and a
world power, the unconquerable outpost of the world (IV, 200).[7]

In spite of all this, it is not as a distinctive national symbol
that the figure of Ólafur Kárason has its deepest meaning. In
this folk poet Laxness has above all given a portrait of the
Poet, in a general sense. As a description of the problems posed
by creative writing the work certainly has no equal in the Scandinavian countries, and may even be unequaled in world literature.

As a poet Ólafur is presented in sharp relief through being
contrasted with poets of a different kind. On the more humorous

level Ólafur is contrasted with his fellow poet Reimar, who with his shallow, transparent eyes is the rhymster "for all waters," with no creative problems; he reels off poetry on subjects of all kinds, without the agony of the true creator. Ólafur, on the other hand, lives through the destinies of his fictional characters, "wrestling, as it were, with the Creator Himself, in the manner of the poet. Thus he would sit up for many a night over a sentence which he later crossed out at the dawn of day, and went to bed cold, tired, and disappointed like a man who has lost everything, and will never experience a happy day again" (III, 76–77). But the struggle also offers causes for rejoicing: "A well-balanced sentence and a faultless line in a poem is a great reward for a day's hunger and a sleepless night," Ólafur maintains. "In the future, when my image has long since faded, no one will ask what the poet ate or whether he slept well at night; but people will ask: did he write good Icelandic? did he compose with purity?" (III, 122).

For all the distress which assails him, Ólafur is one of the elect; he is a vocational and compulsive poet. Through the whole of his life he is accompanied by a wonderful voice which at any moment can be made to sound within him. He perceives it in its highest potency as "the sonic revelation of the deity," and when he, just like Magnús Hjaltason, has experienced for the first time, before the age of nine, what it means to become "a trembling voice in an almighty sound of glory," where the soul seems "to flow together with a boundless sea of higher life, above words and beyond all perception," and the body is imbued with "a foaming light, above all light," he feels an unutterable happiness: "He lay in peaceful ecstasy and felt as if no shadow could ever fall again on his life; that all adversity was as nothing; that nothing mattered any longer; that everything was good. He had perceived the One. His father in heaven had taken him unto his heart here on the edge of the northern sea" (I, 18–19). At different stages of his life he will call the sound of the "harp of the cosmos" (I, 45) by varying names. But basically it is the selfsame experience all the time.

This blissfully intoxicating awareness, this sense of a mystical expansion and ascension of the individual self into the cosmos, is released first and foremost in the heart of the Icelandic countryside. In this work it is striking, too, how often nature is animated, and appears to merge together with the nature of man in a pantheistic and monistic experience of total oneness. The borderline between matter and spirit, between time and eternity, may seem blurred. In the third chapter of *Höll sumarlandsins* there is a description of how Ólafur wanders about in the spring countryside and is rapturously transported by "the Creator's manifold dwelling places." He follows "a virgin brook, a streamlet of clear blue water, like all other virgin brooks; it springs forth in the innermost part of the valley; it flows on with a peaceful, almost religious joy; is a breath from a sphere even higher than this; its joy is of the same kind as the poet's; the brook and the poet, they love; the sun shines on them; death does not exist." And as he lies among the flowers in the grass and looks up at the sky, with the murmur of brooks and the chirping of birds all around him, while the mountains beyond "the gleaming fjord" merge together "into a blue haze of mystery," he realizes that nature is "one loving mother, and that he himself and all that lives are of the selfsame spirit; nothing is ugly any longer, nothing evil" (II, 37).

The poet's strange experiences, and his whole situation and mental *habitus,* make him a unique and solitary character in the fellowship of men. "How shall I be able to say anything, I who stand outside everything" (III, 46), Ólafur says, defending himself, when his opinion on important community problems is asked at a meeting in Sviðinsvík. He explains on the same occasion that "To be a poet is to be a stranger on a far distant coast until one dies" (III, 49).

In the figure of Ólafur Kárason, the poet's ineptitude in worldly matters has been strongly underlined. But although the poet, viewed from without, perhaps seems more vulnerable and defenseless than his fellow creatures, his spiritual experiences, on the other hand, and his status as one of the elect render him unassailable in his innermost being. "There are no blows which can strike a poet," Ólafur says to his pupil Sveinn, who also wishes to become a poet and a learned man. "Poets are stronger than gods, human beings, and horses" (IV, 38). The gift of perceiving what Ólafur on one occasion calls perhaps not "a sound, but rather a light, an inner light, a light of joy, a light of omnipotence; that Light, that Sound which no word has been created to explain" (IV, 35), can make the poet quite indifferent to the usual

interests and passions of men. It can actually seem to Ólafur as
if the life of man were "a matter of secondary importance, almost
nothing": "Beauty is the only thing that matters, and in reality
a poet has no obligations to anyone but her" (IV, 31). And
at the end of the book he surely acts consistently with this
insight. When he walks towards the glacier in the early morning
he is turning his back on the earth and its people forever,
so that he may go to his meeting with Beauty.

A worship of beauty, driven to such lengths, may perhaps
seem inhumanly idealistic; and Ólafur is fully conscious of this.
He once says to the energetic Jórunn, the girl who wishes to
draw him into her vigorous and active life: "Yes, I know you
think me a scoundrel. And you are right: he who contemplates
the heavenly light is a scoundrel. The earth is and remains a
freak of fate in his eyes. Contemplating the heavenly light involves a complete hardening of the heart. Such a person, if he
can be called a person, cannot be saved" (III, 112).

But in spite of the poet's inhuman hardness of heart and
his culpable flight from life, there is a paradox in the fact that
his ruthless longing for beauty seems to draw nourishment from
a love of his fellow mortals and seems, in its turn, to keep
this love alive. Not even when the boy is reduced to bottomless
despair by the meanness and cruelty at Fótur undir Fótarfæti
can he hate or bear ill will towards anybody: "He who has
met the invisible friend, can no longer see any evil in people,
and even if they take everything from him, every smallest joy,
every weakest hope, it makes no difference at all; he will nonetheless do everything to make their joy greater, their hope stronger,
their life more beautiful." He will always "devote what is most
precious in himself to these people," he will "bear the sufferings
of mankind" (I, 180–81).

Compassion "for Ásta Sóllilja on earth," in other words for
defenceless humankind, had already been mentioned in *Sjálfstætt
fólk* as "the source of the highest song" and this thought is not
foreign to Ólafur Kárason, either. "For man is essentially alone,
and one should pity him and love him and grieve with him"
(I, 118–19). He already realizes this as a sickly child dependent
on the parish; and later it is chiefly in his relationship with
Jarþrúður, his betrothed, that his feelings of sympathy are put
to a decisive test. He realizes that he is inseparably tied to

her, because she is a "representative of that generation of mankind of which he himself was an inseparable part, which is bur-
dened with passions and is frail and sorrowful in its attempts to
escape from the darkness and cruelty of its origin" (III, 114).

We can surely see a deeper symbolism in the fact that the
poet is personified as a parish pauper. For in spite of his feeling
of being a complete outsider, he is utterly loyal to the outcasts
and oppressed members of society. "Poets and the rabble are
always friends. And it is an old experience that in time of need
they are one" (III, 212), he explains to his betrothed just before
a political election in Sviðinsvík. A passage such as this may
remind the reader of Laxness' own involvement with politics.
But the parallel must not be pressed too far; for unlike his
creator, Ólafur is no socialist. His idealistic longing is expressed
in more general—even vaguer—terms. It reaches towards an
existence in which goodness has been realized in human cohabitation. The poet does not talk of economic systems or practical
politics. He only knows what the "better world" of his dreams
should be like: a world in which "industry and commerce function of their own accord without anyone trying to steal from the
others"; in that world "which nature has given to men, society
is not a society of thieves, the children are not sickly, but healthy
and contented, and young men and women have their wishes
fulfilled, because that is natural" (III, 49).

V   The House of the Poet

All attempts at fixing in unequivocal formulae the world of
Laxness' literary creation are frustrated, not least of all, by the
markedly dialectical slant which pervades it—which penetrates
the ideational content, the characterization, the design of the
work, and the smallest details of the style. A thesis may suddenly
turn into its own antithesis; and a reserve of irony lurks beneath
the surface of even the most wholehearted pathos. The reader
is never given the opportunity to settle down in safe possession
of an insight or a final judgment. The writer carries the reader
along with him in a continuous discussion of problems to which
form is given in the characters and situations of the narrative.

One of the essential antitheses in the work is the contrast
between Ólafur Kárason and Örn Úlfar. Örn is also a poet,
or rather has been one in the past; his bitter experiences of

life in Sviðinsvík have caused him to burn his poems. This young man will "acknowledge no beauty, as long as human life is a perpetual crime" (II, 125). The contrast between the two friends is most clearly and movingly shown in a night-time conversation at the poet's house, where they were keeping watch over Ólafur's little girl, his dying child. The poet speaks of love and compassion as the guiding stars of man. But Örn has "little respect for that compassion which the coward calls love"; he says he does not even know what love is. In his eyes man has only "one mark of nobility over and above the gods: he chooses justice." "The struggle for justice is the only thing which gives the life of man a rational meaning." But Ólafur has an answer ready: "Örn, has it never occurred to you that it is possible to struggle for justice until there is no longer anyone left on earth? Though the world may perish, justice shall triumph, runs the old saying. It seems to me that there is hardly any saying more suitable as a motto for madmen."

So the whispered dialogue goes on, with its vigorous oscillations between opposing points of view. Ólafur believes that man is a creature of dust who is by nature poor and "lives first and foremost both by and for his imperfection." Örn maintains that man is primarily a fiery being who is by nature rich and "lives both by and for his perfection." It finally seems to the poet as if the distance between him and his friend, as they sit on either side of the girl's sickbed, is "mystical and incredible"— yet they appear to be preconditioning each other's existence, like two polar opposites. Ólafur says: "Tonight, when I listen to our own voices in this strange stillness which is blended with the nearness of death, even though the breeze is playing so innocently on door and roof, I feel as if we were two gods in the clouds of the sky with the dying race of man between us"(III, 159–63).

In this magnificent scene, where the tiny cottage is broadened into a universe and the characters acquire a mystical greatness, the framing of questions asked has been extended far beyond the problems posed by creative writing. The problem discussed here is man's general situation in life. But then the author brings us straight back to the sickroom of here and now. The little girl awakes: " 'Daddy,' she suddenly said loudly, in a clear voice which went like a ray of light through the house and awakened everything to life, and gave brightness to the dull light of dawn after the friends' long and low-voiced conversation, and the faint sighing of the wind. 'Daddy and little Magga are going down to the sea—.'" A few almost imperceptible tremors pass through her body, and her life has sped; but the smile remains on her lips. Her father closes her eyes with his slender poet's fingers. Örn Úlfar sits on the other side of the deathbed and stares into space "without movement or expression, as if this did not concern him; or as if it concerned him too much for him to wish to see it" (III, 164–65).

From the philosophical and metaphysical heights of this conversation on the subject of the great insoluble problems of humanity, we are suddenly brought back into a concrete situation of shocking reality: a child who dies before she has yet begun to live. Why is it that the picture of the little girl gives the episode an exceptional luminous intensity, a new artistic depth? The reason is that in spite of everything it turns the conversation between the two men into something much greater, something much more serious than a dialectical game. It is this individual human destiny with its almost unbearable palpability—the plight of the helpless individual, whom Laxness discusses so often —which thrusts the scene upon us and compels us to experience it with the whole of our being, so that we have to feel that we are involved in this; that we actually *are* Ólafur Kárason, Örn Úlfar, and the dying child.

The two friends part outside the poet's house in the morning. Örn, the socialist agitator, "went off to incite poor people to fight for justice, to the end that children of the future might have the chance to live"; Ólafur "set out in search of the hearts of good people, so that he could bury children" (III, 166). Thus is formulated, once again, the painful, dualistic conflict between aggregate and individual, between looming ideals and immediate human reality.

Ólafur and Örn would often wander about together in the field of Bragi (the god of poetry)—"the field where human destinies receive a meaning" (III, 132). A poem or a work of fiction, however great it may be, cannot solve man's ultimate and most urgent problems. But it can set them before the reader and present them in an artistic creation of such richness that they burn their way into his consciousness with the strength of a revelation. The house of the poet is a humble abode, but has room enough for all essential human experience: "This little house, which in actual fact could hardly be called a house, grew both in width and height until it was as large as the whole world" (III, 79).

CHAPTER 7

Iceland's Bell

I *The Background—Ancient and Modern*

WHEN the final part of the Ólafur Kárason tetralogy was published, the Second World War had become a glaring reality for the Scandinavian countries as well as others. While Denmark and Norway lay within the iron grip of Nazi Germany, Iceland was occupied by British and American troops. The British occupied Iceland on May 10, 1940, and were succeeded there by the Americans after a period of fourteen months. It is true that, as far as Iceland was concerned, the occupation brought no distress or suffering in its train; on the contrary, it was accompanied by increased prosperity for the country as a whole. Nevertheless, a situation where a nation numbering 130,000 provides accommodation in its own country for as many, perhaps, as 50,000 soldiers from a leading power, is not without its problems. It involves great risks for a unique national culture like that of Iceland; and may give rise to much reflection on the general subjects of native and foreign, of freedom and dependence, of right and might.

At this time the Icelanders had another important reason for self-examination. In 1944 Iceland finally detached itself from the personal union with Denmark which had been valid since 1918, and was proclaimed a Republic on June 17 at the historic meeting place of the ancient General Assembly—Þingvellir. The people of Iceland had thus achieved their long and eagerly coveted goal of full national independence, which had been lacking since 1262, when the Icelandic Commonwealth was forced to submit to the king of Norway, largely as a result of disruptive internal conflicts.

During these richly eventful years in the history of Iceland another great work by Laxness was taking shape. This was a novel trilogy: *Íslandsklukkan* (Iceland's Bell, 1943), *Hið ljósa man* (The Bright Maid, 1944) and *Eldur í Kaupinhafn* (Fire in Copenhagen, 1946). From now on the title *Íslandsklukkan* will be used here for the whole work. In the throes of the Second World War, Scandinavian writers often harked back to earlier periods in the lives of their nations. This must have been partly due to the current necessity of disguising certain aims of dangerously topical relevance; it was partly due also, however, to the fact that temporal distance could throw into relief the national and universally human values for which the struggle was being waged. In *Íslandsklukkan* Laxness also turned to his country's past. The action of the novel takes place in the late seventeenth and early eighteenth centuries. It is true that the author avoids any direct dating of its events; indeed, he has prefaced all three parts of the work with the comment that it is not a "historical novel" inasmuch as its "characters, action, and style conform exclusively to the work's own laws." But its gallery of characters, its sequence of events and the description of its setting are closely linked with this gloomy period in the history of the country. The ancient Commonwealth was then being administered as a colony by the absolute monarchy of Denmark. Certain Danish towns had the monopoly of trade with Iceland; and possibilities for the country's economic development seemed altogether precluded. Pestilence and years of famine did not improve the situation. Laxness has, in fact, made himself thoroughly familiar with the history of the time and has very skillfully recreated the atmosphere of the past from historical and legal records and from publications of a rather curious kind.[1]

Íslandsklukkan is dominated by three main characters: Jón Hreggviðsson, the farmer; Snæfríður Eydalín, the lawman's daughter; and Arnas Arnæus, the professor and collector of manuscripts. Their destinies are ingeniously interwoven and together give a manysided picture of the living conditions and dreams of the nation. In the design of the work we may glimpse the author's intention of focusing each part of the trilogy on one of the three leading figures.

II   *The Farmer, the Fair Maid, and the Professor*

The first part of *Íslandsklukkan* receives its stamp from Jón Hreggviðsson. On feeble grounds this penniless farmer has been condemned to death for the murder of His Royal Majesty's executioner. But the night before he is due to be beheaded he escapes from his prison tent at Þingvellir and after an arduous tramp across Iceland manages to get on board a Dutch fishing vessel. The Icelandic farmer's encounter with his new surroundings in the great city of Rotterdam is described with rich humor. His experiences on the Continent, first as a vagabond in Holland and later as a Danish mercenary, develop into a short picaresque novel complete in itself. Yet all the time he has the prospect of his own lawsuit ahead of him; the progress of the case, moreover, is related in accordance with historical events. It is with this lawsuit, which also becomes part of a larger political struggle for Iceland, that the main thread of the work is spun.

Above all, Jón Hreggviðsson develops, in the course of the narrative, into a representative of the starving and ill-treated Icelandic peasantry. He is not an entirely sympathetic character; he cannot afford to be so in his ruthless struggle for survival. His view of his own destiny is quite lacking in pathos and sentimentality; and if qualities of this kind are faintly discernible in his speech, then they may be attributed to the wily farmer's pretence and cunning. But he reveals his human greatness in his stubborn will to endure, in his grim humor which never deserts him in times of adversity or humiliation. "Black" Jón is always ready with a scornful smile of radiant whiteness directed at his tormentors. In the dungeon, in the shadow of the executioner's axe, he indefatigably sings his "Pontusrímur" (Rhymes of Pontus). The "authorities" are the natural enemy of him and his like, and he cares as little for their justice as for their injustice.

In the fantastic crowd of convicts—some of them branded, some of them with their hands cut off—who have been summoned to Þingvellir for the grand judicial assizes, a blind man acts as spokesman for himself and his fellow sufferers: "We are the rabble, the earth's lowest creatures. Let us pray that success may follow every powerful man who comes to help the unprotected. But we shall get no justice until we ourselves become men. Centuries will pass; and the better laws given us by the

last king will be taken from us by the next. But a day will
come. And on that day, when we have become men, God will
come to us and be our warrior" (II, 266). In this prophecy
there is surely a hint of the author's own passion for social
justice.

The archaic title *Hið ljósa man*, which is borrowed from the
Eddic poem *Hávamál* (The Words of the High One), alludes
to Snæfríður. If Jón Hreggviðsson embodies the Icelandic people
—a nation involved to the hilt in its struggle for existence amid
the poverty and ugliness of its everyday life—then the author
has assembled in the figure of the bright maid all that is mysteriously unassailable in the life of the nation: the dream and the
saga above and beyond the grimness of each new day. Despite
the fact that she is herself confronted with the brutal aspects
of life, she is often described as being "absent," as being virtually
independent of material things, and raised above them. Arnas
Arnæus says that he first saw her as a vision, an apparition
different from other human beings (II, 190). The comparatively
few lyrical descriptions of nature in the work are in several
cases associated with her image, as Arnas remembers it (II,
188, 201). Even Jón Hreggviðsson's words become poetry when
he describes Snæfríður, who is also called Íslandssól (Iceland's
Sun) (III, 145–46).

But Snæfríður's nature, for all its lyrical brightness, has much
of the harshness and pride of her forebears, the women of the
söguöld. When Arnas Arnæus deserts her for his passionate desire
to save Iceland's ancient hoard of manuscripts, she marries in
desperation "Squire" Magnús of Bræðratúnga, a "cavalier" type
whose thirst for *brennivín* has reduced him to a complete wreck.
"Sooner the worst than the next best" (I, 123), she says defiantly
to her father, the lawman, who wishes her to marry the canon.
It is perhaps in her conversations with the latter, her "waiting
suitor," that her character stands out in boldest relief. Her self-
assurance and self-will assert themselves against his demands
for humility before God and the authorities.

In *Eldur í Kaupinhafn* Arnas Arnæus finally comes more dis-
tinctly into the foreground than before. The historical prototype
for this character is none other than Árni Magnússon (1663–
1730), the famous Icelandic collector of manuscripts, whose be-
quest of books and manuscripts to the University of Copenhagen

is now known as the Arnamagnæan Collection. Arnas is described as being almost demoniacally possessed by his native country's rich hoard of manuscripts, which in his view preserves the soul of Iceland, and we see something of the work he does to save these irreplaceable cultural documents from decay. The reader accompanies him to Jón Hreggviðsson's farm, where among the rags at the bottom of a bedstead he makes one of his most valuable finds of parchment leaves. A poignant paradox lies in the fact that these spiritual treasures are brought to light in just such a hovel as this, in surroundings of extreme human misery.

Arnas' destiny, however, involves sacrificing his own personal happiness and that of the bright maid for the sake of decayed vellums. The collecting of manuscripts costs money; and he finds that the only way to save his treasures from the hands of usurers is to marry a rich widow in Copenhagen, who is described as "a composite monster, a mixture of troll and dwarf, albeit in a woman's guise" (I, 199)—in every respect a contrast to Snæfríður Íslandssól. And to crown all, this sacrifice turns out in the end to be virtually unavailing. In the fire of Copenhagen, after which the final part of the trilogy is named—and which actually ravaged the city in 1728—a large part of his treasure hoard of books becomes a prey to the flames. Just like the real Árni Magnússon, Arnas Arnæus is strangely tardy in bringing his precious treasures to safety. On being warned that the fire may shortly reach his house, he replies resignedly: "Now it is best that the gods decide. I am tired" (III, 183).

His exhaustion may be partly explained by his failure on the level of law and politics. He has, among other things, been sent out to Iceland as a Royal Commissioner to inspect the administration of justice there and the activities of the merchants. But his efforts to alleviate the hard lot of the peasantry are wrecked by stubborn resistance from both Danish and Icelandic authorities. In the shadow of the king's disfavor he loses his cases before the Supreme Court. A dramatic turning point in the situation transpires when there is talk of Iceland being sold by the Danish crown to the town of Hamburg—and even this remarkable plan is partly based on historical fact. Arnas is offered the post of Governor of Iceland; he is to govern the island for its proposed new owners, and will be free to reside there with Snæfríður, who has recently become a widow, as his wife. In a conversation one night at an inn in Copenhagen the two lovers play with the thought that as Iceland's "lord" and "lady" they will create a new state in which justice and prosperity will reign. "And we shall ride around the country on white horses" (III, 163), adds Snæfríður. But this is just a fleeting illusion. By the following morning Arnæus has already dismissed the temptation with finality. His reply to Herr Uffelen, the emissary from Hamburg, is logical and patriotic: "There is one reason why it is impossible for me to run your errands in Iceland, namely this, that he who is offering to sell the country is not its owner. It is certainly true that I have accepted official duties—though not at my own instigation—from the king who long before my time became the sovereign ruler of my native country by the inevitable decree of chance events and mishaps. But I should be still more to blame, if I now became the trusted servant of those to whom he unjustly wishes to sell this country" (III, 171).

It is a tired and disillusioned Arnas Arnæus who finally accompanies Jón Hreggviðsson, his protégé, to the ship bound for Iceland from Dragör. At least he has finally managed to secure the acquittal of his grizzled compatriot—after judicial proceedings which have lasted, with long intervals, for a period of about thirty years. This is a kind of triumph for Arnas, since Jón Hreggviðsson's protracted lawsuit has occupied something of a key position in a struggle between conflicting interests of a larger kind. When he parts with Jón in Denmark Arnas asks him to show his tousled old head at the *alþingi* back in Iceland: "You can tell them from me that Iceland has not been sold—not this time. . . . And then you can tell them the outcome of your lawsuit" (III, 201).

At this session of the *alþingi* Snæfríður rides across Þingvellir with her formerly despised "waiting suitor," the canon, who is now her husband and the recently elected Bishop of Skálholt. The final scene in *Íslandsklukkan* shows them riding along with their retinue—all of them on black horses.

III   *"The Precious Membranes, the Life of Iceland"*

We may quote an exchange of dialogue from the conversation between Arnas Arnæus and Uffelen of Hamburg, when the latter first brings up the subject of buying Iceland. The Icelander says:

"Have you ever sailed to Iceland, *mein Herr?*"

The man from Hamburg answered: "No, whyever do you ask?"

"So you have not seen Iceland rising up out of the sea, *mein Herr,* after a long and strenuous voyage?" said Arnas Arnæus.

The merchant did not quite understand.

"Storm-lashed mountains rise there from a troubled sea, and glacier peaks wrapped in stormy clouds," said Arnas Arnæus, Professor Antiquitatum Danicarum.

"Quite so," said the German.

Arnas Arnæus said: "I have stood on the lee side of a trading vessel with the same destination as the weather-beaten Norwegian sea rovers who were storm-tossed for days on the sea; until suddenly this sight appears."

"But of course," said the German.

"There is no sight more ominously powerful than Iceland rising up out of the sea," said Arnas Arnæus.

"Well, I don't know about that," said the German rather wonderingly.

"That sight alone gives the key to the mystery of how the greatest books in the whole of Christendom came to be written here," said Arnas Arnæus.

"Well, what of it?" said the German.

"I know that you realize now," said Arnas Arnæus, "that it is not possible to buy Iceland" (III, 24–25).

It is profoundly characteristic that Arnas' poignant tribute to Iceland should end with a reminder of the nation's literary inheritance. The climax of this short exchange seems particularly natural in the case of Arnas Arnæus—a man who like the real Árni Magnússon has devoted his life to the ancient manuscripts of Iceland. But the ancient literature, with its dramatis personae and prevailing spirit, is clearly a source of national consciousness and pride among the ordinary people of Iceland, too. Even a fellow like Jón Hreggviðsson has it in his blood. While being court-martialed in the Danish mercenary army, alone and despised in a hostile environment, he clings firmly to the ancient literature of his native country, to the stories and songs he has heard about famous men in Iceland. Against the colonel's horrifying list of the miserable activities of Icelanders Jón pits his forefather Gunnar of Hlíðarendi, who was "twelve ells tall." And when he is threatened with being broken on the wheel if he should be lying, he repeats and develops his description: "twelve ells. I do not withdraw that statement. He lived to be three hundred years of age. And wore a band of gold about his forehead. The sound of his spear was the most beautiful song ever heard in the North" (I, 194). On the subject of Gunnar of Hlíðarendi he will not take back his words, even though they may cost him his life. And all through the book Jón can be heard easing his hardships by singing the "Pontusrímur eldri" (Older Rhymes of Pontus)—a work which belongs to the singular poetic genre known as *rímur* (rhymed ballads), with its roots in the Middle Ages. The *rímur* may be regarded as a counterpart to the Sagas of Icelanders; their strong element of fantasy contrasts with the sober narrative style of the sagas.

Thus, with their very different qualifications, Jón Hreggviðsson and Arnas Arnæus are each in his own way conscious of the value of their literary inheritance. Jón has a naive and practical attitude to the matter; for him the heroes of Icelandic literature are a weapon with which to hold his own in the face of arrogant foreigners. The ancient writings also fill Arnas with strength and pride; but this is because he is able to estimate the unusual nature of the literary culture and creative power which must have produced them. "There go the books, the like of which will never and nowhere be found till Doomsday" (III, 189), he says, at the sight of his burning bookshelves.

Yet in *Íslandsklukkan* it is Snæfríður, rather than Jón Hreggviðsson or Arnas Arnæus, who is made to plead the cause of Icelandic literature in the most fervent terms. At one point, in the hope of clearing her dead father's name, she comes to Denmark and applies directly to Gyldenlöve, the Governor of Iceland, for a rehearing of an important case which her father had once lost. When the Governor talks of selling Iceland and of placing the island's entire population on the moors of Jutland —a proposal which is also a historical fact, but belongs in reality to the end of the eighteenth century—Snæfríður sits for a long time in silence, and finally says: "There is a verse by an

Icelandic poet of ancient times which runs: 'No matter if you
lose your property and kinsmen and die yourself in the end,
as long as you have won fame' ". When the Governor of Iceland
fails to understand this wisdom from the *Hávamál* she continues
to speak of her forefathers—"kings of both land and sea," bold
seafarers who "came to Iceland at a time when no other people
understood navigation." And their poets "composed lays and
told stories in the language spoken by King Óðinn himself, who
came from Ásgarður, while Europe was speaking the language
of slaves." "Forgive my talking like this," she concludes, "forgive
the fact that we are a saga people and can forget nothing. . . .
We Icelanders are certainly not too good to die. And for a long
time life has been of no value to us. There is one thing only
which we cannot lose as long as one member of this nation, be
he rich or poor, remains alive; not even after death can we be
without it; and that is the thing which is mentioned in the ancient
poem, and which we call 'fame" (III, 125–27).

The Icelanders, she explains to the Governor, are a saga people
who forget nothing. And her whole speech is beautiful evidence
of the close connection between Icelandic literary tradition and
Icelandic national feeling. This subject, moreover, was of the
greatest topical interest during the years when *Íslandsklukkan*
was taking shape. Just before their final separation from Denmark the Icelanders raised, with renewed intensity, the demand
that the old Icelandic manuscripts—including such treasures as
the Codex Regius of the Poetic Edda—should be restored from
Copenhagen to their original home. To many Icelanders these
manuscripts represent the visible sign of their small country's
intrinsic worth, of its right to an honorable place in the circle
of independent nations. There have even been traces of an attitude—not altogether uncommon among Icelandic patriots—that
political independence, however strongly desired, is of limited importance as long as "the precious membranes, the life of Iceland"
(III, 182)—to quote Arnas Arnæus' scribe—still remain in foreign hands. And in 1966, as we have mentioned earlier, the
Danish Parliament decided that the ancient vellums, the subject
of so much controversy, should be handed over into Icelandic
keeping. The decision was greeted in Iceland, with resounding

acclamation, as a magnificent action furthering mutual understanding between the peoples of Scandinavia.

IV Laxness, Hemingway, and the Sagas

Yet it is not only the element of patriotism in *Íslandsklukkan*
that has received a soaring energy from classical Icelandic literature. The style of the work and the storyteller's art also bear
the mark of its influence. Laxness has often emphasized strongly
that for every new work a writer must create a special style
and tone to express the spirit of that particular work. In 1940
he had completed his Ólafur Kárason tetralogy, which is characterized by his richly flowing, often strongly lyrical and subjective
style. The new novel, *Íslandsklukkan*, the subject of which had
long been growing within him, demanded a quite different narrative technique.

It is worth mentioning here that in 1941 Laxness translated
Hemingway's *A Farewell to Arms* into Icelandic, under the title
of *Vopnin kvödd*. According to his preface to the translation,
Laxness finds that certain of "the Anglo-Saxon man's" most
primary and enduring qualities are developed with unusual clarity
in Hemingway's leading characters: "the carefree spirit of play
and merriment in the midst of misfortunes; the naively sincere
honesty coupled with the cool insolence of the gangster; the
realist's precise and objective appraisal of facts despite the general state of turmoil around him, together with a boundless contempt for prolixity and emotional rant; and finally the hidden
certainty, terrifying yet met without fear, that all is in the process
of being lost." Laxness indicates that the constant interplay of
love and death is perhaps the author's principal means of gaining
his effect in *A Farewell to Arms*. Contrasts and parallels are
to be found everywhere in Hemingway, not least of all in *For
Whom the Bell Tolls*, "one of the works of the most terrible
beauty existing in the novel literature of modern times."

It was probably his interest in Hemingway's characteristic style
which first inspired Laxness to translate *A Farewell to Arms*.
He makes clear in the preface that in his view hardly anyone
has contributed as much as this American towards "altering
writers' concepts of the art of narrative in the course of the
last ten to twelve years." Hemingway's style is "the style, *par*

excellence, of the spirit of the times." It performs its task with swiftness and precision like "a perfect modern machine" as he states more specifically elsewhere—in an article where he also says that Hemingway's style shows him to be a "trained newspaper correspondent"; "we must never forget, either, the unique stylistic quality of the telegram" in this style which is, above all, "an expression of the period of functionalism around 1930." Yet, according to Laxness, it is of small avail to search the works of Hemingway for finely fashioned words or "pearls" of wisdom: "We must, as when reading Icelandic sagas, be able to judge of the author's genius from his total stature, as it reveals itself in the work as a whole." [2]

The observation that Hemingway's modern, "hard-boiled" style is reminiscent of the objectivity and tautly restrained narrative art exhibited in the ancient sagas, is not altogether original.[3] But Laxness had a special reason for reflecting on their affinity at this time, when he was confronted with the problem of finding a form for *Íslandsklukkan.* It was in his mind to establish a link, in his own work, with the classical prose of the sagas; and as far as we can judge, his work on the translation of *A Farewell to Arms* harmonized with this intention, and formed part of his serious preparation for the new novel. This is all the more likely in that he not only found a certain formal resemblance to the Icelandic sagas in Hemingway's work; the similarity in narrative technique corresponded to something shared by Hemingway's novels and the sagas in their very spirit and view of life. Laxness' descriptive account of Hemingway's character portrayal, which we have quoted above, might almost be applied, sentence for sentence, to the ancient sagas.

While working on *Íslandsklukkan* Laxness also devoted himself assiduously to the editing of Icelandic sagas in modernized spelling. In 1945 he published a long essay which bears eloquent witness to his profound involvement with the classical saga literature, and also throws light on his own aspirations as a writer of prose in *Íslandsklukkan.*[4] At the end of 1944, when the first two parts of the trilogy had appeared, he gave in an interview a clear statement of the connection between *Íslandsklukkan* and the sagas. He said there that in his efforts to "see things from without instead of from within" he had been able to take Icelandic "novels from the thirteenth century," such as *Njáls saga,* as models. In his terminology they are "objective" (*hlutlægur*) in contrast to the fiction of more recent times, which broadly speaking is "subjective" (*andlægur*). Modern natural science has "overthrown the subjective psychology so that it is no longer possible to regard it as anything other than the relics of a religious philosophy of merely cultural-historical importance. In the subjective psychology things happen in people's 'mental recesses,' in mysterious settings, while the objective psychology explains the result of investigating, through the natural sciences, the nervous systems of men and animals." In this interview Laxness emphasizes that books "like the ancient sagas and *Íslandsklukkan* would be more likely than most others to be based on the view of life characteristic of people who were acquainted with the objective psychology. Thoughts and feelings are expressed in speech and physical reactions; the action does not take place in the recesses of the mind." [5]

His study of Hemingway's style and of modern psychology has thus been a stimulus to Laxness in his renewed consideration of the resources of classical Icelandic prose. Here as elsewhere he shows a remarkable capacity for activating and actualizing his native inheritance with the support of new experiences and approaches to problems. However, we should not stress the element of saga style in *Íslandsklukkan* too onesidedly. It is true that it provides the work with its actual keynote of coolness and purity. But this is made to conflict with certain other stylistic elements. The coldly matter-of-fact mode of expression alternates with a Danicized "officialese" and a religious rhetoric which have borrowed their coloring from contemporary documents. This archaizing dress of language never runs the risk, however, of leaving an impression of patchwork or of a laboriously handled apparatus of learning. It is carried off with sovereign facility and seems to blend quite naturally with the narrative's own rhythm.

CHAPTER 8

The Atom Station

I *Traitors to Iceland*

THE novel cycle *Íslandsklukkan* caused a temporary abate-
ment in the storm around its author's name and gave him
something of the status of a national writer. Its historical subject,
in which the ordinary people of Iceland recognized well-known
episodes from the country's past, furnished Laxness with stirring
symbols of the Icelandic struggle for freedom through the ages.
It is true that scenes of incredible poverty and human degradation
were also to be found there, and that in describing these the
author showed his perception of the class antagonisms in Icelandic society. But such features were obscured by the perspective of time long past and did not necessarily shock the reader,
as in the novels about Bjartur í Sumarhúsum or Ólafur Kárason.
Íslandsklukkan had the quality of a gift from the writer to the
entire nation on the threshold of a new epoch. It responded
to his countrymen's fervent interest in the dissolution of the
union with Denmark, and was made available to them at a
time when they were animated by a spirit of national unity
and enthusiasm seldom seen before or since. Laxness' dramatiza-
tion of the novel, under the title of *Snæfríður Íslandssól*
(Snæfríður, Iceland's Sun) was also one of the three Icelandic
plays with which the new National Theater in Reykjavík was
inaugurated in April, 1950.

Even in *Íslandsklukkan,* however, a kind of "discordant political note" could be heard. In the conversations between Uffelen
of Hamburg and Arnas Arnæus a sensitive ear could catch an
echo of the greatest question in Iceland's foreign affairs since
the dissolution of the union—the request made by the United
States for military bases on the strategically important island

in time of peace as well as war. This request became public
in the autumn of 1945, before Laxness had yet finalized *Eldur
í Kaupinhafn.* Even if the Icelanders accepted the presence of
foreign troops during the actual war years—having, of course,
no military forces of their own—the situation became quite different once hostilities were ended. It had generally been expected
or hoped that the foreigners would then gratefully acknowledge
the loan of Iceland and depart. Instead, the United States made
a formal request for permission to have control, for ninety-nine
years, of the largest airfield and the most important naval base
in the country.

This request gave rise to an atmosphere of agitation in Iceland. By June 17, 1944, the Icelanders had attained their eagerly
coveted goal of becoming the sovereign rulers of their own soil.
There seemed nothing attractive in the instant necessity of grant-
ing the use of their land to foreign military forces and thus
actually acknowledging their dependence on a great world
power—and not this time on a more evenly matched Scandinavian nation. Indeed, the solid opposition in Iceland brought
about a certain reduction of the American request. After a
dramatic vote on October 5, 1946—with thirty-two in favor and
nineteen against—the *alþingi* granted the United States of
America the right to have control of the airfield at Keflavík,
some thirty miles southwest of Reykjavík, for a period of six
and a half years—"for the fulfillment of the obligations assumed
by the United States in connection with the occupation of Germany." This agreement has since been prolonged under the
auspices of NATO, of which Iceland is a member.

Laxness' voice could also be heard in the general storm of
protest surrounding the "base question" in Iceland. Characteristic
of the keynote of agitation—the current blending of contempt
and despair—is a speech he made in November, 1946. The
writer speaks here of "the sorrow which has assailed us all
and almost taken from us our power of speech, deprived us
of the joy of being a nation, and inflicted on every Icelander
an aching wound, so that we are no longer the same people."
On October 5 thirty-two "miserable Icelanders," "just a few
traitors" had succeeded in gambling away the nation's independence of June 17, 1944, and turned Iceland into "an American
air base," in the eyes of both the world and the Icelandic people.

Iceland had had no obligation whatever to meet the demands of the United States: "We lent our country to the Americans during the war, and they estimate the value of that loan at several billion dollars; in return they gave us military protection against the Fascists." With the so-called agreement of October 5 the United States Government had "made special friends and protégés of Icelandic quislings and thus shown scant respect for the Icelandic people." But that does not give the Icelanders any right to accuse the United States, "and for the American nation itself we entertain purely friendly feelings." The responsibility for what has happened must be laid entirely on "the thirty-two." In the summer of 1946 they had artfully contrived to get into the *alþingi* with false electoral promises; their first action when they met in the autumn was to betray their electors and surrender Iceland.[1]

These political events, and sentiments such as these, form the background of the short novel *Atómstöðin* (The Atom Station, 1948). The hotly debated subject of yielding up the military bases in Iceland plays a prominent part in the book. According to a statement in the author's first draft of the work, the narrative is supposed to begin in the autumn of 1945—at the very time, in fact, when the American request came to the knowledge of the public. Laxness began to write his novel shortly after the decision of the *alþingi* came into effect on October 5, 1946. He takes the question of high politics connected with the base and couples it together with the grotesque complications surrounding the bringing home and burial of the body of Jónas Hallgrímsson, the national poet, which had lain at rest for a century in Copenhagen; for this memorable event happened to coincide with the hectic final stages in the *alþingi's* handling of the base question. The action of the leading politicians is given sarcastic comment in the novel, in the refrain: "Sell the country, dig up bones" (260).

II   *Ugla Falsdóttir and Others*

Atómstöðin is presented in a rather unusual way. The entire narrative is placed in the mouth of Ugla Falsdóttir, a young country girl from northern Iceland, who comes to Reykjavík to learn to play the organ. This fictitious narrator can hardly be regarded as thoroughly true to life. Ugla's thoughts sometimes seem improbably mature and artistically formulated. As a type, however, the girl from the north is realistically drawn. The Icelandic country people's traditional book knowledge and thirst for education are not mythical; and among the young people of the present day intellectual curiosity has found new aims and pursuits. When Ugla of Eystridalur reflects on modern music and sculpture, she represents Iceland as it really is, albeit in a stylized way.

In order to earn her living in Reykjavík the girl from the north takes the post of domestic help in the house of Búi Árland, political economist, wholesale merchant, and member of Parliament. In his house she gains an insight into the life and mentality of the country's leading circles. But she also comes into contact with other aspects of life in the capital. At the house of her eccentric organ teacher, whom she visits in the evenings after her working hours, she is introduced to an environment in which thieves, harlots, police constables, and country parsons can meet together in an atmosphere of mutual tolerance. This new and strange world stands out in bold relief against the background of Ugla's isolated home valley.

Búi Árland is described as an intelligent and kindly representative of the upper middle class. He seems to be endowed with everything a human being can desire: good looks, the power to charm, education, and wealth. But his character is marked by a tired skepticism; he lacks faith in life. He awaits with equanimity the collapse of his social class and of its capitalistic culture. For a moment he can toy with the idea of starting a new life with the girl from the north, whom he calls his life's truth, and of running away with her to "Patagonia" (241–51). But these, of course, are fantasies which basically serve merely to underline his sense of rootlessness. And indeed, when it really comes to the point he continues to play the part imposed on him by his environment and position. In the last pages of the book we find him at the wretchedly attended funeral of the Beloved Son of the Nation, helping a few high-ranking mourners to carry the coffin containing the great poet's mortal remains, recently exhumed in Denmark. The procession is followed by jeering cries from the onlookers in the street about selling the country, digging up bones.

In Dr. Árland's wife and children Ugla is confronted by various aspects of middle-class culture in disintegration. The lady of the house is an egocentric hysteric who, in contrast to her husband, upholds her position and her class interests against supposed conspiracies in a manner both narrow-minded and cynically candid. She regards serious educational pursuits in women as being detrimental to true womanhood and as testifying, moreover, to "communism." "Look at me," she says to her servant, "I am qualified for university studies, but it doesn't show" (13).

According to the organist, the children of the family react to their environment in a manner wholly consistent with it: "One cannot get away from the fact that a thing which lies in salt water will soak up salt" (67). There is the eldest son, the university student, who is brought home one evening to his father's house, dead drunk and muddy, with vomit down his front. On another occasion he appears amid the luxury of his parents' home, hunched up in a miserable heap, with his cigarette smoldering between his lips and the whites of his eyes showing, as "a living picture of the despair current at the time, a refugee, homeless, at a hopeless station" (132). There is "Fruit-blood," as Ugla calls her, the recently confirmed daughter, who with a hazy look in her eye and a cigarette in a holder glides through the rooms of the house in the manner of a film star, plays the piano with nervous alternations between Chopin and wild jazz, digs her dark-lacquered nails deep into the servant girl's arm or else embraces her, bites her, and says "you devil" (138); who becomes pregnant by a married "Americanized jitterbug" (141) twice her own age, and is taken by her father to a doctor: "He drove iron things up inside me. He killed me. There were bloody scraps of something in the bowl" (175). There is the schoolboy who in the company of his cousin amuses himself by stealing fifty minks from a farm, killing a few of them and then letting the rest of the dangerous vermin loose.

But the author also shows, in an unforgettable way, the unsullied core of these stray young souls of the upper class. In the middle of an orgiastic party which the children have arranged in the absence of their parents, among drunken couples jitterbugging and slobbering over each other "in a general promiscuous mix-up" (141), amid patches of vomit and the roar of the amplifier, Ugla happens to look into a clothes closet with its door ajar. Inside, the two little mink thieves are squatting over a chess board opposite each other, at an infinite distance from all that is going on around them. They neither answer when Ugla addresses them nor look up, even though she stands for a long time at the door of the closet, watching them: "And at this sight I was once again filled with a sense of that security of life, that radiance of the mind's depths and those healing powers of the heart which no misfortune can reduce. For a time I contemplated the civilized calmness of the chess game amid the din from the American radio station and the four phonographs in various parts of the house, a few saxophones, and a drum; then I went up to my room, locked my door, and lay down to sleep" (142).

When the maiden Fruit-blood returns home from her abortion, still in a semi-dazed state, she finds comfort and security in the girl from the north, who watches at her bedside. Fruit-blood's affected attitude has left her; she becomes the child she is and asks to hear something about the country, about the lambs—: "I saw twitches of weeping come into the girl's eyes; and then came tears. And he who weeps does not die; weeping is a sign of life: weep, and your life is worth something again. So I began to tell her about the lambs" (176).

III   The Organist and the Immortal Flowers

Ugla Falsdóttir acts as Búi Árland's foil; her natural anchorage in the real life of the people, and her uncorrupted sense of what is right stand in contrast to his melancholic nihilism. She is a sister to Salka Valka; these two country girls both embody the indestructible powers of the nation. Ugla has a healthy and "unblasé" longing for education and independence. When she comes back to Reykjavík after giving birth to her child in Eystridalur during the summer she explains to Búi Árland that she wishes to "become a human being": "Neither an unpaid bondwoman like the wives of the poor nor a bought 'madame' like the wives of the rich; still less a paid mistress; nor the prisoner of a child which society refuses to acknowledge. A human being among human beings: I know that it is ludicrous, contemptible, shameful, and revolutionary that a woman should not want to be some kind of slave girl or harlot. But that's how I'm made" (239).

Atómstöðin has the following dedication: "This book is written
in memory of Erlendur í Unuhúsi (died February 13, 1947).
To no one do I owe a greater debt of gratitude." In the character of the organist Laxness has immortalized certain essential
qualities of this unusual man, Erlendur Guðmundsson of Unuhús
(1892–1947), who from the very beginning of Laxness' literary
career had not only been a support to him, but had also represented, in Laxness' view, an ideal of broadminded humanity.
The author endows him with an inner freedom which seems
to make him virtually independent of material things—one of
those few "who use this world as if they used it not." The organist shows a kind of universal understanding for everything
human and a quite unconventional, smiling objectivity in his
view of people's actions.

The character of the organist is perhaps most beautifully and
clearly revealed in an episode involving him and Ugla. After
returning from the country, where she has spent the summer,
she is given temporary accommodation at her teacher's house.
The father of her child, a young ex-policeman, has ended up
in prison after optimistically collecting orders and receiving payment for goods he had not yet obtained. A very large sum
of money is needed to set him free. Once the organist is certain of the girl's loyalty to her child's father he hands her,
without further ado, a large bundle of bank notes. While she is
accepting this fortune, overwhelmed, he begins to cut the most
beautiful flowers from among his potted plants and to arrange
them in a bouquet. At their parting it comes to light that he
has sold his house and intends to move:

"Where will you go?" I said.
"The same way as the flowers," he said.
"And the flowers?" I said. "Who will look after them?"
"Flowers are immortal," he said, and laughed. "You cut them in
the autumn and they grow again in spring — somewhere" (273).

Shortly afterwards Ugla stands in the square and witnesses
Búi Árland playing his part as a coffin bearer in the drama
which centers around the remains of the Nation's Beloved Son.
Sell the country, bury bones. "I looked around for the quickest
way out of this square, pressed my bouquet of flowers closer

to me and started to run. What would life have been worth to me if there had not been these flowers?" (276).

The final meeting between the organist and Ugla testifies to the mysticism which in Laxness conflicts so peculiarly with his harshly rational view of society. In these key characters of the novel he has found expression for his faith in the future of man. The organist's flowers—these immortal flowers—in the arms of this girl from northern Iceland indicate the futility of every kind of treason against humanity; they are a symbol of life's indestructibility. Indeed, the author at one stage thought of giving this book the title of "Ódauðlegu blómin" or "Ófeigu blómin" (The Immortal Flowers, The Undying Flowers).[2]

IV   Atómstöðin *and Reality*

Atómstöðin was undoubtedly a spear thrown with the warrior's intention of wounding and killing—if indeed we should not rather compare it with a bomb. Certain circles within Icelandic society were deeply offended by it, for all their attempts to see it as nothing but an uncontrolled outburst of fury, a *roman à clef*, and a political lampoon.

In spite of this, however, *Atómstöðin* in no way betrays any prejudiced kind of political inspiration or purpose. As far as we can judge, the atom station is, broadly speaking, the symbol of a certain disintegration or explosion of accustomed ideas and associations. The Reykjavík of the war years, with its trade boom and its hectic life of business and pleasure, offered a background favorable to all kinds of picturesque types and eccentricities. And indeed, *Atómstöðin* has a rich array of characters, some of which are exceedingly bizarre: the two "gods," for instance—Benjamín, "the atom poet," and Briljantín (Brilliantine), the father of the twins—or the spiritualist medium, Óli fígúra. For all of these the author has models in the external world, some of which are more obvious than others. The very action of the book also has elements of fantasy—even though the author, as we have already indicated, perhaps keeps closer to real life in Iceland than may seem apparent to an outsider.

But photographic realism has certainly never been Laxness' main concern, and in spite of all its reminiscences of real people and events it would be absurd to regard *Atómstöðin* as a kind of *roman à clef*. The author is bent on presenting a synthesis, an artistically intensified experience of things. His tendency towards bold stylization culminates sharply in this book, which thus acquires a fiercer rhythm than the broader narrative flow of the epic in *Sjálfstætt fólk* or *Íslandsklukkan*, for example. But this is exactly the way in which Laxness, with brilliant intuition, has captured the scattered and hectic features of the environment he wishes to describe.

CHAPTER 9

The Happy Warriors

I   *"The Ancient Books" and "the Hidden Sources"*

WITH *Atómstöðin* Laxness had plunged directly into the Icelandic world of his own times. His next novel, *Gerpla* (The Happy Warriors), which was published in 1952, deals with Vikings of around the year 1000. It testifies in its own way to the contrasts and vigorous oscillations in his art; although in Iceland it is not unusual to find the old and the new in close and direct proximity to each other. In *Atómstöðin* Laxness had also given bold play to the contrast between modern Reykjavík and Ugla's native heath in northern Iceland. For the few farmers remaining in Eystridalur the heroes of ancient Iceland are ever-living characters. These farmers see their own existence in the light of the *söguöld*.

For a long time past, the Icelandic sagas have acted as a stimulus for Scandinavian fiction, both in style and choice of subject. Iceland's own writers have, of course, been no exception to this. As a model of style the sagas must, for them, have a deeper meaning than for writers of other nations. This is primarily due to the fact that the Icelandic language itself has to such a remarkable degree preserved its link with the past. The Icelanders do not, as do other Scandinavians, have the feeling of moving in a linguistically foreign world when they read their medieval literature in its ancient linguistic form.

When Laxness followed in the footsteps of the saga writers with his *Gerpla* he did not go to work unprepared. He devoted four years to his new work from the time that he began it in Rome in the autumn of 1948. But the idea of writing something in the manner of *Gerpla* is probably older. *Íslandsklukkan*, indeed, may in some measure be regarded as a stopover on the road leading back to the Icelandic saga. It is true that *Íslandsklukkan* deals with a much later period; but as we have mentioned before, it was in connection with this work that Laxness found a reason for renewing and deepening his acquaintance with the stylistic ideal of classical Icelandic prose. In the essay on the Icelandic sagas which he published in the spring of 1945 he explains by way of introduction that it has not been his intention to compete with specialists in this field of study; his primary excuse for dabbling in the subject, he says, is that "an Icelandic writer cannot live without constantly having the ancient books in his thoughts." [1] This essay mainly draws its illustrative material from *Njáls saga*. In another long essay, dating from 1949, which discusses the traditions relating to outlaws in Iceland in past times, we are given a penetrating account of Grettir Ásmundarson—Grettir the Strong—the most famous of all Icelandic outlaws and the hero of one of the greatest sagas.

As a twenty-one-year-old devotee of the cloister Laxness had, in his day, made a clean sweep of Snorri and those "old Icelandic fogeys" in a letter to a good friend: "On the whole I do not think it is possible to learn to write Modern Icelandic from Old Icelandic; something else is needed." But thirty years later he has followed this up by placing himself under the strict discipline of the ancient writers and writing a new Icelandic saga. This is as fine a testimony as any to the living power and continuity of Icelandic culture, and to its hold on one who has grown up under its wing.

In his own heroic saga Laxness has allied himself with the native Icelandic tradition both ambitiously and consistently. The name of the work already reminds us of an Icelandic practice much in use where the sagas are concerned. The name *Gerpla* is taken from the word *garpur,* meaning "warrior" or "hero," just as the saga title *Grettla* was earlier taken from *Grettir,* and *Njála* from *Njáll.* Laxness has actually wished to write his saga on the same basis as the ancient writers, and for this reason he records meticulously, in the very beginning of the book, the sources from which he has drawn his knowledge. But even if he has made careful use, in his subject, of earlier materials—drawn in particular from *Fóstbrǽðra saga* (The Saga of the Foster-brothers) and Snorri Sturluson's *Ólafs saga helga* (The Saga of St. Olaf)—he does, of course, work as a novelist and not as a historian, and his opening section is primarily an artistic stroke made with the purpose of arousing the reader's confidence in the narrative to follow. And when he finally alludes to many "hidden sources" (8), we may suspect that this is an ingenious expression for the hidden springs of the author's own imagination.

It is also clear that in spite of everything Laxness is not writing this Icelandic saga from the same angle of approach as his fellow writers of the Middle Ages. Had this been the case his own work would merely have become a pastiche, a rehashing of traditional material, and not a new saga, with its own set of problems. The author's own times show through in his work in many different ways, even though it might perhaps be necessary to subject it to a searching scrutiny in order to see that this is true. Thus, certain of the sophistic or unintentionally cynical declarations on the subjects, for instance, of war and peace and the right to burn churches, etc., which he places in the mouths of bishops and other persons of authority, have been inspired by the countless proclamations of heads of state, cabinet ministers, prelates and others on nuclear weapons and similar current topics during the years of the Cold War. The author's drafts and manuscripts give further and more precise information on the connection of this novel with his own times.

II   *Paganism and Christianity—Þorgeir Hávarsson*

The author has got the actual idea for his work from *Fóst-bræðra saga,* which describes the fortunes of the two foster-brothers Þorgeir Hávarsson and Þormóður Kolbrúnarskáld, including their relations with Ólafur Haraldsson, king of Norway, later known as "Ólafur helgi" (Saint Olaf). On the whole, Laxness has retained in his work the dramatis personae of the saga and their basic traits of character. But naturally enough, he has also, on many points, linked together the threads of the action in a new way, in order primarily to achieve a stronger continuity and a greater inner tension.

One of the features peculiar to *Fóstbræðra saga* is its medieval author's effort to reconcile a markedly Norse ideal of heroism with his Christian faith. There is no lack of ingenuity in the way he sets about doing it; of one of the foster-brothers we read as follows: "For the author of the world's origin had created

and placed in Þorgeir's breast a heart so tough and dauntless
that he could not be afraid, and in every trial that beset him
was as fearless as a lion. And since all good things are created
by God, so also is fearlessness created by God and placed in
the breasts of courageous men, together with the freedom and
power to do as they wish, whether good or evil. For Christ
has made Christian men his sons but not his slaves; and he
shall reward every man according to his deserts." [2]

In his essay on the ancient sagas Laxness for his part maintains that paganism and Christianity ran side by side in Iceland, but were as little able ever to be united as cold water
and molten lead. We are given a strong impression of the incom-
patibility of these two elements when we hear what Þorgeir
Hávarsson has to say in *Gerpla:*

"I have learned from my mother that many of the finest men have
challenged the White Christ to single combat, but that he has not
dared to fight with anyone. He must be craven, and I would wish to
serve almost any king but him. My mother has also told me that the
strength which thrives in men and gods is called earth power and is
made up of the hardness of stones, of the juice contained in grasses,
and of the cruelty which dwells in the tooth of the wolf; and I know
for certain that Christ has not acquired that power, and that other
gods have decayed and withered when they lost it; and such, surely,
is the case with men" (48).

This faith in the inherent power of matter provides the sharpest
possible contrast to the Christian belief in the triumphant super-
iority of spirit to matter. On the whole, the confrontation of
Christianity and the paganism of the North has provided Laxness with a rewarding literary motif which he has handled well.

In *Gerpla* Þorgeir Hávarsson has been made into an arche-
type of the ancient heroic ideal of the North, which in his character is given an absurd strain of robot-like stiffness and lack
of compromise. Originally enough, he is described as the victim
of an unrealistic and perverse upbringing. After his father has
been slain in an inglorious manner without managing to raise
a finger in his own defense, Þorgeir's mother never tires of ex-
tolling the insignificant Hávar, in the presence of the boy, as
"a dauntless warrior who had gone forth over the lands with
fire, and fought in the forefront of the host in battles between

glorious kings" (25). On her son she impresses the qualities which should distinguish the true hero: "A man's capability in conflict, his strength and his cunning, those are what make him a man. Whether his life be long or short, whether he stands or falls in the fight matters not at all, if only the splendor of fame may fall on his deeds. . . . Never should a man of true worth bring on himself the disgrace of choosing peace, if strife should be there for the taking. His mother also said that a good Viking should never spare a woman or a child in warfare. The name of every man who followed this good advice would live among the peoples of the world, as long as the world-serpent lay in bonds" (25–26).

A richly humorous contrast develops when the young man is supposed to start putting into practice the words of wisdom he has earlier imbibed on the subject of kings, gold, heroes, norns, and valkyries in the guise of swans. When he and his foster-brother Þormóður establish themselves as Vikings in their own home district and make coastal raids in the fjords in a barely seaworthy vessel, their story turns into a parody of the Viking life.

Þorgeir Hávarsson unswervingly espouses a heroic ideal which is already outdated and in ruins at the time of his youth. The gulf between reality and the dream world in which he lives is so great that it provokes ridicule. In this respect he reminds us of the Knight of the Sorrowful Countenance. He and that knight also resemble each other inasmuch as their ideals are inspired by literature. Just as Don Quixote had read too many chivalric romances, the Icelandic warrior has from babyhood been fed to excess on his mother's sagas of heroes.

Þorgeir is a comic figure when, like a lemming, he pursues his direct course onward over the rugged winter landscape; he asks his less heroic companion Lús-Oddi (Louse-Oddi), who is inclined to make detours round the worst natural obstacles, if he does not know which way Hlórriði (a name of Þór—the god Thor) traveled with his goats (116). He is comical also when he sleeps sitting upright in his bed with his shield in its strap, with one hand round its handle and the other round his sword hilt, and the axe in his lap. "He believed that heroes slept in that position and did not lie down" (62).

For Þorgeir's brutal lack of feeling Laxness has had perfect
models in *Fóstbræðra saga* itself. Famous, for instance, is the
episode in which Þorgeir, riding by on his horse, cuts off the
head of a quite harmless shepherd, just because the wretched
man happens to be standing "in such an excellent position to
receive the blow." On another occasion in the saga he rides
alongside a river and sees a man approaching on the opposite
bank with a load of brushwood on his back. He calls out to
the man who does not hear him, however, for the wind is rustling
in the twigs of his burden. Þorgeir tires of calling out and grows
angry—"for beforehand he was out of humor," we are told. He
rides over the river and thrusts his spear through the man.[3]
In *Gerpla* we find this story again, filled out with concrete details which make it no more edifying.

Ironically enough, the mighty warrior is given, in his new
saga, the most ignominious end that could possibly befall him.
He is decapitated in his sleep by people of such insignificance
that it is hardly worth the trouble to take revenge on them;
and in any case his foster-brother Þormóður, for all his tremendous efforts, never lays hands on the culprits. In contrast
to his prototype and namesake, Þorgeir has to lie unavenged—
a bitter fate for a Northern hero.

III   *War and Peace*

Laxness has himself called *Gerpla* a book about war and
peace, and has thus touched upon what could be called the
purpose of the work, and the pathos which trembles beneath
its severe and cold external form. In his view the remote period
which he describes is not so homogeneous as it may seem to
be in the ancient sagas. Deep within itself the society of the
söguöld contains powerful tensions between different interests
and ideals—not least between the ruler and his subjects, where
a remorseless antagonism may prevail. Haraldur lúfa (better
known as Haraldur hárfagri—Harald Finehair), we read, "took
the name of king according to the custom which some learned
men believe to have been prevalent in the North: that such
would be the name of the powerful man who with longest
endurance and most success could flay the peasantry in any
country" (288). In a passage of bitter irony about King Aðalráður
(Ethelred) of England we read that he was "a king so peace-

loving that he never went to war with any but his own subjects"
(270). He is always ready to buy himself peace from the Viking
hordes with enormous sums of ransom money, which he extorts
from his own people, and he often takes the invaders into his
service in order to keep his subjects in check. He fears nothing
so much as the possibility that the actual inhabitants of the country will rise up and put their foreign oppressors to flight—for they
would then become conscious of their strength and form a threat
to the king's authority and rule.

The nations desire to live at ease with their peaceful occupa-
tions, or, as an old woman in Normandy is made to express
it: "But Christ has created all men as peaceable beings, even
though overlords and heroes continually wish to kill us" (257).
She drives Þorgeir Hávarsson out of her house with the words:
"Be off with you now, and busy yourself with work that befits
a warrior: setting fire to people's houses and killing, in the
service of your sea kings or overlords, all that draws the breath
of life; and then ruling the world" (260).

In the home environment of the foster-brothers in Iceland
the activities of these overstrung young fellows come close to
provoking ridicule, at least among people of more settled character; it is only boys and maidens who stand gaping with admiration as the warriors fare forth in their warlike accoutrements.
Þorgeir's kinsman, the wealthy farmer Þorgils Arason, who pleads
the cause of common sense and peaceful work, has little understanding of the two rogues and their ideals: "Harm and bad luck
have always resulted from warriors and skalds getting together;
and people without home or property need to train themselves
in flounder fishing and seal hunting rather than in weapon clash-
ing and word rattling" (56). The bond of foster-brotherhood,
which is solemnly sealed with a mingling of blood beneath
frozen turves of grass, calls forth the sarcastic comments of the
people in the neighborhood: "Christian folk laughed at them and
said that they had never heard the like of these two frost-turf-
brothers sharing equally the lice which crawled upon them both,
and that it would surely be a long time before wretches such as
they had any other property to share" (76).

In the poetry of the skalds, on the other hand, the poetry
which celebrates kings and heroes, it is customary never to mention a peaceable farmer "otherwise than as vermin, which people

kill in their shirts" (301). Þorgeir and Þormóður also agree
to "live the life of warriors and always to hold cheap the opinions
and thoughts that gaffers and slaves might have on the subject"
(55). It need hardly be said that the slave, in particular, is
as far removed from the heroic ideal as he could possibly be;
it simply was not considered suitable for people of the North
to take the part of a beaten slave (36). It is thus especially
interesting to see what the same ideal looks like from the point
of view of Kolbakur, the Irish slave. This man gives the daughter
of his Icelandic taskmistress an insight into his life and destiny.
The girl asks why it is that so splendid a man as he should
be a slave and not become a hero and a skald:

"It was heroes and skalds who came to my home in Ireland," he
said.
"Why do you not weep when you are beaten?" asked the girl.
"The reason why I do not weep, young woman," he said. . . ,
"the reason why I do not weep is that heroes and skalds burned my
house; they cut down my father in his field and put a spear through
my grandfather, a man enfeebled with age. My grandmother was on
her knees . . . , and a man struck her dead with the head of his axe;
and that is the reason why I do not weep. They also took my baby
brother, unwound his swaddling clothes and threw him naked to
each other on their spears; and they dragged my mother and my
young sister, both of them screaming, away to their ships; that is the
reason, young woman, why I do not weep" (39).

Kolbakur says that while fishing with one of the old farm-
hands he has learned a kind of wisdom which is not "so hard-
laid as to frighten the fish: the hobbler rides horses, the handless
man herds" (44). These words from the Eddic poem *Hávamál*
formulate the dull art of everyday living, a life free of any
illusions. On another occasion, in a conversation with Þormóður,
Kolbakur repeats what he has learned at home in Ireland: "that
only men of craven heart place their trust in steel" (332). Þormóður seems to waver in the face of this maxim, but does
not give up his own ideal: "It may be," he said, "that you
are right in what you say and that slaves shall inherit this land,
when we heroes and skalds have fallen into oblivion; my children,
if they like, may learn from you the wisdom of the saying that
only the craven place their trust in steel. I am glad that I shall

be dead, however, at the time when the specious wisdom of you Irish succeeds in running the world" (333).

Þormóður clearly has a premonition that the slave Kolbakur, with his peace-loving ideals, represents those who shall finally inherit the earth. We may point out that in his novel about Ólafur Kárason, the parish pauper and folk poet, Laxness allows Pétur Pálsson Three Horses, the dominant representative of the economic system, to pay bombastic homage to his forefathers' ideals of Viking heroism. His opponents in the social conflict, on the other hand, the poor day laborers, who at length begin to unite in the struggle for conditions more worthy of human beings, are called "Irish slaves"—the traitors and baseborn inhabitants of the nation. In *Heimsljós,* as in *Gerpla,* the slaves are conceived as a threat to the ideology and supremacy of the leading social class. We need hardly doubt that in the one case as much as in the other Laxness stands with head and heart on the side of the slaves. In both cases it is the socialist who has joined forces with the writer. In a speech made shortly before the novel was published Laxness characterized "socialist peace, the working man's peace" as "the highest ethical power of our time": "In the face of socialist peace it is as if the murderous weapons of capitalism were losing their strength; and that is because the peace which socialism offers is one and the same thing as human ethics; socialism is humanity's moral imperative." [4]

The ideal of peace is most beautifully depicted in the description of the Eskimos in Greenland, where Þormóður has landed in the course of his futile hunt for the murderers of his foster-brother. The timeless idyll of their existence has left its heart-stirring mark on these primitive people who do not understand the notion of striking a man dead, and therefore have no conception of revenge and matters connected with it. The Scandinavians in Greenland regard it as their duty to slay such tedious half-men wherever they come in contact with them. Þormóður, who has been partly responsible for starting a massacre of them, happens to break his leg and ends up among the surviving Eskimos. These uncivilized creatures do not strike the white man dead; instead they take him into their care and heal his broken leg. But Þormóður lies there all the time regretting that it is not possible to come to Greenland with a king and heroes so as to make an end of this absurd race of men. Seldom have violence and war been placed in so merciless a light as in this description of the peaceable Eskimos. As far as we can judge, this section has been inspired in no small measure by the policies of the white race in relation to colored peoples through the ages. In the speech just mentioned Laxness also speaks with disgust of the Korean War which was current at the time and in which "the warmongers of capitalism" were trying "to harass the life out of this wretched and penniless people with whom they have no cause to quarrel, on that far distant peninsula of theirs."

IV *Þormóður the Skald*

As a skald, Þormóður complements Þorgeir the hero and espouses the same ideals as he does; both of them dream of the great leader and king, whose blazonry they shall follow even unto death. In the presence of Ólafur Haraldsson himself we find Sighvatur the skald giving the following account of his own and his fellow poets' mission: "And we skalds are the voice of the king's good fortune and the heralds of that hero who wins kingdoms unto himself" (299). Nevertheless, the court poet is no freer than the hero from the author's biting irony. Sighvatur's lofty declaration of his mission as a skald is given rich comment in an exchange of dialogue between Þorgeir Hávarsson and the skald Þórður. The latter has composed a poem about the glory won by Þorkell hávi (Þorkell the Tall) and his Vikings in taking London. Þorgeir, however, who himself took part in this adventure, finds little truth in the description given in the poem: "And you babble about our having won London with valor; yet you know better than anyone that when we were there we had urine and pitch poured over us, and they cut us into slices with meat knives as if we were shark meat; and those who did this to us were women and doddering old men." Old Þórður replies to Þorgeir's naive honesty in tones of cynical opportunism: "It is always the same with kings as with savage dogs—they lie down on their backs when you scratch their bellies: such is the lot of skalds" (227).

Thus the skalds in *Gerpla* chiefly stand out as notorious liars and falsifiers of reality. Hero and skald exercise an evil influence on each other. Or as Þorgils Arason said of the two foster-brothers: "Harm and bad luck have always resulted from warriors and skalds getting together" (56). The foster-brothers, however, are already well differentiated in the ancient saga and despite the fact that Laxness gives them a common ideal in *Gerpla* he has further deepened the dissimilarity in their characters and destinies in life. Þormóður is more human and not so like a robot as Þorgeir. The difference between them is clearly shown in their attitudes towards women. *Fóstbræðra saga* itself characterizes Þorgeir as being little interested in women: "He said that it was shameful to his manly strength to crawl to women." [5] This feature has been taken up in *Gerpla* and used with effect in several comic episodes.

The life of Þormóður, on the other hand, is dominated by Woman to a considerable degree. While Þorgeir considers it a better fate to fall before the enemy's weapons than to bow the knee to a woman, Þormóður regards as most blessed with happiness the man who spends a night awake in the company of his love (167–68). On either side of Þormóður stand two women: Þórdís, the young and fair valkyrie figure; and Kolbrún, who is older, dark and witch-like. If the former represents Þormóður's bright and wholesome happiness on earth, then Kolbrún, the woman "who lives in the underworld" (132, 151), is the symbol of the darkly irrational but irresistible current which runs through his character and destiny.

The tense struggle between the two forces dominating Þormóður's life is set forth in symbolically concentrated form when he witnesses in a vision the fair woman and the dark woman throwing to each other a little egg, the *fjöregg* or "life egg," with which his fate is associated. [6] At the same time each of them is talking about the gifts she has intended for him. The fair one will give him a home and possessions and will bear him two daughters—the one as beautiful as the moon, the other as fair as a star; and she herself will be the sun of his life. But the dark one says

"I shall give him the greatest poverty to be found at the outermost edge of the world, and by him I shall beget the daughters who most resemble Hel, and their names shall be Night, Void, and Silence. But in my embrace he shall experience that wonder which neither heaven nor earth can match or surpass until the world is at an end and the gods are dead."

With these words this woman stood up and went into the rock, taking with her the life egg of Þormóður Kolbrúnarskáld. (151)

An extremely beautiful description is given of Þormóður's life as a peace-loving farmer with Þórdís, the love of his youth, the fair and bright woman in his life, and their fair and curly-haired daughters. The two little girls have their own way of rousing their father from sleep; one of them kisses his foot in the bed and the other presses her forefinger against his nose. And Þormóður always remembers the supple toes of his daughters. Details such as these are given a special luminous intensity against the background of the tough heroic ideal. His idyllic family life is bathed in an atmosphere of warm sunshine, which is the more moving in that it is threatened by the dark shadow of Þormóður's coming fate.

Early one summer morning when the people of the farm are going out to work, a terrible sight meets their eyes: the head of a man, impaled on a pole, with the face turned towards the farm. Þórdís comes out with her daughters and sees this diabolical thing. The slave Kolbakur asks whether he should make haste to bury the head before Þormóður, the master of the house, has awakened, or wait until he appears: "Then he shall choose between your head and this" (318). But Þórdís resigns herself; she has expected this and knows that her husband's destiny must run its full course. When Þormóður recognizes the head of his foster-brother on the pole it becomes clear that he is still under the curse of his foster-brotherhood and of the heroic ideal. He sacrifices everything for the sake of revenge, both for Þorgeir's sake and for Ólafur Haraldsson, the king to whom they have both sworn allegiance. After a time he departs, leaving his home and his wife for ever to the slave Kolbakur, and goes abroad in order to track down Þorgeir's assassins. His attempts to do so, however, are quite fruitless and after undergoing monstrous hardships he arrives in Norway, a broken man.

On the day before the battle of Stiklastaðir, Þormóður's long desired moment has come at last: he stands before Ólafur Haraldsson and asks if he may recite him a poem. But the king replies that the trolls may take the Icelandic skalds: "I have had more trouble from them than from most, and I am weary of the bragging of Icelanders" (482). And when Þormóður tells him of the great but futile sacrifices he has made to avenge Ólafur's greatest warrior, Þorgeir Hávarsson, the king fancies that the wretched Icelander must be out of his mind. He cannot even remember having heard the name: "But it may be that some Icelandic blockhead of that name drifted into our band in the past, when we were engaged in Viking warfare" (483). And with this the king turns away.

In the course of the following night Þormóður is to experience yet another bitter disappointment. He happens to witness King Ólafur lying prostrate in the grass, believing himself to be alone, dreading the outcome of the morrow and uttering prayers of anguish to the powers that be. This is not the dauntless and forthright hero whom the foster-brothers have seen as their ideal. The king discovers the listening man, and asks who he is:

> The man replies: "I am the Icelandic skald."
> "Welcome, skald," says the king; "did I hear right earlier on, that you have composed a poem about me?"
> "That is true, my lord," says the man, "I have composed a poem of much worth about the warrior who is become the finest in the North—and about you, his king. The price of that poem was my happiness and the sun of my life; also my daughters, the moon and the star; and my own beauty and health, my hand and foot, my hair and tooth; and finally my loved one herself who lives in the under-world and keeps the egg of my life."
> "Well, skald, divert your king awhile," says Ólafur Haraldsson, "and sing your poem, Gerpla, by the mound here tonight."
> The skald answers, somewhat reluctantly: "Now I remember that poem no longer"—and then he rises slowly, limps away with his stout stick and disappears behind the mound.
> By then the moon had gone down and night covers valley and hill at Stiklastaðir and the late-flowering bird-cherry (492–93).

Thus *Gerpla* ends. The atmosphere of this meeting between king and skald in the night of late summer is charged with fate. We know from other sources what happened to them—both of them were slain the following day in the battle against the peasant army of Norway. Þormóður's destiny affects the reader in a manner quite different from Þorgeir's, because Þormóður, in contrast to his foster-brother, has actually been faced with a choice and had to sacrifice everything in order to go the way he does. And when he reaches his goal everything turns out to be an illusion. The reason why the figure of Þormóður has become so very much alive may be that Laxness the writer has in some way felt himself to be sharing in the fate of the skald, has felt himself disillusioned by his own commitments and his own idols. This conjecture seems to find gradual confirmation in a close study of Laxness' life and work.

V Gerpla *as a Tribute to the "Immortal Books"*

We can hardly be mistaken if we find that *Gerpla* implies, among other things, a stern criticism of the romance attached to "germanisches Heldentum" and the like. We read of Þorgeir that he would be given iron by the other men of the household in exchange for his weekly ration of butter, because he found it unmanly (*lítilmannlegt*) to eat butter: "Iron is more to our taste" (29). Here we undoubtedly have a comical echo of Hermann Goering's slogan about guns before butter. Once and for all, the author has wished to make a clean sweep of what he regards as a misuse, at once naive and dangerous, of his country's glorious literary inheritance—its ancient literature.

Paradoxically enough, however, it turns out that Stiklastaðir does not merely imply the collapse of an ideal of conquest and heroism which is both sterile and inimical to life. In fact, Þormóður's view of Ólafur Haraldsson's greatness is not altogether mistaken. For Ólafur was one day to become "the only Northern king who is superior to Knútur hinn ríki [Canute the Great] in reputation and praise", and was to win, as St. Olaf, as much praise in heaven as on earth. Yet to none would he become so dear as to Icelandic skalds, "as is shown by the fact that never in the world has there been written a book about kings, not even about Christ Himself, which even halfway compares with that which Snorri the Learned has written and which is called the Saga of St. Olaf" (474).

This work to which Laxness the saga writer here pays tribute is the principal source for his own portrayal of Ólafur Haraldsson who, after Þorgeir and Þormóður, is the third leading character in *Gerpla*. And of Þormóður himself we read: "But Ice-

landic saga writers have clothed with honor the death of Þormóður Kolbrúnarskáld at Stiklastaðir in immortal books, to the
end that the fame of the skald should live as long as that of
the king whom he sought and found" (490).

A despised and fugitive king tries to reconquer his country
with an army of mercenaries and falls in battle against a spon-
taneously mustered army of peasants. An Icelandic skald falls
with him, after losing everything and denying all values save
his ideal of heroism. In reality this is perhaps a dismal fate. But
in literary documents both king and skald shine with the glory
denied them by life. Thus *Gerpla* may also be read as an inspired tribute to classical Icelandic literature, to the art which
becomes a *monumentum aere perennius.*

As a work of art *Gerpla* itself is an unusually powerful achievement. Laxness has not transposed his subject into a modern
key; he has chosen to preserve a close link with the style of
the ancient sagas. He has been able to take over, virtually word
for word, a number of pithy expressions from *Fóstbræðra saga,*
and in the speeches of Snorri's account he has had perfect models
for Ólafur Haraldsson's rhetoric. Even the syntactical peculiarities
of the saga prose—for example the freer linkage of clauses within
the sentence—are sometimes effectively applied. Of course, Laxness has also allowed himself some obvious and conscious devia-
tions from the form of the classical sagas. Yet in spite of this, it
is surprising indeed how closely he has managed to follow it.
The saga style of *Gerpla,* while having its own highly individual
character, is not seriously at variance with that of the ancient
sagas. The writer has managed to give the impression that the
tradition of saga writing is quite unbroken.[7]

CHAPTER 10

After the Nobel Prize. New Departures

I "Spiritual Freedom, Absence of Fear"

IN 1955, when Halldór Laxness was awarded the Nobel Prize at the age of fifty-three, he was one of the younger literary prize winners over the years; and he has since managed to add a creditable number of new works to the general picture he presents as a writer. Up to the time of writing, in October, 1967, it is the following books which chiefly concern us: the novels *Brekkukotsannáll* (The Fish can Sing, 1957) and *Paradísarheimt* (Paradise Reclaimed, 1960); the collection of short stories *Sjöstafakverið* (The Book of Seven Signs, 1964); the plays *Strompleikurinn* (The Chimney Play, 1961), *Prjónastofan Sólin* (The Knitting Workshop called "The Sun," 1962) and *Dúfnaveislan* (The Pigeon Banquet, 1966); the book of literary memoirs *Skáldatími* (A Writer's Schooling, 1963) and its little complement *Íslendíngaspjall* (An Essay on Icelanders, 1967); and the two collections of articles and speeches written for various occasions, *Gjörníngabók* (Documents, 1959) and *Upphaf mannúðarstefnu* (The Beginning of Humanism, 1965).

What is essential, however, is not this testimony, so heartening in itself, to the writer's unbroken productivity. More interesting is the fact that these new works reveal, on certain points, a reorientation on Laxness' part. His attitude towards, on the one hand, the artistic and literary problems which face the writer, and on the other to the great political and social questions of his own time, seems to have undergone a marked change. We may well be right, therefore, in tentatively regarding the Nobel Prize as a kind of milestone in his development. The present chapter should be regarded as a highly preliminary account of this later period, covering just over ten years. The individual works will also be treated more summarily here, and chiefly as being symptomatic of certain artistic principles or of certain attitudes to the culture of our time.

Right up to the time of his receiving the Nobel Prize Laxness stood out, politically, as a strongly left-wing writer. In his home country, radical circles with demands for a socialistic remolding of society had long regarded him as a figurehead. He had made many harsh pronouncements on Western politics, having recently become internationally involved in the so-called World Peace Movement, the chairman of which was Frédéric Joliot Curie, the French physicist and Nobel Prize winner, and which has often been associated with communism. On the political level in particular, Laxness has, since the Nobel Prize, given clear expression to his reconsideration of earlier standpoints. There might perhaps have been no reason for any special delay here over this aspect of his development if it had not had important consequences, also, for his creative work. But that it actually has done so is hardly a matter of the slightest doubt.

One tangible result of the Nobel Prize for Laxness was an extensive journey to various parts of the world, his having received invitations from many countries, west and east, including the United States, China, India, and Israel. In these and other countries he was able to appear as a kind of cultural ambassador for Iceland. It is clear that if a man more or less voluntarily assumes a role of that kind, it cannot fail to set its mark on his public image. A person whose various activities involve welcoming the King of Sweden on an official visit to Iceland, sending a message of congratulations to the Soviet Union on its fortieth anniversary, greeting America with a speech at The American-Scandinavian Foundation in New York, and speaking as the guest of honor at a banquet in Peking before the Chinese People's Association for Cultural Relations with Foreign Countries, must surely regard it as a matter of common courtesy to avoid too controversial subjects. In itself the situation seems calculated to dampen all acutely personal expressions of opinion, especially, perhaps, where sensitive political questions are concerned.[1]

This does not prevent Laxness the writer and speaker from injecting some rather openly expressed criticism into his appeals. In the message just mentioned, in which he congratulates the Soviet Union on its fortieth anniversary, and which is dated

New York, November 1957, he calls himself "a writer who for about thirty years has called himself a socialist because he believed that socialism stood for a better life, and still thinks that if socialism does not mean the wellbeing of the people, it is an empty word." And further: "My wishes to the USSR at present as before are for all-round prosperity of its people in our day, spiritual freedom, absence of fear, an unhampered growth of the arts and sciences, a peaceful blossoming of the multicolored flower of civilization; for all the things that should make a socialist state a place where life is richer and the people happier than elsewhere, a place where most people would want to stay and nobody want to leave by his free will" (186).

This thinly disguised criticism is hardly made any the less severe by being formulated as a wish for prosperity. And in Peking a public which presumably was faithful to Marxism was given, among other things, an emphatic warning against absorbing "a single doctrine to the extent of making you forget to use your commonsense"; still less advisable is it to become "so petrified by an orthodoxy as to forget humanity itself" (194).

Laxness has grown more and more into the habit of demonstrating his skepticism of rigid ideologies so as to emphasize instead, and the more strongly, actual practice and concrete results on the one hand, and the freedom and rights of the individual on the other. It is thus characteristic that he should rate Mao Tse-tung's China as "the only regime in Asia which not only feeds and clothes its citizens, and keeps them busy; but also the only Asiatic government that is not sitting in tears by the roadside, sticking out a begging hand towards the United States of America." And then, bearing in mind the rest of the Orient—and India, perhaps, most of all, he asks himself "whether the Red brainwash is not preferable to a lot of philosophy and religion, and whether those latter conveniences are not in some of those countries a sheer product of misery, mainly serving as a substitute for ordinary consumers' goods."[2]

Nevertheless, his increasing distaste for doctrinaire viewpoints has also shown itself, to a considerable degree, in a gradual modification of his earlier commitment to the Soviet Union and the communist states in general. It is not just a case of his having avoided in recent years all criticism of the United States and the policies of NATO. Elements of that kind are conspicuous

by their absence from his two collections of speeches and articles since the Nobel Prize: *Gjörningabók* and *Upphaf mannúðarstefnu;* and in the same way Laxness has not, surprisingly
enough, publicly repudiated the American war in Vietnam, unlike
so many other writers and intellectuals of the Western world both
within and outside the United States.

His attacks in the other direction, however, have become all
the more frequent. On November 30, 1958, for instance, he
sent off a telegram to Nikita Khrushchev in consequence of "malicious onslaughts of sectarian intolerance upon an old meritorious
Russian poet Boris Pasternak." [3] But more important than isolated
protests of this kind—which in themselves might be reconcilable
with feelings of sympathy for the general politics of those addressed, or at least for the socialist system as such—are, of course,
his more fundamental and exhaustive statements. The contribution which has attracted most attention and discussion among his
countrymen is to be found in the book of memoirs *Skáldatími.* A
large part of that work is taken up with a retrospective survey
of the author's two educational visits to the Soviet Union in
the early and late thirties. At that time he had, of course, recorded his impressions in two travel books, which in all essentials
were strongly in favor of the communist revolution and regime.

The slant in *Skáldatími* is now quite different, and the negative
sides of the system are brought out with a glaring intensity.
Laxness points out with particular emphasis that a sterile kind
of Marxist jargon was used to cover up the deficiencies of actual
practice. He also directly repudiates now his depositions given
in the thirties. He explains them by saying that he, like many
others, was led astray partly by the influence of his Soviet Russian
guides, and partly by the tendency to see and believe what one
wishes to see and believe. An excuse was found for manifest
drawbacks of the regime in the appalling difficulties which had
assailed the great Revolution at the outset; all shadows vanished
in the light streaming from the vision of the future realm of
socialist bliss.

This late apology for political aberrations—which at least is
what this account would seem to be—naturally aroused attention,
as we have said, among the author's countrymen. Many of his
faithful admirers and "comrades in arms" in radical circles were
greatly offended. In the opposite camp, on the other hand, people

made little secret of their triumphant joy that the left-wing contingent had now lost what had been one of its principal trump cards through the years. Laxness has in fact taken no public stand in relation to this struggle for his personal support. On the contrary, he has dissociated himself from it, irritated by what he regards as an instance of provincial and political bickering. But it cannot be doubted that he has now reached a stage very far removed from the most radical of his earlier positions. Illuminating in this connection is a passage like the one quoted below from an essay written in 1964, the title of which, "Upphaf mannúðarstefnu" (The Beginning of Humanism), became that of the book in which the essay later appeared. Part of this essay is taken up with a discussion of the middle class as a bearer of Renaissance culture today, while the Middle Ages, in Laxness' view, was marked by the authoritarian and dogmatic power of the church. But all the time the author has his sights fixed on the age in which he lives and suddenly he writes, in clear allusion to the Marxist view of the middle class: "Many speak of the middle class as if it were Ku Klux Klan number Two, and some, indeed, as if it were Ku Klux Klan number One, or as people used to speak of the devils in the Middle Ages. It is to be feared, however, that in the places where it is eliminated the Middle Ages will return with their popes, with their ban on freedom of speech and on literature, art and politics; with the Inquisition and the burning of heretics; to be followed by state capitalism, the kind of capitalism which attracts dictatorship and tyranny and which alone is more merciless than the many-headed capitalism of the middle class" (26).

A convinced socialist would hardly express himself thus. On the whole, the juxtaposition of political and religious dogma has become something of a regular device in Laxness' criticism of his times. Writing in reply to the editor of a Soviet cultural review he warns against "the medieval custom of quoting scripture, i.e. referring to 'autores' instead of saying what you think yourself." [4] In another article dating from the following year (1958) we read that Christianity is of its very nature "an Oriental ideology, but Communism is an English religion [which] originated in the English experience of the 19th century Industrial Revolution and [was] evolved by a German-writing London Jew. Orthodox Marxism manifested in the slogan 'Proletarians unite,' derives its strength to a great extent from being almost as simple and ingenuous as the central Moslem idea: Allah is Allah." [5]

We notice that Christianity is here called an ideology, while Marxism, on the other hand, is called a religion. With this exchange of labels Laxness of course wishes to underline the fundamental similarity of all doctrinal systems of any kind whatever —whether political, philosophical, or religious. In this connection we may draw attention to a drastic observation made in 1961, where he maintains that German philosophy has been "a national scourge in the cultural life of Scandinavia all the way from Lutheranism to Freudianism." [6] That Freud is also included here is of course due to the fact that Freudian psychology presents itself to Laxness' view as a doctrinaire system. Elsewhere he maintains that "the whole of Freud's great work" would hardly seem to contain "a single indisputable clinical fact"; and Alfred Kinsey is apostrophized as a refreshing contrast to Freud because he has studied human sexual life "with clinical methods," on a strictly empirical basis. Ironical treatment is given to Freud's strange idea of "forcing psychology into a pattern derived from the plays of ancient Greece; compare the Oedipus complex, with all its absurd flights of fancy"; his theory of sublimation is characterized as the "freakish moral notions tinged with asceticism," which are "common to Judaism and Catholicism." This settling of accounts with Freud culminates in the following characteristic juxtaposition: "The gibberish of Freud competed with that of Marx to cripple the language in the days of my youth. Today it is best to be on one's guard against this blight on spoken and written language so as not to become branded as a reactionary, now that psychology, just as much as sociology, has become a subdivision of physics and chemistry." [7]

Briefly: in recent years Laxness has pointedly repudiated all doctrinal systems complete in themselves. All his mature writing— and in this respect his essays are no exception—is characterized by a sharply emphatic and paradoxical mode of expression which in his work represents something of a stylistic principle. But the reason, perhaps, why his argumentation on the point now under discussion has become so arrogant and lacking in nuances is that Laxness himself has felt strongly attracted towards two powerful systems of thought, one religious and the other social—

Catholicism first and then socialism. The case before us is largely that of a man who is coming to terms with himself.

Disillusioned by his past experiences, Laxness now seems to have adopted a skeptical attitude of noninvolvement as his guiding star.

II   *The Reclaiming of Paradise*

This attitude has inevitably left its mark on his creative writing. In an article dating from 1962 in which Laxness rejects every kind of universal prescription for the art of novel writing, he says at the end that actual "facts, just any facts in creation, come closest to being the voice of God for the novelist." This statement may be supplemented by a longer quotation from the same article. For a novelist, says Laxness, truth is a concept taken from metaphysics:

> The very word "truth" as such involves an unattractive ideal of orthodoxy which demands acknowledgment, once and for all, on the basis of some sort of monopoly. In the cases when truth does not mean a myth about facts, it means a myth without facts. Concepts in general, and ready-made definitions in particular, are of little concern to a good novelist. It pleases him to look upon the world not as the mound where the Revelation manifested itself but as the place where facts occur; and he makes use of facts, by degrees, as they come his way—one fact at a time. A storyteller who forgets facts because of his interest in the Revelation or the proclamation of truth runs the risk of ending up among the number of legend writers.[8]

There would seem to be special reasons for particular mention being made here of a mound (*hóll*) as the scene of the Revelation. To judge from all our evidence Laxness is thinking here of Cumorah Hill in the state of New York, where in the spring of 1820 Joseph Smith as a young man had the revelation which is said to have led to the finding of the Book of Mormon and the foundation of the Mormon sect. Indeed, Laxness had for several years had reason to probe somewhat deeply into the unique community of the Mormons in Utah. This was in connection with his work on the novel *Paradísarheimt* (Paradise Reclaimed).

This book may seem very remote from the author's own set of problems. As often before, Laxness here makes use of authentic Icelandic material as a warp in the web of the narrative; for the life and fortunes of Steinar Steinsson, the leading character, are directly modeled on reality. When the thousand-year anniversary of Iceland's settlement was celebrated in 1874, King Christian IX visited the island. A farmer from the southern part of Iceland, Eiríkur Ólafsson á Brúnum (1823-1900), then had occasion to sell a beautiful Icelandic pony to the sixteen-year-old Prince Valdemar. The acquaintance thus begun continued through the following autumn and winter with an exchange of letters between the Prince and Eiríkur. When in the summer of 1876 the farmer made a journey to Copenhagen he once more sought the company of royalty, and was well received. In 1879 Eiríkur settled down in Mosfellssveit—Laxness' native heath—a few miles east of Reykjavík. There he became a Mormon—chiefly, it would seem, under the influence of a work written by his countryman Þórður Diðriksson: *Aðvörunar og sannleiksraust* (The Voice of Warning and Truth, 1879). He traveled to Utah in 1881 and stayed there for eight years, and during that time he was sent back once to work as a missionary in Iceland. In 1889 he broke with the Mormons and returned home from Utah.

Eiríkur Ólafsson wrote a few short works about his experiences. The one which deals with his journey to Copenhagen and his meeting with royalty has become a classic of its kind. With a keen and naively straight-seeing eye the unschooled Icelandic farmer records his impressions of the foreign environment. The confrontation has many amusing points of detail. In the outlines of the story Laxness has followed Eiríkur Ólafsson's life history rather closely and drawn a delightful period picture of late nineteenth-century Iceland. But he has also commented on his own work in a manner which indicates a deeper involvement in the life and destiny of the Icelandic farmer.

He does so in a declaration entitled "The Origins of Paradise Reclaimed," made in connection with the American edition of the novel which came out in 1962. He says there that the subject had lain and grown within him ever since the autumn of 1927, when he stood for the first time before "the straight up-and-down, stern, and simple forms of the Mormon Temple of Salt Lake City, and the flat Tabernacle opposite made to look like the Mouth of God," and then remembered an Icelandic book from his childhood reading, "the story of the long peregrinations of the little man through the kingdoms of the world in search of the Promised

Land." Nevertheless, the writer says that for a long time he was unable to give form to this subject, in spite of repeated attempts: "the real thing, the Promised Land of God, did not get into focus!" And the truth is, he says, that in order to accomplish that task it is necessary for oneself to have been possessed by the dream of the Promised Land, to have sought and found it. It is necessary to have shared in the hardships, at least "figuratively speaking," on the way thither. What he is chiefly alluding to here is the Mormons' remarkable westward migration across the American continent at the close of the 1840's, under the leadership of Brigham Young. In *Paradísarheimt*, too, the reader's attention is drawn to these hardships, which lasted for years; Steinar asks his countryman Þjóðrekur, the Mormon missionary, what it has cost him to become a Mormon, and receives the following answer:

"Only the man who has sacrificed everything becomes a Mormon," he said. "No one comes to you with the Promised Land. You yourself must wander through the wilderness. You must bid farewell to your native land, your family, and your possessions. That man is a Mormon. And if you own nothing in your home save the flowers which people call weeds in Iceland, then you must bid them farewell. You lead your young and rosy-cheeked beloved out into the wilderness. That man is a Mormon. She carries your child in her arms and clasps it to her breast. You walk and walk day and night, week after week, month after month with your bundles on a handcart. Do you wish to become a Mormon? One day she sinks to her knees from hunger and thirst, and dies. From her arms you take your little daughter who never learned to smile; and she looks at you questioningly in this wilderness. A Mormon. But a child does not get warm from leaning against the ribs of a man. . . . Now you walk for a long time alone through the wilderness with your daughter in your arms. Until one night you notice that her little body has ceased to move in the cold. That man is a Mormon. You dig a grave for her in the sand with your hands and make a cross out of two straws which blow away in the same moment; he is a Mormon . . ." (55–56).

Pathetically, the speaker here confesses to the notion of sacrificing everything for an idea or an ideal, of staking everything on one card. But the experience of the new kingdom for those who reach it—their varying degrees of enthusiasm, fanaticism, and immunity to all criticism or, on the other hand, of skepticism, discomfort, and disillusionment—is described in "The Origins of Paradise Reclaimed" in words which seem more applicable to a politically social reality than to a religious one. This, of course, is in keeping with the author's habit, during recent years, of seeing political and religious ideologies and creeds from the same angle of approach. But when Laxness speaks of his personal experience as a precondition for the origin of *Paradísarheimt*, there is no doubt that he is alluding primarily to his own strong and long-standing political commitments. We might very well have ventured to draw this conclusion without having been given additional confirmation on the subject in his own spontaneous words.

The final scene in *Paradísarheimt* shows the Icelandic farmer Steinar Steinsson, alias Stone P. Stanford, Mormon and brick maker, by his old farm. Now he stands here again after the "long peregrinations" that had taken him "through the kingdoms of the world". But everything has changed. The farm is deserted and virtually razed to the ground. He himself is alone: his wife died on the voyage across the sea to the Promised Land, and when he received his daughter and son over there, the long separation had made them strangers to each other. His mission among his own countrymen has been met with lukewarm enthusiasm and good-natured teasing; no Icelanders can be bothered to persecute the Mormons now and there is no prospect of even the most ordinary kind of martyrdom. In the late afternoon Steinar Steinsson takes off his hat and jacket, and begins to gather up fallen stones and repair his boundary walls which formerly were famous. "There was plenty of work here for a solitary man. Such stone walls as these, in fact, require the full-time help of their builder if they are to stand." A traveler passes by and asks who it is who is busy working away at the stone walls on this deserted farm:

The other replied: "I am the man who found Paradise again after it had long been lost, and gave it to his children."
"What is a man like you doing here?" asked the wayfarer.
"I have found the truth and the land in which it dwells," said the wall builder more explicitly, "which of course is worth a good deal. But the main thing now is to build up this stone wall again."

Then Steinar the farmer went on as if nothing had happened,
laying stone upon stone in those ancient walls, until the sun had gone
down on Hlíðar undir Steinahlíðum (300–301).

In his return there is an element of melancholy and resignation, which as far as we can see has no equivalent in Eiríkur
Ólafsson's authentic account of his own life and may therefore
be attributed to Laxness himself. The book of memoirs, *Skáldatími*, expresses directly, aggressively, and onesidedly the author's
disillusionment with the political ideology he had earlier
espoused. In the work of fiction, *Paradísarheimt*, the same experience is reflected in a many-shaded, ingenious, and hidden way.
It would be a gross oversimplification to read this novel primarily as a kind of summing up of Laxness' political commitments.
The melancholy and the sense of void seem to have their utmost
origin in an experience of a more primary and more universally
applicable nature: the experience of the flight of time, of our
own and our fellow mortals' mutability.

III *The Annals of Brekkukot*

Steinar Steinsson, home again at last at his old farm at the
foot of the mountain and starting to pick up fallen stones, is
perhaps a symbol of the writer's homecoming—in the widest sense
of the word—to Iceland, a return bringing many profound and
to some extent bitter experiences with it. There is much in Laxness' most recent works which bears witness to an intensified
experience of the Icelandic heritage, not merely as a literature
but also as a personal attitude to life and an art of living,
a humanism with its roots among the people of his native land.

The social satire which Laxness has lately been cultivating
can hardly be said to have a clearly defined political purpose
any longer. In plays like *Strompleikurinn, Prjónastofan Sólin,*
and *Dúfnaveislan* it is aimed against all kinds of humbug in
the social and cultural life of modern times. In counterbalance
and contrast to this life of pretence figure people who are honorable in a sterling, old-fashioned way. They certainly bear laughing at—for, after all, the plays in which they appear are "com-
edies"—but with their balance, their unalterable scale of values,
and their lack of pretentiousness they represent something genuine in the midst of all swindle, in the midst of the hectic dance

around the golden calf. One of them, for example, is Ibsen Ljósdal, the editor of the publication known as "The Banqueting Table," in *Prjónastofan Sólin;* another is the old pants-presser in *Dúfnaveislan.*

The novel *Brekkukotsannáll* provides what is perhaps the most clear and manysided expression of this new tendency in Laxness' art. The entire narrative is here placed in the mouth of a certain Álfgrímur. This technique is not entirely new in the author's work; he had used it earlier in *Atómstöðin.* But its effect in the two cases turns out to be rather different. In the earlier work the country girl Ugla is conceived as one commenting on the action while standing in the very midst of it. The reader of *Atómstöðin* is given a strong impression of nearness and direct experience—as is fitting in a book with such a smolderingly topical and inflammable subject. Álfgrímur, on the other hand, looks back on the years of his youth from a distant viewpoint in time. His remoteness from the action is emphasized from the very beginning. The little turf cottage where he was born and spent his childhood and early youth was situated "south of the churchyard in what was later to become our capital city" (7).

The dating of the narrative may easily be deduced from the book itself. It emerges from many allusions to conditions and events in Iceland, and also from occasional references to the world without: "This happened around the time shortly after the Boer War when the age of barbed wire was beginning in Iceland" (45). The mention of Iceland's barbed-wire epoch—which is discussed in further detail and illustrated by a comic episode —is characteristic of the whole book. Álfgrímur's chronicle of reminiscences has an element of the cultural historian's devoted reconstruction of the past. Things great and small, important and unimportant—or the things which are conventionally interpreted as being so—are treated with the same respect.

The cottage of Brekkukot itself, with its unique inmates and its unlimited hospitality, seems, even in its own time, to be a place altogether apart—a kind of cultural reservation for the people. When in the last chapter Álfgrímur, who is now qualified for higher education, leaves his childhood home for ever in order to go abroad and continue his studies there, he tells us that "We walked out through the turnstile at Brekkukot where the boundary runs between two worlds" (313). Brekkukot, then, is another world; but it is also a vanishing world. It vanishes quite literally, since to pay for Álfgrímur's studies his old "grandfather" Björn has sold the cottage, "our house which was to be razed to the ground tomorrow" (316).

It is surely extremely likely that this episode also has a symbolic meaning: Brekkukot and its soul belong to an Iceland of the irrevocable past. It has, of course, never actually existed as it does in this book; it is a writer's vision, a nostalgic dream. It is true that *Brekkukotsannáll* is carefully localized in time and space, and Álfgrímur and Halldór Laxness would seem to be more or less the same age, both of them having been born around the turn of the century. Even so, it is perhaps not only the Iceland of his childhood which the author has wished to recreate here. He has sought, rather, to give a quintessence of those features of the Icelandic psyche and of Icelandic culture that have affected him most deeply. When Álfgrímur is about to take final leave of his home, he finds it good "to have been able to stay at Brekkukot, this little cottage of turf which was the justification for all other houses on earth, at the house which gave other houses a purpose" (312). Bearing in mind what Brekkukot represents, we may surely venture to assume that Laxness has written these words as much from his own as from Álfgrímur's point of view.[9]

The soul of Brekkukot is embodied first and foremost in the head of the household, the old fisherman Björn í Brekkukoti, whom Álfgrímur calls his grandfather. He is a man totally devoid of fanaticism in religious as well as other matters, and never divulges any information on the subject of his faith. Álfgrímur imagines that Björn of Brekkukot would very likely not have been "different in any important respect if he had lived here in Iceland in heathen times or if his home had been in some part of the world where people do not read Jón Vídalín's *Book of Sermons* but believe in the bull Apis, the god Ra, or the bird Colibri" (25).

It is surely no coincidence that a link is here established with certain Oriental creeds. In fact, one of the Eastern philosophies, Taoism, plays an essential part in the description of Brekkukot and its inmates. When Álfgrímur alludes on one occasion to his "Chinese book" (133), the book in question must be the famous *Tao-te-king* (The Book of Tao, the Book of the Way) of Lao-tse. Laxness himself acknowledges that this book has fascinated him strongly ever since the years of his youth, perhaps more than any other. The concept of Tao already figures in the early, unpublished manuscript of *Rauða kverið*, and *Tao-te-king* is praised in *Alþýðubókin* as the book which the author "esteems most highly of all books about the soul," even though he "does not understand what is written in it" (30–31)—"the most remarkable book which has ever been written in the world" (35). Taoistic ideas have their part to play in the story of Ólafur Kárason and to a considerable extent also in *Atómstöðin*, where the character of the organist has many of the features of Tao.

It is not easy to condense or pin down in a few sentences the teachings of Lao-tse, which after all are expounded aphoristically rather than systematically. But he seems to conceive Tao as a mysterious elemental power which pervades and dominates everything, even though its nature is tranquil, humble, and passive. The consciousness of Tao gives rise to a kind of quietistic ethic, the basic principle of which is that "the soft overcomes the hard" and "the weak the strong"; and in which universal goodness, gentleness, and humility are seen as the highest virtues.

Perhaps Laxness, personally, has been attracted by the paradoxical and mystical strain in Taoism, by its elements of what could be called escape and mockery. He himself has occasionally sought to interpret the doctrine as the expression of a skeptically relativistic view of things—an attitude which he has clearly felt to be allied with his own.[10] Above all, however, he has been inclined to see Icelandic country people—and particularly old people, with experience of life—in the light of the Tao concept, as he has interpreted it. And when he has done so, the stress has been on a natural humility, goodness, and tolerance, combined with a marked reticence in any display of emotion and the strictest kind of moderation in speech and choice of words. These people are also characterized by a profound harmony and balance of mind, by an intense solidarity with the world in which they live; the very objects around them become, as it were, animated. Their work somehow seems to be carried on without purpose and without effort, as if nature itself were at work. Of old Björn of Brekkukot we read that "he always had something on hand yet he never seemed to be really working." For Álfgrímur it is like "lying at anchor" to have him pottering about nearby; "In him the soul possessed the security which it desired" (13). His experience of the old woman of the house, his "grandmother," and of her presence which is so much a matter of course, is of a corresponding nature: "But if she were likened to the heart of the home, then much the same thing could be said of her as is said of healthy hearts in general—that the person who has such a heart in his breast does not know that he even has a heart" (33).[11]

The old pants-presser in *Dúfnaveislan* also embodies certain elements of the Taoistic ideal, being as it were invulnerable and finally triumphant in his humbly natural mode of existence. In the editor Ibsen Ljósdal in *Prjónastofan Sólin* we find a rather similar view of life consciously formulated and put into practice. Many of the words of wisdom which he lets fall are clearly Taoistic and occasionally are even direct quotations from *Tao-te-king*. As far as we can gather, the concept above all involves behaving with a calm and unwavering trust in the inherent rightness and beauty of existence. When the denouement of the play has occurred and the "French villa" has been blown up, Ibsen Ljósdal appears there in the early morning. When he comments on the devastation in his concluding words, he is clearly as unruffled as ever, and as sure in his faith: "It will be a beautiful morning. It is true that the French villa has been burnt down and that the knitting workshop no longer exists. But what about the man who crawls out of the ruins, what does he hear? He hears the nightingale sing. Whatever may happen, this One, and no other, is capable of victory. Farewell" (122).

It would obviously be wrong to interpret Björn of Brekkukot, or the pants-presser or Ibsen Ljósdal as direct embodiments of the author's own ideals. For one thing, they are very different from each other as people; and above all, the two characters in the plays have been given the pronounced profiles of caricatures, and are thus effectively contrasted with their environment. They are characters in a type of comedy which has many bizarre features. But even as caricatures they reveal to a large extent the kind of attitude which Laxness seems, in recent years, to have come to value especially highly. Peace of mind, humble dignity, and the absence of all doctrines and all aggressiveness are some of the qualities which characterize them. In the midst of a world of swindle and hollow "ideology" they represent the sure foundation of life, the true dignity of man—or, if we like, the principle of humanity. It is perhaps no coincidence that they are old people and to some extent strangers in their own times. They seem more in harmony with the past than with the future.

IV *From the Novel to the Drama*

The change on the level of ideas which we may observe at this present stage of Laxness' writing also has its equivalent on the level of style, in a broad sense of the word. Along with ideologies of various kinds he has also—and characteristically enough—discussed with enthusiasm the esthetic problems of writing. Thus Álfgrímur remembers the books in his home at Brekkukot, most of them "unclaimed property," which over the years had been left behind by visitors and lodgers at the hospitable cottage. The little library testified to the fact that among these guests there had been "more devotees of heroes, knights, and long sea voyages than admirers of Danish novels—for that was our name for modern literature in general and especially for the kind which had an element of hysteria. When we spoke of Danish novels I believe we had in mind vague ideas about Dostoevsky and other storytellers who seem to have spilt a great quantity of tar which then flows out in a shapeless mass and through its force of gravity finds its way into every nook and cranny" (71).

The designation of "hysteria" (*móðursýki*) is an obvious allusion to subjectivism and emotional effusion. This becomes fairly clear when the "Danish" novels are later contrasted with the books that were read aloud, and with the art of oral narrative which was practiced at Brekkukot: "The stories were legion. But most of them had one thing in common: the method of telling them was directly opposed to the one we associated with Danish novels—the storyteller's own life had nothing to do with the story; his opinions had still less to do with it. The plot of the story was allowed to speak for itself. . . . Cool and lofty, the story lived its own life independently of its telling—rather like Nature, in which the elements have complete dominion" (71–72).

We need hardly have any doubt as to which of these two diametrically opposed narrative methods has the sympathy of Álfgrímur. It is just as clear, too, that on this point the author himself shares Álfgrímur's judgment. Many statements made by Laxness in recent years reveal his irritation with "this nauseating
trash that calls itself modern novel-writing." The phrase quoted
is to be found in his reply to a questionnaire on the future
of the novel in the 1958 Spring Number of the American periodical *Books Abroad*. In Laxness' contribution, which is full of
strong feeling, there is talk of "the hysterical, alcoholic, erotoman-
iacal etc. profession that passes for story-telling nowadays, in
an out and out psychopathic age," and the bulk of modern
novel writing is described as "some sort of sickening subjec-
tivist expectoration." We notice here among other things the epi-
thet "hysterical"; certain "Danish" novels are also characterized
as hysterical in *Brekkukotsannáll* which was published in the
same autumn as that in which Laxness dated his reply to *Books
Abroad*—September 7, 1957.[12] The genuinely Icelandic narrative
art which is practiced at Brekkukot seems to have its origin in a
humanity and style of living which are as far removed from everything "psychopathic" as they could possibly be.

In summary it may be said that as far as the novel is concerned, Laxness is resisting everything which savors partly of
personal effusion and partly of proclamation and propaganda—
all of which, he believes, would clash with the spirit of narrative
art. But neither does the new French "anti-novel" (*anti-roman*)
come up to the standard he requires. It is true that it implies
a logical reaction against surrealism and the literary phenomena
resulting from it. Yet unfortunately it has set about "trudging
in the footsteps of the old realists on the tedious, well-worn
paths of the descriptive style." The writers of this movement
"strive to avoid main outlines . . . , or a story, an adventure,
or a framework, and seek their world where things have the
minimum feasible amount of mutual connection." No masterpiece
has so far appeared in the genre and therefore "the phenomenon"
has "unfortunately advanced no further than becoming one of
these many centrifugal movements which are endemic in the
modern literature of France."[13]

It is Laxness' opinion, perhaps, that Scandinavian novelists
ought to look nearer home for models and patterns for their

work. In any case, he praises in this connection Snorri Sturluson and others like him as the creators of an unsurpassed kind of epic prose. His descriptive account of their narrative art stands out in particular relief against the background of what he has said about the modern novel's besetting sins, namely its subjectivism and weakness for "ideologies" of one kind or another:

It may well be that the authors of the ancient sagas were learned and gifted men, perhaps even philosophers and psychologists. But if this was the case they have done all they can to avoid letting it become apparent. They never speak of themselves in what they write and do not show how many strings they have to their lyre. Even if they know Latin they hide it like a shameful secret. Vis-à-vis the subject, which by reason of its greatness compelled them to take up the pen, they considered it tactless to demonstrate in the saga any of their accomplishments apart from their skill in setting the matter forth "in the right way." They did not even leave their names on the books they wrote.[14]

Of Snorri's *Heimskringla* we read elsewhere in the same essay: "In spite of the storyteller's constantly impassive attitude the story itself is never without a certain strain of finely developed irony [*kaldhæðni*], which is hidden below the surface" (69). It may thus seem as if this very strain of ironic distance were the only evidence of the author's personal presence that Laxness finds properly consistent with "good form" in epic prose.

There are probably several reasons why Laxness, as a well established and award-winning epic writer, has enthusiastically embarked on the writing of plays in recent years. One of the reasons, however, is that he has found his novels—with their copious elements of dialogue—growing closer and closer to "the naked drama." The step from the novel to the drama thus appeared as a logical consequence of his development as a writer. Its connection with his orientation towards a more and more objective or "impersonal" attitude as an author is obvious, and is also illuminatingly illustrated in several passages where he argues from an esthetic point of view.

Thus Laxness has characterized as "Plus X" the novel's inescapable attendant spirit: ". . . Plus X . . . the anonymous parasite of dubious identity who is constantly present, like a Peeping Tom, at whatever page one opens a novel," and who

is not satisfied with less than "the seat of honor near the center
of the narrative, even in a story where the author is at great
pains not to identify himself with the narrator." It is clearly
this Plus X—alias the writer himself with his hopeless subjectivity
and his own particular interests—who has a distracting effect in
the novel, and prevents the action from developing undisturbed,
in accordance with its own inner logic. Not so in a play, where
"various factors which seek to lead the person in charge of
the novel astray" find no place: "There Plus X has vanished
like dew before the sun—and in his place we have a packed
auditorium. The spatial limits of a play are as narrowly constructed as those of a chessboard or a crossword puzzle. There
is no room left on the stage for any additional effects which
the author may possibly introduce." [15] It is clearly this stricter
artistic "objectivity" which has attracted Laxness to the drama
as an art form.

   It can hardly be maintained that he penetrates especially
deeply in his discussion of the novelist's art and of the drama.
Patiently and subtly blended shades of opinion are not, on the
whole, his main concern. With his often drastic phraseology, on
the other hand, he throws basic problems into sharp relief in a
brisk and provocative manner. And besides, his view of these
esthetic questions has a far greater strain of refinement than is
superficially apparent. His discussion of the parasite Plus X, for
example, may seem a trifle naive or over-robust, but basically
Laxness is fully conscious of the fact that a writer can never
escape from his own shadow: he is necessarily present in everything he writes, however "objective" or "impersonal" his work
may appear. Strictly speaking, it is surely only in a formal
and technical sense that one can speak of Plus X as being to a
greater or lesser degree active in a work of the imagination; as
the author's alter ego he of course remains, in spite of all, the creator and stage manager of the whole. Steinn Elliði, the main character of Laxness' early novel *Vefarinn mikli frá Kasmír*, had
already declared himself to have "sufficient experience to know
that it is impossible to write about anything but oneself" (317).
And in his essay Laxness now modifies his reflections on the subject of Plus X with the following questions: "But if Plus X is sup-
perfluous in the novel, is not then the novel superfluous in literature as a whole? The fact is that, phrased in this manner, the

question rapidly becomes absurd. Perhaps it would be more correct, then, to phrase it the other way round and ask in a general way whether the author is not the only person of any significance in a novel, just as much as in other books? And was not that the case in the ancient sagas too, when all is said and done?" (74–75).

Having thus briskly reversed his outlook and demonstrated his insight into the complications of the subject the author resumes the main line of the argument. Laxness has at all events given us a very clear statement of his present literary ideal, which as we have seen is marked in no small degree by a strong emphasis on artistic control and discipline. Not for nothing is mention repeatedly made of the author's "self-denial" (76) and the "personal yoga" (69, 79), which form an indispensable condition for his creative endeavor. And among the various aspects of the writer's work his bond with the classical Icelandic tradition of the sagas is both manifest and conscious. This applies just as much to the more formal aspects of the work, such as economy and precision in choice of words, as to the writer's actual attitude to his subject—an attitude involving distance, cool objectivity, and the absence of any kind of message.

It may seem as though Laxness were now aiming at a certain kind of timeless art, independent of all the turns and changes of fashion, and perhaps his reasoning on this point is similar, *mutatis mutandis,* to that of the pants-presser in *Dúfnaveislan.* To the interviewer's question as to what changes have taken place within the pants-pressing business since he started in it, the old man answers: "Some people say that everything goes backwards. Others say that everything goes forwards. In the case of the pants-pressing business the state of affairs is quite different; and the reason for that is that all people have been created two-legged for time and eternity. Not even the zipper makes any difference" (100). This is an attitude which contrasts strikingly with the proclamations of the young avant-gardist at the time of his work on *Vefarinn mikli frá Kasmír.* In an article on contemporary fashions and culture, dating from May, 1925, he urged that the writer should be "a child of his own time bearing the mark of its highest culture, or blatant nonculture; his clothing should correspond to the demands for form made by his own time": "Only those who were the greatest people in their own times, the mightiest champions of the fashion which set its mark on their time—only they will live in the culture of the future. Classical literature is richly instructive and remarkable for the simple reason that at one time it was modern literature." [16]

Yet it is not certain that Laxness would wish to abjure today the words he uttered at the age of twenty-three, the words which apparently—but only apparently—were altogether at variance with his present values. Imitative writing in its conventional forms, against which he was chiefly protesting in the article of 1925, is of course something different from the ideologically unrestricted, nonorthodox art which he now has in mind. He might with perfect justice maintain that he, with more intensity than most, has lived through his own time's "systems of ideas" and tested their possibilities. If he, for his own part, is now going—or considering himself to be going—against the current, then this is the fully conscious reaction of a "modern" writer and man—and one way, also, of speaking for his own time.

V   Art and "The World's Creation"

This pointed skepticism of all forms of orthodoxy, all "doctrines," which has characterized Laxness during this later stage of his writing is, of course, no isolated phenomenon at the present time. On the contrary, it has been possible to discern in many quarters tendencies towards a kind of ideological "zero position." On the level of fiction this has involved, among other things, a more or less radical removal of the writer's claim to stand forth as the promulgator of truths—not to mention the Truth. In a more resigned and unpretentious way the writer has been willing to rest satisfied with being an observer and explorer of the reality we experience. And this being the case, he has sought to go to work without preconceived opinions, to approach things directly and simply. Writers have done this, to be sure, in all periods of literature, though formerly more intuitively perhaps, and less systematically. What has happened in our time is that this attitude has acquired the character of an effectively employed method, or principle, or philosophy, or—we might be tempted to say—ideology.

Thus in some ways Laxness has been in harmony with trends in contemporary literature; but in all essentials his reorientation has its preconditions and sufficient basis in his own past—and not least of all, perhaps, in his fruitful involvement with the native Icelandic cultural tradition.

If Laxness' recent discussions of literary subjects have clearly been aimed against "ideologies" of all kinds, we should not, however, simply interpret this as if he were in the process of isolating himself from currently controversial issues and freeing himself of all responsibility for what is happening in the world. His passionate concentration on the work of the artist is still complemented, as it was before, by a strong consciousness of the fact that art lives and works in the midst of a social and political reality. Most recently, Laxness has formulated his credo as a writer in a little work in Danish on the subject of the Icelandic painter Svavar Guðnason (born 1911). It is true that this passage, as it is worded, refers to pictorial art; but there is surely nothing unsuitable in applying it to art in general:

No forecast can be made about where the roads are leading within art as a whole. No new code has yet crystallized within the realm of modern painting. So many efforts in the world without seem to suffer beneath the yoke of frustration and depression, general cultural torpor, sick humor and demoralization—which find their dismal expression in, among other things, a phenomenon such as pop: a hopeless surrender not only of artistic morality but of all principles and positions within art; a pastime for soldiers who are determined to fight for the world's destruction. The situation is not a new one. People have been in it before. Never forget that the world is not yet created, it is being created; and we are part of a process. While politicians seek to bring about the destruction of the world, art takes up the cause of the world's creation. Such has been the case before, and so it is still.[17]

The words testify to a feeling of aversion in the face of certain tendencies in contemporary cultural life, but they in no way imply a defeatist attitude on behalf of art. They seem to be written by a man who believes in the purpose and future of art as a creative force in our existence.

Notes and References

Chapter One

1. The cardinal's opinion may be found in Sturla Þórðarson's *Hákonar saga Hákonarsonar,* printed in *Icelandic Sagas and other historical documents* . . . . Vol. II. *Hakonar saga and a fragment of Magnus saga* . . . . Edited by Gudbrand Vigfusson, London 1887, p. 252.
2. Stefán Einarsson, *A History of Icelandic Literature* (New York, 1957), pp. 215–17.
3. *Íslendíngaspjall* (Reykjavík, 1967), pp. 78–79.
4. *Heiman eg fór* (Reykjavík, 1952), pp. 20–24.

Chapter Two

1. The quotations on the subject of Laxness' childhood are taken from one of Laxness' letters to his compatriot Stefán Einarsson, dated October 13, 1929, Los Angeles.
2. Letter from Laxness to his compatriot Einar Ólafur Sveinsson, dated October 28, 1921, Leipzig.
3. Letter to Einar Ólafur Sveinsson, dated March 15, 1922, Berlin.
4. Letter to Stefán Einarsson, dated October 13, 1929, Los Angeles.
5. Letter to Father Jón Sveinsson, dated February 4 (Sexagesima), 1923, St. Maurice de Clervaux.
6. Letter to Einar Ólafur Sveinsson, dated December 27, 1922, St. Maurice de Clervaux.
7. Letter to Einar Ólafur Sveinsson, dated December 27, 1922, St. Maurice de Clervaux.
8. Letter to Einar Ólafur Sveinsson, dated March 5, 1923, St. Maurice de Clervaux.
9. Letter to Einar Ólafur Sveinsson, dated July 12, 1923, St. Maurice de Clervaux.
10. Letter to Jón Helgason, dated October 13, 1923, St. Maurice de Clervaux.

11. "Úr circus menningarinnar" is dated December 6, 1924, and printed in the newspaper *Morgunblaðið*, Reykjavík, December 14, 1924.

12. Konrad Simonsen, *Dostojewski* (Copenhagen, 1924), originally a series of lectures given at the University of Copenhagen in October, 1922.

13. Letter from Laxness to the editor of *Morgunblaðið*, printed in *Morgunblaðið* May 10, 1927, and dated May 6. The origin of the discussion was an editorial comment on *Vefarinn mikli* in the same newspaper on April 24.

14. Laxness had published in *Morgunblaðið*, on October 31, 1923, a translation of the chapter in question, which is entitled "Antinatura" in Papini's original version.

15. "Richard Becker *in Memoriam*," here translated from the German text in *Gjörníngabók* (Reykjavík, 1959), p. 178, and there dated June, 1956.

16. Interview with Laxness in *Morgunblaðið*, May 22, 1926.

17. *Vefarinn mikli frá Kasmír*, Önnur útgáfa (2nd edition), (Reykjavík, 1948), p. 381.

18. Letter to Einar Ólafur Sveinsson, dated March 12, 1926, St. Maurice de Clervaux.

19. Letter to Father Jón Sveinsson, dated May 15, 1925, Brighton, England.

20. Letter to Einar Ólafur Sveinsson, dated April 17, 1923, St. Maurice de Clervaux.

21. In a letter to Einar Ólafur Sveinsson from St. Maurice de Clervaux, dated December 29, 1925, Laxness says that he is anxious to lend his addressee "a book called *Satan conduit le Bal*, by Anquetil": "It's a book and a half!"

22. The article was first printed in the weekly journal *Folket i Bild* (Stockholm), No. 4, January 23, 1949, and later in the collection of essays *Reisubókarkorn* (Reykjavík, 1950), pp. 319–21, there dated December, 1948.

23. Letter to Einar Ólafur Sveinsson, dated December 20, 1925, St. Maurice de Clervaux.

24. *Kvæðakver*, Önnur útgáfa aukin (2nd edition, augmented), (Reykjavík, 1949), p. 142.

Chapter Three

1. Letter to Father Jón Sveinsson, dated May 15, 1925, Brighton, England.

2. Cf. my work *Den store vävaren. En studie i Laxness' ungdomsdiktning* (Stockholm, 1954), especially pp. 335–62.

3. The series of articles was printed in nine numbers of the newspaper *Alþýðublaðið*, March 8–30 (inclusive), 1927.

4. *Alþýðubókin*, Þriðja útgáfa (3rd edition), (Reykjavík, 1949), p. 9.

5. Letter to Jón Helgason, dated April 12, 1928.

6. Article in the newspaper *Vörður*, May 7, 1927.

7. Letter to Ingibjörg Einarsdóttir, dated March 27, 1928.

8. On Laxness' study of Spengler see *Alþýðubókin*, Þriðja útgáfa (3rd edition), (Reykjavík, 1949), p. 9.

9. Letter to Kristín Guðmundsdóttir, dated September 8, 1929, Los Angeles.

10. Letter to Jón Helgason, dated April 12, 1928, San Francisco.

11. For example, in a letter to Einar Ólafur Sveinsson from St. Maurice de Clervaux, March 5, 1923: "Indeed, the business of novel writing is only for hysterical or corrupt old maids or students—and then people of a sixth or seventh class way of life—who are quite worthless."

Chapter Four

1. The collection has since come out in a new edition, which, however, has been augmented with later poems, most of them published as component parts of Laxness' novels: *Kvæðakver*, Önnur útgáfa aukin (2nd edition, augmented), (Reykjavík, 1949).

2. Letter to Erlendur Guðmundsson, dated February 3, 1926.

3. Interview in the newspaper *Verklýðsblaðið* (The Workers' Paper), May 10, 1932.

4. A review by Kristján Albertsson in *Morgunblaðið*, September 25, 1932, dealing with both parts of the novel. It has been reprinted in his book *Í gróandanum. Greinar og ræður* (In Springtime. Articles and Speeches), (Reykjavík, 1955), pp. 62–68.

5. Einar Olgeirsson's article in the periodical *Réttur* (Justice), 1932, pp. 95–117; on Laxness pp. 99–102.

6. Article by Laxness, written at the age of nineteen: "Síðasta bók Hamsuns" (Hamsun's Latest Book) in *Morgunblaðið*, September 15, 1921.

7. Quoted from *Alþýðubókin*, p. 228.

8. The short story in question is "Og lótusblómið angar . . ." (The Fragrance of the Lotus . . .), first printed in the periodical *Eimreiðin*, 1930, pp. 161–78, later to be incorporated in the collection of short stories *Fótatak manna*, 1933.

9. Letter to his wife Ingibjörg, April 20, 1931.

Chapter Five

1. This draft, which is still preserved, is discussed—with exhaustive quotations—in my article "Heiðin. Fyrsta uppkastið að skáldsögunni Sjalfstætt fólk." *Tímarit Máls og menningar*, 1955, pp. 280–323.

2. "Eftirmáli" (Postscript) to *Sjálfstætt fólk*, Önnur útgáfa (2nd edition), Reykjavík, 1952), p. 472.

3. Letter to his fiancée Ingibjörg, dated March 27, 1928.

4. On this manuscript cf. my work *Skaldens hus. Laxness' diktning från Salka Valka till Gerpla* (Stockholm, 1956), p. 238.

5. Quoted from the "Eftirmáli," (p. 471), mentioned in note 2.

6. Laxness' *Þakkarávarp* was printed in the newspaper *Alþýðublaðið*, July 3, 1934.

7. Quoted from the "Eftirmáli" (p. 471) mentioned in note 2.

8. Grettir Ásmundarson is the hero of one of the great Sagas of Icelanders, *Grettis saga Ásmundarsonar*, which was written around 1300.

9. The *rímur* (sing. *ríma*) constitute an Icelandic poetic genre of epic type, which originated in the fourteenth century. The elaborate formal structure of these poems is derived from that of Old Norse skaldic poetry, while their content is often based on earlier prose works.

10. On Laxness' reminiscences of his grandmother cf. my work *Skaldens hus*, p. 270 et seq.

11. Letter dated February 3, 1926.

Chapter Six

1. *Heimsljós* (Reykjavík, 1955).

2. The relationship between Magnús Hjaltason's diaries and Laxness' novel is examined in further detail in my work *Skaldens hus*, pp. 314–46.

3. Interview in the newspaper *Þjóðviljinn* (The Will of the People), Reykjavík, August 31, 1937.

4. This foreword is reprinted in Icelandic in the collection of articles *Gjörníngabók* (Reykjavík, 1959), and there entitled "Bókin um skáldsnillínginn" (The Book on the Poetic Genius).

5. Quoted from Eva M. Martin's translation of Dostoevsky's *The Idiot* (Everyman's Library, London, 1963), pp. 443–44.

6. Quoted from the section entitled "Einn dag í senn. Vasabókarblöð" (One Day at a Time. Pages from a Diary) in the collection of essays *Dagleið á fjöllum* (Reykjavík, 1937), p. 321 et seq.

7. Bremerholm was the name of a greatly feared prison in Denmark, to which Icelanders as well as Danes were sent for serious offenses.

Chapter Seven

1. The elements of contemporary history in the novel trilogy are exemplified in my work *Skaldens hus*, p. 412 et seq., as well as in my article "Íslandsklukkan í smíðum. Um handritin að skáldsögu Halldórs Kiljans Laxness," *Árbok Landsbókasafns Íslands 1955–56* (Reykjavík, 1957, pp. 139–78).

2. These quotations are from the article "Málið" (Language), printed in the collection of essays *Vettvangur dagsins* (Reykjavík, 1942) and there dated 1941; the opinions on Hemingway are expressed there in connection with Laxness' defense of his principles as the translator of *A Farewell to Arms*—for his Icelandic translation had met with petty linguistic criticism in certain quarters.

3. The comparison has been made by Sveinn Bergsveinsson, for example, in an article in the Norwegian literary periodical *Edda* (1942): "Sagaen og den haardkogte Roman," (pp. 56–62).

4. The essay is entitled "Minnisgreinar um fornsögur" (Notes on the Sagas). It was first printed in the periodical *Tímarit Máls og Menningar* (1945), pp. 13–56, and later in the collection of essays *Sjálfsagðir hlutir* (Reykjavík, 1946).

5. Interview in the newspaper *Þjóðviljinn*, Reykjavík, December 23, 1944.

Chapter Eight

1. This speech was given on November 7, 1946, and is here quoted from the collection of articles *Reisubókarkorn* (Reykjavík, 1950).

2. More detailed information on the subject of the drafts and manuscripts of *Atómstöðin* may be found in my article "Úr vinnustofu sagnaskálds. Nokkur orð um handritin að Atómstöðinni. (*Tímarit Máls og Menningar*, 1953, pp. 145–65).

Chapter Nine

1. Quoted from the collection of essays *Sjálfsagðir hlutir* (Reykjavík, 1946), p. 9.

2. Quoted from *Íslenzk fornrit*, VI (Reykjavík, 1943), p. 133.

3. Quoted from *Íslenzk fornrit*, VI (Reykjavík, 1943), p. 153.

4. Quoted from the collection of articles and speeches *Dagur í senn* (Reykjavík, 1955), p. 156.

5. Quoted from *Íslenzk fornrit, VI* (Reykjavík, 1943), p. 128.

6. The concept of the "life egg" does not, as far as I know, belong to the world of the Icelandic sagas but to that of the Icelandic folk tales, where it is associated with the lives of giants or trolls. Cf. Jón Árnason's collection of Icelandic folk tales *Íslenzkar þjóðsögur og æfintýri, I-II* (Leipzig, 1862–64).

7. On the language of *Gerpla,* and the relevance of this novel to modern times, see now my article "Halldór Laxness' *Gerpla.* Einige Bemerkungen über Sprache und Tendenz," in *Scientia Islandica (Science in Iceland),* Anniversary Volume 1968, pp. 31–40.

Chapter Ten

1. The speeches mentioned in this paragraph are printed in *Gjörníngabók* (Reykjavík, 1959), to which page references are made in the following paragraphs. The English in the congratulatory message to the Soviet Union and in the speech at the banquet in Peking is Laxness' own.

2. The article "Eastern Lessons" (February, 1958), here quoted from *Gjörníngabók,* p. 202.

3. The telegram is here quoted from the English text in *Gjörníngabók,* p. 237.

4. Quoted from Laxness' own English text in *Gjörníngabók,* p. 170.

5. "Eastern Lessons," *Gjörníngabók,* p. 201.

6. The article "Ísland, Norðurlönd og Evrópa" (Iceland, Scandinavia and Europe), here quoted from *Upphaf mannúðarstefnu* (Reykjavík, 1965), p. 85.

7. *Skáldatími* (Reykjavík, 1963), p. 54–55.

8. The article "Persónulegar minnisgreinar um skáldsögur og leikrit" (Personal Notes on Novels and Plays), here quoted from *Upphaf mannúðarstefnu,* p. 73 and p. 70 respectively.

9. In his autobiographical work *Íslendíngaspjall* (Reykjavík, 1967) Laxness, while discussing poor but hospitable homes ("supernatural places"), recalls his words about Brekkukot: "I have made so bold as to recall in print a place of this kind from my own experience: the house which gives other houses a purpose" (101).

10. Cf. in particular the article "Bókin um veginn" (The Book of the Way), written in connection with a new Icelandic translation of *Tao-te-king;* the article, which dates from 1942, is reprinted in *Sjálfsagðir hlutir* (Reykjavík, 1946).

11.   Cf. further my article "Litla bókin um sálina og Halldór Laxness" (Halldór Laxness and the Little Book about the Soul), (*Tímarit Máls og Menningar,* 1962, pp. 119–31).

12.   The reply to the questionnaire, in Laxness' own English, is included in *Gjörníngabók* (Reykjavík, 1959), p. 185.

13.   The quotations on the subject of the *anti-roman* are from the article mentioned in note 8. (*Upphaf mannúðarstefnu,* p. 72.)

14.   *Op. cit.,* p. 71.

15.   *Op. cit.,* p. 73 and p. 75 respectively.

16.   The article "Tíska og menning. Um ljóð" ((Fashion and Culture. On Lyrical Poetry), printed in *Morgunblaðið* (Reykjavík) May 21, 1925. Cf. my book *Den store vävaren* (Stockholm, 1954), pp. 201–202.

17.   Quoted from *Svavar Guðnason. Et udvalg af billeder med indledende tekst af Halldór Laxness.* Vor Tids Kunst 67. (Copenhagen: Gyldendal 1968.)

Selected Bibliography

I. THE GENERAL BACKGROUND

ANDERSSON, THEODORE M. *The Icelandic Family Saga. An Analytic Reading* (Harvard Studies in Comparative Literature, XXVIII). Cambridge, Mass., Harvard University Press, 1967.

ANDRESSON, KRISTINN E. *Íslenzkar nútímabókmenntir 1918–1948.* Reykjavík, Mál og menning, 1949 (Swedish translation by Rannveig and Peter Hallberg: *Det moderna Islands litteratur 1918–1948.* Stockholm, Kooperativa förbundets bokförlag, 1955).

BECK, RICHARD. *History of Icelandic Poets 1800–1940 (Islandica,* Vol. XXXIV). Ithaca, New York, Cornell University Press, 1950.

CRAIGIE, SIR WILLIAM A. *The Art of Poetry in Iceland.* The Taylorian lecture, 1937. Oxford, at the Clarendon Press, 1937.

CRAIGIE, SIR WILLIAM A. *Sýnisbók Íslenzkra Rímna* (Specimens of Icelandic Rímur from the Fourteenth to the Nineteenth century). In three volumes. Introductions in English: Vol. I, pp. 281–306; Vol. II, pp. 315–331; Vol. III, pp. 402–409. London, Thomas Nelson and Sons, Ltd., 1952.

EINARSSON, STEFAN. *History of Icelandic Prose Writers 1800–1940 (Islandica,* Vols. XXXII and XXXIII). Ithaca, New York, Cornell University Press, 1948.

EINARSSON, STEFAN. *A History of Icelandic Literature.* New York, The Johns Hopkins Press for The American-Scandinavian Foundation, 1957.

GISLASON, BJARNI M. *Islands litteratur efter Sagatiden.* Copenhagen, Aschehoug Dansk Forlag, 1949.

GJERSET, KNUT. *History of Iceland.* New York, The Macmillan Company, 1925.

HALLBERG, PETER. *Den isländska sagan* (Verdandis skriftserie, 6). Stockholm, Svenska bokförlaget, Bonniers, 1964 (second edition) (English translation by Paul Schach: *The Icelandic Saga, Translated with Introduction and Notes.* Lincoln, University of Nebraska Press, 1962).

HALLBERG, PETER. *Den fornisländska poesien* (Verdandis skriftserie, 20). Stockholm, Svenska bokförlaget, Bonniers, 1964 (second edition).

HOLLANDER, L. M. *The Skalds: A Selection of their Poems with Introduction and Notes.* Princeton, Princeton University Press, 1945. Reprinted as an Ann Arbor Paperback (Ann Arbor: Michigan University Press, 1968).

KER, W. P. *Epic and Romance. Essays on Mediaeval Literature.* New York, Dover Publications, Inc., 1957. (A republication of the second revised edition published by Macmillan and Company, Ltd., in 1908).

PHILLPOTTS, BERTHA E. *Edda and Saga.* London, Thornton Butterworth, Ltd., The Home University Library, 1931.

TURVILLE-PETRE, G. *The Heroic Age of Scandinavia.* London, Hutchinson's University Library, 1951.

TURVILLE-PETRE, G. *Origins of Icelandic Literature.* Oxford, at the Clarendon Press, 1953.

II. THE WORKS OF HALLDOR LAXNESS

(a) *Works in the Original*

Barn náttúrunnar (Child of Nature). A love story. Reykjavík, at the author's expense, 1919; and Reykjavík, Helgafell, 1964.

Nokkrar sögur (Some Stories). Reykjavík, Ísafoldarprentsmiðja, 1923.

Undir Helgahnúk (Under the Holy Mountain). Reykjavík, Ársæll Árnason, 1924. Second edition: Reykjavík, Helgafell, 1967.

Kaþólsk viðhorf (From a Catholic Point of View). A defense of Catholicism. Reykjavík, Ársæll Árnason, 1925.

Vefarinn mikli frá Kasmír (The Great Weaver from Kashmir). Reykjavík, Acta, 1927. Later editions: Reykjavík, Helgafell, 1948, 1957.

Alþýðubókin (The Book of the People). A collection of essays. Reykjavík, Alþýðuflokkurinn, 1929. Later editions: Reykjavík, Helgafell, 1947, 1949, 1955 (Mál og menning), 1956.

Kvæðakver (Poems). Reykjavík, Acta, 1930. Later editions (much enlarged): Reykjavík, Helgafell, 1949, 1956.

Þú vínviður hreini (O Thou Pure Vine). Reykjavík, Bókadeild menningarsjóðs, 1931.

Fuglinn í fjörunni (The Bird on the Beach). Reykjavík, Bókadeild menningarsjóðs, 1932.

Salka Valka (*Þu vínviður hreini* and *Fuglinn í fjörunni* published together in one volume). Reykjavík, Helgafell, 1951, 1959.

Í Austurvegi (Going East). Impressions of a visit to Russia. Reykjavík, Sovétvinafélag Íslands, 1933.

Fótatak manna (Steps of Men). Seven short stories. Akureyri, Þorsteinn M. Jónsson, 1933.

Sjálfstætt fólk (Independent People). An epic in two volumes. Reykjavík, E. P. Briem, 1934–35; and Reykjavík, Helgafell, 1952, 1961.

Straumrof (Short Circuit). A play. Reykjavík, Heimskringla, 1934.

Þórður gamli halti (Old Þórður the Lame). A short story. Reykjavík, offprint from *Réttur*, 1935.

Dagleið á fjöllum (A Day's Journey in the Mountains). Essays. Reykjavík, Heimskringla, 1937, 1938; and Reykjavík, Helgafell, 1962.

Ljós heimsins (The Light of the World). Reykjavík, Heimskringla, 1937, 1938.

Gerska ævintýrið (The Russian Adventure). Impressions of Russia. Reykjavík, Heimskringla, 1938.

Höll sumarlandsins (The Palace of the Summerland). Reykjavík, Heimskringla, 1938.

Hús skáldsins (The House of the Poet). Reykjavík, Heimskringla, 1939.

Fegurð himinsins (The Beauty of the Skies). Reykjavík, Heimskringla, 1940.

Heimsljós I–II (World Light). *Ljós heimsins* (under the new title of *Kraftbirtíngarhljómur guðdómsins* (The Revelation of the Deity)), *Höll sumarlandsins, Hús skáldsins* and *Fegurð himinsins* published together in two volumes. Reykjavík, Helgafell, 1955; and 1967 (one volume).

Vopnin kvödd. A translation of Hemingway's *A Farewell to Arms* (1929). Reykjavík, Mál og menning, 1941.

Sjö töframenn (Seven Enchanters). Short stories. Reykjavík, Heimskringla, 1942; and Helgafell, 1962.

Vettvangur dagsins (The Contemporary Scene). Essays and articles. Reykjavík, Heimskringla, 1942. Second edition: Reykjavík, Helgafell, 1962.

Íslandsklukkan (Iceland's Bell). Reykjavík, Helgafell, 1943, 1945; Skálholt, 1965.

Hið ljósa man (The Bright Maid). Reykjavík, Helgafell, 1944.

Birtíngur. A translation of Voltaire's *Candide* (1759). Reykjavík, Helgafell, 1945.

Eldur í Kaupinhafn (Fire in Copenhagen). Reykjavík, Helgafell, 1946.

Íslandsklukkan (Iceland's Bell). *Íslandsklukkan, Hið ljósa man* and *Eldur í Kaupinhafn* published together in one volume. Reykjavík, Helgafell, 1957, 1961.

Sjálfsagðir hlutir (Obvious Things). Essays and articles. Reykjavík, Helgafell, 1946.

Atómstöðin (The Atom Station). A novel. Reykjavík, Helgafell, 1948, 1961.

Snæfríður Íslandssól (Snæfríður, Iceland's Sun). A play. Reykjavík, Helgafell, 1950, 1956.

Reisubókarkorn (A Little Diary of Travels). Reykjavík, Helgafell, 1950, 1963.

Heiman eg fór (From Home I Went). A portrait of the artist as a young man. Reykjavík, Helgafell, 1952, 1956.

Gerpla (The Happy Warriors). A saga. Reykjavík, Helgafell, 1952 (twice), 1956.

Þættir (Short Stories). *Nokkrar sögur, Fótatak manna* and *Sjö töframenn* published together in one volume. Reykjavík, Helgafell, 1954.

Silfurtúnglið (The Silver Moon). A play. Reykjavík, Helgafell, 1954.

Dagur í senn (A Day at a Time). Articles and speeches. Reykjavík, Helgafell, 1955.

Smásögur (Short Stories). Reykjavík, Bókaútgáfa menningarsjóðs, 1956.

Brekkukotsannáll (Annals of Brekkukot. English translation under the title: *The Fish can Sing*). A novel. Reykjavík, Helgafell, 1957.

Gjörníngabók (Documents). Essays. Reykjavík, Helgafell, 1959.

Paradísarheimt (Paradise Reclaimed). A novel. Reykjavík, Helgafell, 1960.

Strompleikurinn (The Chimney Play). A comedy. Reykjavík, Helgafell, 1961.

Prjónastofan Sólin (The Knitting Workshop called "The Sun"). A comedy. Reykjavík, Mál og menning, 1962; Helgafell, 1962.

Skáldatími (A Writer's Schooling). Literary reminiscences. Reykjavík, Helgafell, 1963.

Listahátíð 1964 (Festival of Art, 1964). Inaugural speech. Reykjavík, Helgafell, 1964.

Sjöstafakverið (The Book of Seven Signs). Seven short stories. Reykjavík, Helgafell, 1964.

Upphaf mannúðarstefnu (The Beginning of Humanism). Essays. Reykjavík, Helgafell, 1965.

Dúfnaveislan (The Pigeon Banquet). A comedy. Reykjavík, Helgafell, 1966.

Veisla í farángrinum. A translation of Hemingway's *A Moveable Feast* (1964). Akureyri, Bókaforlag Odds Björnssonar, 1966.

Íslendíngaspjall (An Essay on Icelanders). Literary reminiscences. Reykjavík, Helgafell, 1967.

Kristnihald undir Jökli (Christianity in Snæfellsness). A novel. Reykjavík, Helgafell, 1968.

Svavar Guðnason. Et udvalg af billeder med indledende tekst af Halldór Laxness. Vor Tids Kunst 67. Copenhagen, Gyldendal, 1968.

Vínlandspúnktar (Some Remarks on Vinland). Essays. Reykjavík, Helgafell, 1969.

Innansveitarkronika (A Parish Chronicle). Reykjavík, Helgafell, 1970.

(b) *Translations of Novels and Short Stories.*

Salka Valka. Tr. by F. H. Lyon (from Gunnar Gunnarsson's Danish translation of the original Icelandic). London, George Allen & Unwin, Ltd., 1936; New York—Boston, Houghton Mifflin Company, 1936; and London, George Allen & Unwin, Ltd., 1963.

"Lily. The Story of Nebuchadnezzar Nebuchadnezzarson in Life and in Death." Tr. by Axel Eyberg and John Watkins. In Richard Beck, *Icelandic Poems and Stories,* Princeton—New York, 1943. pp. 302–15 ("Lilja. Sagan um Nebúkadnesar Nebúkadnesarson í lífi og dauða," a short story published in *Fótatak manna,* 1933.)

Independent People. Tr. by J. A. Thompson. London, George Allen & Unwin, Ltd., 1945; New York, Alfred E. Knopf, 1946; and New Delhi, People's Publishing House, 1957 (*Sjálfstætt fólk*).

The Happy Warriors. Tr. by Katherine John. London, Methuen & Co., Ltd., 1958 (*Gerpla*).

The Honour of the House. Translator not named. Reykjavík, Helgafell, 1959 (*Ungfrúin góða og Húsið,* a "long short story" dating from 1933).

"New Iceland." Tr. by Axel Eyberg and John Watkins. In *Seven Icelandic Short Stories.* Reykjavík, The Ministry of Education, 1960; and in Loftur Bjarnason, *Anthology of Modern Icelandic Literature, Vol. II,* University of California, 1964, pp. 153–58. ("Nyja Ísland," a short story published in *Fótatak manna,* 1933.)

The Atom Station. Tr. by Magnus Magnusson. London, Methuen & Co., Ltd., 1961; and London: Brown, Watson, Ltd. (a Digit Book), 1961 (*Atómstöðin*).

Paradise Reclaimed. Tr. by Magnus Magnusson. London, Methuen & Co., Ltd., 1962; and New York, Thomas Y. Crowell Company, 1962 (*Paradísarheimt*).

"The Defeat of the Italian Air Force in Reykjavík 1933." In Hallberg Hallmundsson, *An Anthology of Scandinavian Literature.* New York, 1965, pp. 259–67. ("Ósigur ítalska loftflotans í Reykjavík 1933," a short story first published in 1937).

The Fish can Sing. Tr. by Magnus Magnusson. London, Methuen & Co., Ltd., 1966; and New York, Thomas Y. Crowell Company, 1967 (*Brekkukotsannáll*).

World Light. Tr. by Magnus Magnusson. Madison, Milwaukee and London, The University of Wisconsin Press, 1969 *(Heimsljós).*

III.   ON HALLDOR LAXNESS AND HIS WORK

ANDRESSON, KRISTINN E. *Íslenzkar nútímabókmenntir 1918–1948.* Reykjavík, 1949, pp. 279-343 (Swedish translation by Rann-veig and Peter Hallberg: *Det moderna Islands litteratur 1918–1948.* Stockholm, 1955, pp. 190–238).

EINARSSON, STEFAN. *History of Icelandic Prose Writers 1800–1940.* Ithaca, 1948, pp. 219–29 *(Islandica,* Vol. XXXII-XXXIII).

EINARSSON, STEFAN. *A History of Icelandic Literature.* New York, 1957, pp. 317–19.

EINARSSON, STEFAN. *Íslenzk bókmenntasaga 874–1960.* Reykjavík, 1961, pp. 411-16.

EINARSSON, STEFAN. "Halldór Kiljan Laxness". In *Skáldaþing,* Reykjavík, 1948, pp. 417–34.

ESKELAND, IVAR. *Halldór Kiljan Laxness: Menneske og Motiv.* Oslo, 1955.

FRIDJONSSON, GUDMUNDUR. *Sveitaómenningin í skuggsjá skáldsins frá Laxnesi.* Reykjavík, 1937.

GISLASON, BJARNI M. *Islands litteratur efter sagatiden.* Copenhagen, 1949, pp. 139–51.

HALLBERG, PETER. *Halldór Kiljan Laxness.* Stockholm, Bonniers, 1952 (Icelandic translation—Reykjavík, Helgafell, 1955).

HALLBERG, PETER. *Den store vävaren. En studie i Laxness' ungdoms-diktning.* Stockholm, Rabén & Sjögren, 1954 (Icelandic translation: *Vefarinn mikli* I–II. Reykjavík, Helgafell, 1957–60).

HALLBERG, PETER. *Skaldens hus. Laxness' diktning från Salka Valka till Gerpla.* Stockholm, Rabén & Sjögren, 1956. (Icelandic translation of the first half: *Hús skáldsins* I. Reykjavík, Mál og menning, 1970).

HALLBERG, PETER. "Laxness vid skiljovägen." In *Edda,* 1967, pp. 297–345 (Icelandic translation: "Laxness á vegamótum". In *Tímarit Máls og menningar,* 1968, pp. 37–82).

(For additional works on Laxness by Peter Hallberg, see under Notes and References.)

JONSSON, JONAS. "Fólk í tötrum." In *Nýja Dagblaðið,* February 16–March 8, 1936.

JONSSON, RAGNAR (ed.). *Afmæliskveðjur heiman og handan:* essays to commemorate Laxness' 60th birthday. Reykjavík, Helgafell, 1962.

KARLSSON, KRISTJAN. *Halldór Kiljan Laxness* (contains a bibliography by Haraldur Sigurðsson of Laxness' works in Icelandic and other languages: "Skrá um bækur Halldórs Kiljans Laxness á íslenzku og öðrum málum"). Reykjavík, Helgafell, 1962.

KÖTZ, GÜNTER. *Das Problem Dichter und Gesellschaft im Werke von Halldór Kiljan Laxness. Ein Beitrag zur modernen isländischen Literatur. (Beiträge zur deutschen Philologie,* 35, Giessen, 1966.)

MAGNUSSON, PETUR. *Nóbelskáld í nýju ljósi.* Reykjavík, published by the author, 1962.

MARKEY, T. L. "Sjálfstætt fólk, Hamsun and Rousseau. A Note." In *Edda,* 1967, pp. 346–55.

Index

This index includes personal names and book titles, the latter in italics. Halldór Laxness' own writings are all indexed under his name.

DATE DUE
